WARS AND SOLDIERS IN THE EARLY REIGN OF LOUIS XIV

Volume 7 – Armies of the German States 1655-1690 Part 2

Text and Illustrations by Bruno Mugnai

'This is the Century of the Soldier', Fulvio Testi, Poet, 1641

HELION & COMPANY

Helion & Company Limited
Unit 8 Amherst Business Centre
Budbrooke Road
Warwick
CV34 5WE
England
Tel. 01926 499 619
Email: info@helion.co.uk
Website: www.helion.co.uk
Twitter: @helionbooks
Visit our blog http://blog.helion.co.uk/

Published by Helion & Company 2025
Designed and typeset by Mary Woolley, Battlefield Design (www.battlefield-design.co.uk)
Cover designed by Paul Hewitt, Battlefield Design (www.battlefield-design.co.uk)

ISBN 978-1-804514-47-4

British Library Cataloguing-in-Publication Data.
A catalogue record for this book is available from the British Library.

For details of other military history titles published by Helion & Company Limited contact the above address or visit our website: http://www.helion.co.uk.

We always welcome receiving book proposals from prospective authors.

Contents

1

Introduction: The German Trade of Soldiers

If we duly consider 'the Genius of this Nation', which inhabits this great Empire, it is most evident, that this Nation ever since the memory of Men has been very brave, and addicted to War; and that Germany has been an inexhaustible Source of Soldiers, since there is scarce ever any want of Men, who are ready to serve for Money: and if they are once well Disciplined, they are not only good at the first onset, but are very fit to endure the hardships and inconveniences of a long war. There are not in any other Nation so many to be met withal, that are ready to list themselves in Foreign Service for Money; neither is there any Country in Christendom where greater Forces both of Horse and Foot may be raised, than in Germany.

Samuel von Pufendorf, *Einleitung zu der Historie der Vornehmsten Reiche und Staaten, so itziger Zeit in Europa sich befinden* (Frankfurt am Main: 1695), p.347.

Unlike Pufendorf, non-Germans were not quite so flattering of the part that German arms played in the wars of the seventeenth century. The French military writer Guibert was not alone when he spoke of the 'mania of all these little [German] sovereigns to have battlements and troops.'[1] A contemporary English travel book described Germany as the *officina gentium,* the great nursery of the North, from which swarms of men have been drawn in all ages.'[2] This warlike character took the form, not of a German bid for European domination, for Germany itself was divided into a large number of states, but of providing trained contingents for the armies of the great powers, in return for pay. This commerce in soldiers went back to the breakup of the medieval German Empire. The feudal levy had ceased to turn out, but there was no bureaucratic state apparatus for raising, equipping, paying, and maintaining men, nor for collecting the taxes to support them.

1 François-Apolline de Guibert, *Journal d'un Voyage en Allemagne fait en 1773* (Paris: 1803), vol. I, p.121.

2 Thomas Nugent, *Travels through Germany* (2 vols. London, 1768), vol. I, p.136.

The soldiers were recruited from uprooted people who had mainly drifted into towns, and who, in the old phrase 'took their skins into the market' and enlisted in return for the *Handgeld* (bounty money). The heyday of the military entrepreneurs was the Thirty Years' War, with the arch-practitioner, of course, Wallenstein. He raised an army of 100,000 men, nominally under the Emperor, but actually under his personal command and his mercenary captains. For every Wallenstein, there were hundreds of small scale operators who made war profitable, both by raising men and quartering them over areas from which he could exact *Kontribution.*[3] Some were successful, received titles and became 'millionaires' from their profits and booty, but even more met with violent deaths.

Portrait of a German mercenary officer, *c.* 1670, artist unknown. (Author's collection)
Negative stereotypes of 'mercenaries' emerged from early modern moralistic literature and then were reinforced by state-building historians of the nineteenth century. Rather than seeing the seventeenth century as a moment of the emergence of modern states and military organisations, the contemporary historiography stresses continuities in state development and military organisation.

In the second half of the seventeenth century, when the size of armed forces grew exponentially, armies typically ranked among the largest employers within a state. Thus, soldiers constituted the most numerous unified labour force within Europe.[4] Germany, was among the first in this ranking, becoming the most specialised locality for recruiting professional soldiers. It was actually the net of recruitment which confers this leadership on Germany. A major change about the recruitment of mercenaries emerged in this period.

From the second half of the seventeenth century, methods of recruitment developed in a number of significant ways. In the first major development, states made greater use of involuntary recruitment. They continued to draft criminals and other less socially desirable people in larger numbers than before, since 'the army must inevitably consist of the scum of the people, and of all those for whom society has no use.'[5] This

3 Fritz Redlich, *The German Military Enterpriser and his Work Force: A Study in European Economic and Social History*, bande I and II (Wiesbaden: Viertelsjahrschrift für Sozial- und Wirtschaftsgeschichte, nrs. 47 & 48, 1964–5). Redlich's little-known work discusses military entrepreneurship as a form of nascent capitalism.

4 Frank Tallet, 'Soldiers in Western Europe, *c.* 1500–1790' in E. J. Zürcher (ed.) *Fighting for Living. A Comparative History of Military labour, 1500–2000* (Amsterdam: Amsterdam University Press, 2008), p.136: 'A consideration of troops within the framework of labour history is accordingly both appropriate and also long overdue, especially since in certain circumstances soldiers acted very much like modern workers.'

5 Louis Ducros, *French Society in the Eighteenth Century* (London: G. Bell & Sons, 1927), p.294; quotation attributed to Comte de Saint Germain.

did not end altogether after 1648, but it changed markedly, especially with regard to the main actor: the general contractor. These figures, who had figured so prominently in the Thirty Years' War, diminished in number but did not disappear from the scene, although they were gradually replaced by the Princes. These latter, unlike private contractors, did not have to offer bounty money to attract recruits; they merely called up their farm boys to fill out the ranks at the exercise season and in time of war. Thus they could underbid their rivals. German Princes also turned to 'military entrepreneurs' – who, in return for cash fee per head recruited, the right to keep booty and to traffic in arms and equipment as well as men – raised levies of troops.

For the period of about 1660–1720, there was almost constant war or threat of war amongst England, France, Austria, and the Dutch Republic. The demand for troops was frequent, but intermittent. Even the strongest states were financially unable to keep as many troops permanently under arms as were needed in war. It was easier and cheaper to pay retainers to the German Princes, who were willing to keep soldiers ready 'on call', as it were, for their paymaster. The German Princes, by keeping outsized armies, also helped to save themselves from being swallowed up by the bigger powers, as the latter were interested in the Princes' survival as a source of manpower in exchange for the subsidy.

Traditionally, the subsidy treaties of these princes have been regarded as a *Soldatenhandel* (soldiers' trade) whereby the princes sold their subjects to foreign powers 'to increase their revenues and satisfy their desire for luxury.'[6] This interpretation has profoundly influenced the historical view of the lesser German princes and their role within the Empire and the European states system.[7] The root of the misunderstanding lies in a failure to distinguish between the recruitment of foreigners directly into an army and their temporary hire under a subsidy. The former was always illegal within the Empire and the subject of frequent condemnation by publicists.[8] Later writers have often mistaken these for attacks on subsidy treaties. By the second half of the seventeenth century, such treaties were regarded in a largely positive light. Some even welcomed them, believing that they led to a decline in the direct recruiting of soldiers by foreign powers in the Reich. The jurists agreed that the treaties conformed to the Peace of Westphalia which gave the Princes

Schütze (shooter), from a German print dating to *c.* 1660. (Author's collection) German militiamen were embodied as emergency field units to supplement the mercenaries or, as they were increasingly from the 1660s, used as a recruitment pool for what were becoming permanent field formations as happened in Brandenburg, Celle and Württemberg. The mercenaries, meanwhile, were subjected to greater central control by subordinating the private military contractors, who recruited them, to princely authority.

6 Friedrich Kapp, *Der Soldatenhandel deutscher Fürsten nach Amerika* (Wolfenbüttel: Melchior, 2006), p.20.

7 Peter H. Wilson, *War, State and Society in Württemberg, 1677–1793* (Cambridge: Cambridge University Press, 1995), p.74: 'Only recently has it begun to be revised. So far these revisionist attempts have failed to escape from a particularist standpoint which re-evaluates the treaties of a particular state but leaves intact the traditional interpretation of those of other states.'

8 France began payments to a number of German princes in the 1650s as part of its moves to win backing against a potential Habsburg revival, but the first treaty for offensive purposes was made by England with Münster on 13 June 1665.

A military career offered an attractive method of advancement to junior members of princely houses who often served in a considerable number of armies. Prince Philipp Florinus von Pfalz-Sulzbach (1630–1703) was the youngest son of Augustus, Count Palatine of Sulzbach and Hedwig of Schleswig-Holstein-Gottorf. He began his military career in the Army of Lorraine. Then he joined the Swedish army and fought under King Charles X Gustav of Sweden against Poland, and later in the war of 1657–60 and the Ottomans, where he lost the disastrous Battle of Nyborg, and had to save his life by fleeing at night. After the death of the King of Sweden, Pfalz-Sulzbach went to Venice where he took part in the Cretan War of 1645–1671 against the Ottoman Turks. But he left Venice in 1662 and entered the service of Austria. He played an important role as *Feldmarschall* and commander of the cavalry in the successful Hungarian campaign of 1664 under Montecuccoli.

the right to make foreign treaties as long as these allowed him to provide his contingent to the *Reichsarmee* and were not directed against the Emperor or the Empire. These rights had been confirmed in subsequent election promises, the *Wahlkapitulationen*, by the Emperor.[9] From the Peace on, the subsidy treaties developed a number of different forms, but always retained the same basic characteristic: one party provided military assistance in return for financial or political advantage from the other. This has been one of the most misunderstood areas of early modern international relations. The market was gradually developing by which Princes would rent parts of their army to other states, as a way to fill tax coffers while keeping precious troops and officers occupied and giving them experience. Most of these Princes were German, although the Guelph Dukes, the Prince of Lorraine and several others also participated in some way calling the fee for their service a subsidy.[10]

As in the past, military entrepreneurship was not an easy job. The risk to life was considerable and the income uncertain. Often a prince could not pay the money to the entrepreneur: a circumstance that was all too frequent. For this reason, entrepreneurs usually required an advance payment of the first three months' wages. Alongside the risks deriving from the encounters with the enemy, there were those deriving from disease. Of the 1,500 entrepreneurs of all nationalities in the seventeenth century, 214 died in battle or of wounds received. This death rate is about 17 percent, which probably includes deaths from accidents on campaign and from disease. Besides the risk of death, there was also the possibility of capture, which would entail having to pay a ransom. The number of entrepreneurs who survived and prospered, and ended the wars with a great profit, such as Waldeck or Degenfeld, were very small.[11]

9 Peter H. Wilson, *War, State and Society in Württemberg, 1677–1793* (Cambridge: Cambridge University Press, 1995), p.75.

10 David Parrot, *The Business of War: Military Enterprise and Military Revolution in Early Modern Europe* (Cambridge: Cambridge University Press, 2012), pp.21–22.

11 Bruno Mugnai, *Wars and Soldiers in the Early reign of Louis XIV, volume 7: German Armies 1655–1690, part 1* (Warwick: Helion & Company, 2024), pp.7–13.

Most enterprisers served until almost the end of their lives, if they did not die on campaign, but some did retire to a well-feathered nest. Below the rank of colonel, however, only crumbs remained: the pay for captains dropped by half after 1648, denoting a gradual change in the military condition, and the mercenary motive alone cannot explain the attraction of such careers.

Georg Friedrich of Waldeck-Pyrmont (1620–1692), in an engraving by Jacques Bloneau. (Author's collection)
Waldeck was a very talented military commander and statesman who achieved an important role in German policy of the second half of the seventeenth century. He belonged to the Eisenberg branch, and his complete titles were Prince of the Holy Roman Empire, Prince of Waldeck-Pyrmont, Count of Cuylenburg, Baron of Pallant and Mittenwerth, Cathedral Provost of Halberstadt, Senior of the Order of St John and Commendator of Logau, *General Fieldmarschall* of the Empire and The United Provinces of The Netherlands, Governor of Maastricht. In 1634, at the age of 14, George Friedrich had already had a taste of military action by witnessing the victorious resistance of the town of Arolsen against the Spanish. In 1640, he entered the service of the Dutch Republic and began to learn his trade. Prince Philipp Theodor's death in 1645 put him in the line of succession. Like the House of Nassau, his family already had relatives in The Netherlands and he married Countess Elisabeth Charlotte of Nassau-Siegen, daughter of *Fieldmarschall* Wilhelm of Nassau-Siegen. In 1651, Georg Friedrich entered the service of Brandenburg, where he reached the highest rank as a minister of the Crown. During this period, he initiated a significant reform of the Brandenburg administration and began his very active correspondence with the ruling princes of Europe and their ministers. Since 1651 he had been in continuous contact with Cardinal Mazarin. In 1656 he arranged an alliance with Sweden, and commanded the Brandenburg cavalry in the Battle of Warsaw against Poland (1656). He was dismissed in 1657 after the peace between Brandenburg and Poland. Then he served under Charles X Gustav of Sweden against Denmark, and later as *Feldmarschall* in 1664 at Szentgotthárd in the *Deutsche Allianz*. Again in Dutch service in 1672–79, in 1683 he commanded the *Reich*'s troops during the campaign to relieve Vienna. After Prince William of Orange left for England in 1688 to claim the English throne, Waldeck was appointed *Veldmaarschalk* (Field Marshal) of the Dutch Army. He pursued a foreign policy trying to forge a coalition with the Protestant princes against the Emperor, but in the 1680s, he changed to the Austrian Habsburgs side.

Count Heinrich VI of Reuss (1649–1697), in a portrait dating to the 1680s
The military career was attractive and profitable but dangerous. Count Heinrich entered the military profession in 1672 as a military entrepreneur for Münster, Austria and for other states. In 1684, he was appointed *Generalwachtmeister* of the Imperial Army, serving until he died of wounds received at the Battle of Zenta, fought on 11 September 1697. (photo Author's collection. Current location of the portrait unknown)

2

The German Chessboard

In 1648, the Peace of Westphalia brought an end to the Thirty Years' War, and in the legislators' wishes there was above all an intention of preventing any future recurrence of similarly disastrous conflicts in Germany. The war had deeply scarred the consciences of the contemporaries, and the literature published in those years bears witness to the fact that, at least in the more educated classes, the horrors caused by the conflict generated an actual anthropological mutation in Germany comparable to the World War Two. The settlement had forced a drastic change in the Empire's structure in order to prevent the Habsburgs from controlling the Imperial 'Military' and repeating the disasters of the Thirty Years' War.[1] Now, the Empire was to constitute a system to guarantee the collective security of its members and the resolution of internal conflicts, within which the different traditions, religions and orders were to coexist.[2]

For the diplomacies of seventeenth century Europe, this set-up was also to preserve the Empire from outside attack without becoming a danger to neighbouring states. All decisions concerning the use of troops were to be made by the *Reichstag* (the Imperial Diet), leaving the Emperor only a formal right of veto over the resulting resolutions. The Emperor was also obliged to consult the Electors before issuing a decree against any foreign powers. The confirmation of the sovereignty of the Electors and other princes consolidated the monopoly of local powers, although leaving many questions concerning their international legal status unresolved. This ambiguity allowed many princes to carve out a role for themselves with increasing autonomy and also permitted the birth and consolidation of regional armed forces that were completely independent and detached from the original military context of the *Kreis*, which were transformed after 1648 into an instrument

1 Peter H. Wilson, *German Armies. War and German Politics, 1648–1806* (London: UCL Press, 1998), p.14: 'Collective security only emerged as a major issue from the early sixteenth century, for until the appearance of the Ottoman threat on the eastern frontier, the greatest danger to peace appeared to come from the internal feuding of knights and princes.'

2 Gerhard Papke 'Von der Miliz zum Stehenden Heer. Wehrwesen in Absolutismus' in G. Papke and W. Petter (eds) *Deutsche Militär-Geschichte. 1648–1939* (Munich: Bernhard & Graefe, 1983), vol. I, p.19.

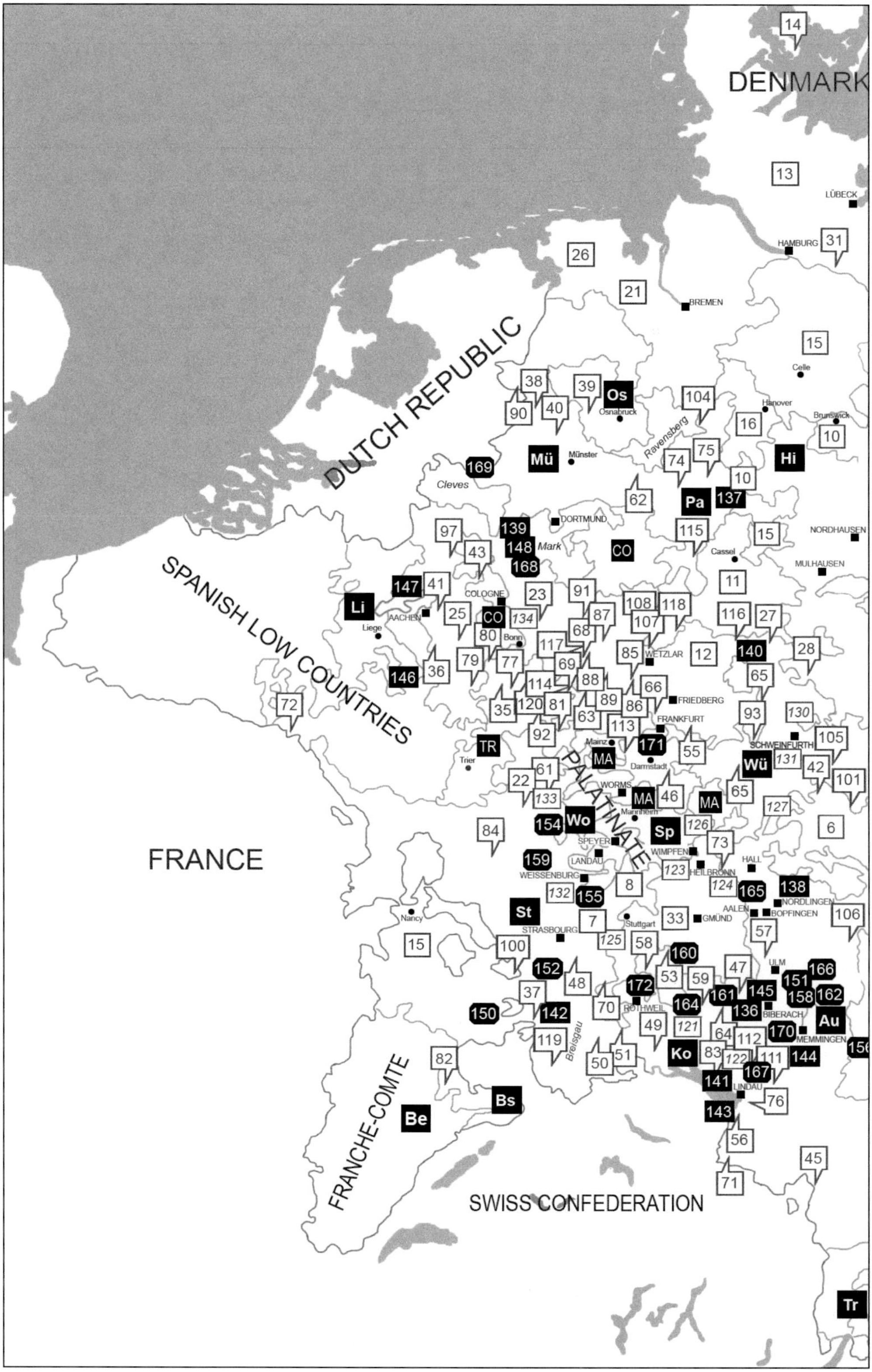

The German Empire: The 'Immediate States' in 1649.

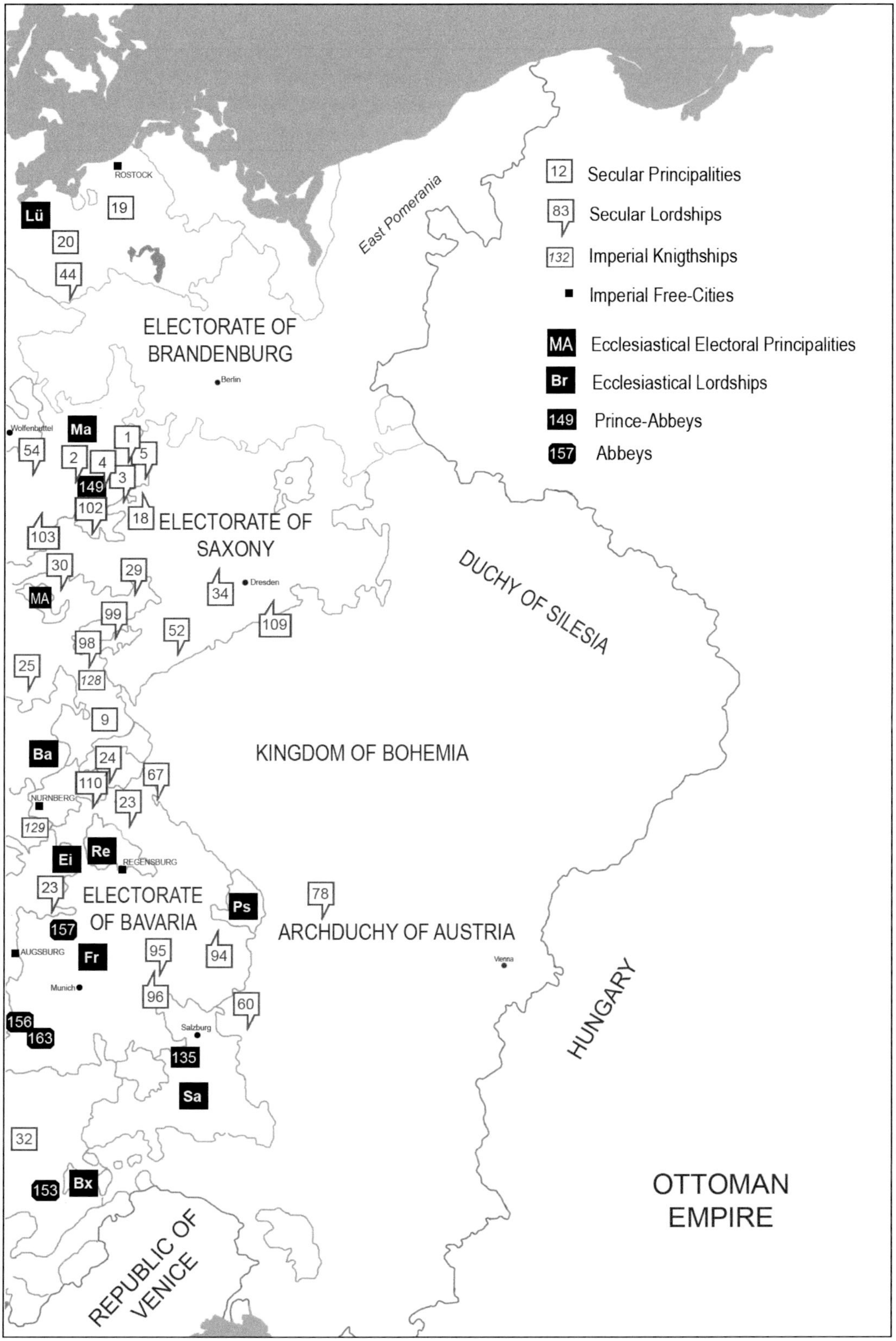
12 Secular Principalities
83 Secular Lordships
132 Imperial Knigthships
Imperial Free-Cities
MA Ecclesiastical Electoral Principalities
Br Ecclesiastical Lordships
149 Prince-Abbeys
157 Abbeys
ROSTOCK
East Pomerania
Lü
19
20
44
ELECTORATE OF BRANDENBURG
Berlin
Wolfenbüttel
Ma
54
1
2
4
5
3
149
102
18
103
ELECTORATE OF SAXONY
30
29
MA
34
Dresden
109
99
52
98
25
128
9
DUCHY OF SILESIA
Ba
24
KINGDOM OF BOHEMIA
110
67
NURNBERG
23
129
Ei
Re
REGENSBURG
23
ELECTORATE OF BAVARIA
Ps
78
157
ARCHDUCHY OF AUSTRIA
AUGSBURG
Fr
95
94
Vienna
Munich
96
60
HUNGARY
156
163
Salzburg
135
Sa
32
153
Bx
OTTOMAN EMPIRE
REPUBLIC OF VENICE

to control relations between states.[3] Prohibitions to this effect were written into the *Wahlkapitulationen* (electoral agreements) containing concessions wrung from each new Emperor by the Electors, while the *Instrumentum Pacis Osnabrugensis* (the section of the Westphalian Settlement dealing with Germany) imposed additional restrictions obliging the Emperor to seek *Reichstag* approval before sanctioning a full *Reichskrieg* effort (Imperial War). Federalism and Imperial absolutism threatened this emphasis on peaceful adherence to accepted norms and collective neutrality because they both contained elements of particularism inclined to belligerence. In an example of how German political development could move in opposite directions simultaneously, both the Westphalian settlements also gave federalism a boost by confirming princely territorial sovereignty, but nonetheless, the princes were identified as the sole representative of their territories. Moreover, territorial rulers were permitted to make treaties with foreign powers provided these were not directed against the Emperor.

Landgrave Georg II of Hessen-Darmstadt with his wife and children in a print by Johann Schweitzer. (Author's collection) Far from being the 'cut-price Louis XIVs' of popular mythology, German Princes did not seek political change in emulation of foreign models but refashioned their territories by internal administrative consolidation and exclusion of external influence only when they encountered obstacles to the achievement of their ambitions. None of these went as far as desiring full independence since even the strongest prince still derived his security and prestige from continued membership of a polity ruled by Europe's premier monarch. What each sought was an adjustment of the territorial and political balance in his favour, while denying similar advantages to his rivals.

3 Peter H. Wilson, *German Armies. War and German Politics, 1648–1806* (London: UCL Press, 1998), p.12.

Engraving by Johann Stephan Burgermeister, from the *Codex Diplomaticus Equestris cum Continuatione, oder Reichs-Ritter-Archiv* (Ulm, early eighteenth century), representing the various circles of the *Reichs-Ritterschaft* (Imperial Knightships). Among the less powerful Princes of the Empire, the Imperial Knights occupied a special position for they did not achieve representation with *Sitz und Stimme* (seat and talk) in the Diet or in the assemblies of the Circles. During the sixteenth century, the knights had developed increasingly formal corporative bodies, culminating in the establishment of three *Ritterkreise* – in Swabia, Franconia, and the Rhineland. These were subdivided into cantons each with its own director, directorate, or ruling council, and non-noble legal and clerical staff. A *Generaldirektorium*, which represented the interests of all the Imperial Knights at Vienna and kept a vigilant eye on the composition of the higher courts of the *Reich*, rotated between the three *Ritterkreise*. They provided both a means of making collective representations to the Emperor and a way of organising the contributions that the knights collectively paid to him. At the same time, the fact that these monies were not agreed via the Empire's Diet or the Circle assemblies further set the Imperial Knights apart from the Imperial Estates, for the Knights insisted that their payments were voluntary contributions, rather than taxes. Attempts by the Knights to become Imperial Estates in the 1650s, and the 1680s failed. As Princes of the Empire, they could contribute to the Empire contingents, as the Swabian Imperial Knights did in the 1680s. They consented to the inclusion of their 220 infantry in the *Reichsarmee*, although they were under no obligation to cooperate

Confirmation of territorial sovereignty consolidated the princes' monopoly of domestic power but left their international status still in doubt. The ambiguous status of the lesser German dynasties as autonomous vassals of a man still claiming European overlordship made their position acutely vulnerable. Increasingly, it seemed that possession of a Royal title, whether created within the Empire or acquired by inheritance or conquest outside it, offered the surest way to securing a place alongside the other sovereign powers, and this explains what has been labelled the 'monarchisation' of German dynastic ambition in the later seventeenth century.[4] In this scenario, the Princes began to exclude local bodies like the estates, which claimed the right to conduct internal and external relations. Competition for status was not confined to the most powerful states. It was also characteristic of the ecclesiastical territories, such as Münster, Cologne, Mainz and other smaller principalities. Achievement of such goals required resource mobilisation fuelling the growth of princely absolutism, and as a result, German involvement in international conflict continued after 1648, and it was the very dynastic-territorial situation of the Empire that made Germany an ideal battleground. The presence of a multitude of 'immediate' states with hundreds of small enclaves appeared as a kind of land Tortuga, into which the ambitions and strategies of neighbouring powers could easily intrude.

Leagues and Alliances

The outlook of the Westphalian settlements was not promising at first, since the dislike of the Habsburgs remained strong among the German Princes, and the common desire for security led many into regional alliances that were also anti-Austrian in their basic tendency. In Lower Saxony, Westphalia, the Upper Rhine, and Franconia there was an early revival of the existing Circle organisations, with a particular anti-Habsburgs impetus particularly in Lower Saxony. Other principalities also formed leagues and unions. In August 1650, the Elector of Mainz proposed an Association of the Electoral Rhenish and Upper Rhine principalities to secure the region from the Franco-Spanish war still going on immediately to the west. The plan was welcomed and in the spring of 1651, Mainz, Trier, and Cologne formed the 'League of Frankfurt' with some princes and republics of the Upper Rhine Circle. Similar agreements came about in the following years with the initiatives of the Princes of Brunswick and others, notably the omnipresent Prince-Bishop Elector of Cologne, Maximilian Heinrich von Wittelsbach.[5] In December 1654, the Northern and Rhineland Catholic states formed the 'Alliance of Cologne', comprising Electoral Cologne, Trier, Münster, and Pfalz-Newburg, and were joined the following year by the Electorate of Mainz. All these treaties were defensive, binding the signatories only to hold

4 Evan Luard, *The Balance of Power: the System of International Relations, 1648–1815* (London: Palgrave Macmillan, 1992), pp.149–173.

5 See also Bruno Mugnai, *Wars and Soldiers in the Early reign of Louis XIV, volume 7: German Armies 1655–1690, part 1* (Warwick: Helion & Company, 2024), pp.20–21.

troops in readiness to prevent possible Austrian assistance from interfering in the Burgundian Circle, which was essentially a Spanish territory.

All the alliances that involved the Rhineland territories were short-lived, but in some ways they were more successful than the Protestant associations in the north. There were three reasons for that. Firstly, many of these territories felt themselves to be acutely vulnerable, as they were close to the continuing conflict between France and Spain in the Low Countries. Many were also either small or were fragmented, which generally made them more dependent on the *Reich* than larger and more consolidated territories. Secondly, the most important ruler of such a fragmented territory was Johann Philipp von Schönborn (r. 1647–1673), Elector and Archbishop of Mainz. As director of the administration of the *Reich*, Schönborn saw himself as the representative of all the Imperial Estates, the figurehead of the Empire in the sovereign constitutional entity of *Kaiser und Reich*.[6] As the official 'number two' in the *Reich*, Schönborn was the natural leader of all gatherings and alliances in Germany that did not involve the Emperor. It was therefore logical that Schönborn perennially sought to consolidate the various alliances and leagues in order to provide security against a Habsburg revival and to ensure that the *Reich* was not dragged into a new conflict on behalf of Spain.[7]

Prince-Bishop Elector Johann Philipp von Schönborn, engraved by Caspar Merian in the *Beschreibung und Abbildung Aller Königl. und Churfürstl. Ein-Züge, Wahl und Crönungs Acta* (Frankfurt am Main: 1657)
Proclaimed as 'the Caton of Germany' or 'the German Solomon' by his contemporaries, he came from a family of officials with a tradition of service in Mainz and Trier. His temperament inclined him towards peaceful resolution of conflict by acceptable compromises. The Elector also played an important part in negotiating the final settlement of Westphalia. Though Johann Philipp initially worked with France to counter Austrian Habsburgs influence in the *Reich*, he became a reliable ally of the Emperor after the dissolution of the Rhenish League in 1668, thus establishing a tradition followed by successive generations of the Schönborn family, and the family developed into a fundamentally pro-Habsburg dynasty, which occupied important positions in the Imperial Church in successive generations. Promotion of other members followed, and the dynasty produced another Elector of Mainz and a number of Ecclesiastical and Imperial office-holders over the next century.

6 Georg Mentz, *Johann Philipp von Schönborn: Kurfürst von Mainz, Bischof von Würzburg und Worms: 1605–1673*, band 1, (Jena: Gustav Fischer, 1896), p.54.

7 Joachim Whaley, *Germany and the Holy Roman Empire. Vol. 2: from the Peace of Westphalia to the Dissolution of the Reich. 1648–1806* (Oxford & New York: Oxford University Press, 2012), p.11.

The third reason, the influence and involvement of France, acted as a stabilising factor during the 1650s. Under Mazarin, until his death in 1661, French policy sought influence in, rather than expansion in, the Empire. As for concerns over the Swedish presence in Northern Germany, this became sensitive after 1655, when Sweden and Brandenburg attacked Poland and in turn Denmark intervened to support the Polish Commonwealth. The scenario became very sensitive, since some Lower Saxony principalities offered their support to Sweden for expelling the Danes from Bremenwörde. Though Imperial institutions cooperated with the northern German principalities in declaring most of Lower Saxony neutral,[8] it proved impossible to prevent the conflict spreading to Mecklenburg and Holstein-Gottorf, particularly as the Emperor himself was a belligerent from 1657.

The key objectives were thus creating security and stability on the western and northern frontiers, preventing the resurgence of Habsburg authority in Germany, and preventing their intervention in the ongoing conflict with Spain, which was eventually concluded by the Peace of the Pyrenees in 1659. The interests of Mazarin and Schönborn were thus well aligned, and reached their most perfect expression in the formation in 1658 of the *Rheinbund*, or 'Rhenish League', which was dedicated to collective security and the Empire's reform.

The immediate impetus for the League's formation was the interregnum after the death of Ferdinand III in April 1657. The election of Leopold I the following August secured the continuity of Habsburg rule, but it was immediately countered by a league formed by Mainz, Cologne, Pfalz-Neuburg, Hessen-Kassel, Brunswick-Lüneburg-Celle and Calenberg (Hannover), and Brunswick-Wolfenbüttel. One year later, on the initiative of Cardinal Mazarin, France joined the League – as the guarantor of the Westphalia Treaty – and later Sweden, as the ruler of the territories of Verden and Bremen, became a member as well. Brandenburg and others joined in the coming years bringing the number of members to 18 in all; by 1665, all of the leading Princes of the Empire, except the Electors of Bavaria, Saxony, and the Palatinate were members. The two Margraves of Baden also applied but were refused membership because of their exorbitant demands. [9]

Schönborn diplomacy skills succeeded in combining both Catholics and Protestants in a Union dedicated to upholding the Peace of Westphalia. Although this, the *Corpus Catholicorum*, even directed by the Elector of Mainz, was dominated by a majority of Catholic bishops and prelates who remained fundamentally loyal to Vienna.[10] The 'military' members contributed money and/or men to a peacekeeping force of 10,000 men (including 2,400 French soldiers) that was also intended to block any attempt to send Imperial troops to the Spanish Low Countries. This secured the Empire until the Peace of the

8 Peter H. Wilson, *German Armies. War and German Politics, 1648–1806* (London: UCL Press, 1998), p.37.

9 Peter H. Wilson, *German Armies. War and German Politics, 1648–1806* (London: UCL Press, 1998), p.171.

10 Joachim Whaley, *Germany and the Holy Roman Empire. Vol. 2: from the Peace of Westphalia to the Dissolution of the Reich. 1648–1806* (Oxford-New York, NY: Oxford University Press, 2012), p.12.

Pyrenees in 1659, but just one year later, a new agreement was established to raise a field force of 4,120 horse and 8,500 foot, which had to remain separate from the Imperial Circle system, and was assigned to separate commanders.[11] At first sight there seems little to connect the Rhenish League with either the earlier or later leagues and associations, and it has often been dismissed simply as a device to advance French interests in the Rhineland, but since its beginnings the Rhenish League appeared as very strong and cohesive, and the members had good reason to stay with it: France was welcomed by the Catholics as a counterweight to Sweden; the Brunswick duchies were persuaded to join because France backed their policy of neutralising the Lower Saxon Circle during the Second Northern War of 1655–1660 to prevent either Brandenburg or Denmark establishing a larger territorial presence there; the ecclesiastical Electorates took advantage of the network of relations to impose more restriction on the Emperor; Sweden achieved the express aim of politically paralysing the Habsburgs, or at the very least keeping the Emperor in check; France could penetrate into German affairs more deeply, favouring the activity of French agents at many German courts, as proved in the 1650s and 1660s by the appointment of envoys at Dresden and Berlin.

Archduke Sigmund Franz of Habsburg-Tyrol (1630–1665), Prince of the Empire and last sovereign of Tyrol and Anterior Austria, portrait by Giovanni Maria Morandi. (Kunsthistorisches Museum, Vienna. Public domain). Appointed Bishop of Augsburg in 1646, in 1653 he also became Bishop of Gurk, and in 1659 Bishop of Trent, all despite never being ordained as a priest or consecrated as a bishop. In 1662, after the death of his brother Ferdinand Carl he returned to Innsbruck to assume the title of Archduke, but with his early death in 1665 the Tyrolean line of the Habsburg House ended, and the territories passed to the senior line of Austrian Habsburgs. In 1648, Archduke Ferdinand Carl sold the territory of Breisach to France, which retained it until 1697. Thanks to this enclave, the French could easily move troops in the Empire, threatening Swabia and Anterior Austria.

In 1662, as the situation in the war against the Ottomans in Hungary worsened, Austria became increasingly vulnerable to pressure from the German Princes, who rallied behind Schönborn and made their military allegiance a condition of the convening of a new *Reichstag*. Scheduled originally for June, the assembly finally met on 20 January 1663. Exploiting his capacity as Arch-Chancellor (*Erzkanzler* in German and *Archicancellarius* in Latin) to subvert procedural rules, Schönborn tabled a reform of collective security for discussion alongside Leopold's simple call for increased cash contributions. Using the existing framework of the Rhenish League as a model for a new army, independent

11 Peter H. Wilson, *German Armies. War and German Politics, 1648–1806* (London: UCL Press, 1998), p.172.

of direct Imperial command, Schönborn proposed revising the matricular system to support a force of 4,000 cavalry and 10,000 infantry controlled by a war council to be based in Frankfurt. The Alliance immediately issued detailed instructions to its members to regulate transit, billeting and all matters of supply and payment of their contingents. Articles of War were issued to provide the basis of a disciplining code, while a general auditor was appointed to oversee a common system of martial law. Provisions were also made for unified command.

Discussions were further complicated by a parallel debate on other matters,[12] but the panic following the rapid Ottoman advance and the Tatar raids in summer 1663, transformed the political situation. Although suspicious of the Austrian Habsburgs, the League members realised that it was better to deal with a weak Austrian Emperor, rather than a powerful Ottoman Sultan and, therefore, consolidated their efforts to set up military support for Hungary. Even the French envoys no longer believed the Emperor was merely trying to turn the crisis to his political advantage. Emperor Leopold I was compelled to compromise, agreeing to the Rhenish League's terms on 11 July 1663, permitting the members to field their contingents as a separate army, which would be immediately sent to the front. Before the end of the year, the Imperial Diet convened at Regensburg. In a brilliant piece of stage management, Leopold I broke the deadlock by arriving in person on 22 December in Regensburg. Encouraged by his presence, and alarmed by the Ottoman advance, the other Princes followed suit, gathering in the Imperial Free City for personal talks with Leopold. By publicly thanking Schönborn for his efforts, and promising further discussion on outstanding issues, Leopold avoided the need for a final decision and secured substantial support from those territories that had not already sent troops to the *Deutsche Allianz*.[13]

In early 1664, infantry from Celle, Hessen-Kassel and Trier marched to Hungary, where they were attached to the troops already under the command of *Generalleutnant* Wolfgang Julius von Hohenlohe.

This contingent headed to Croatia, participating, in conjunction with the *Grenzer* forces and Croatian-Hungarian militia of count Miklós Zrínyi, at the siege of Szeged.[14] Other units reached the theatre of war in the following spring, increasing the *Deutsche Allianz* forces available to a field strength of just under 8,000 men.[15] The last troops to arrive in Hungary camped between Komárom and the Schutt, under Georg Friedrich von Waldeck, at that time one of the arch-enemies of the Habsburgs. These troops had been recruited mainly from Mainz, Lower Saxony and Münster; among the

---

12 Whaley, *Germany and the Holy Roman Empire*, p.67. The separate matter concerned the permanent electoral capitulation. A proposal was being pushed forward, by the Protestant princes to define the powers of future Emperors in a single document. If the proposals were not considered, they threatened to withdraw.

13 *New Cambridge Modern History*, 'The Ascendancy of France, 1648–1688' (Cambridge: Cambridge University Press, 1968), vol. V, p.491.

14 Gustav Payer, *Armati Hungarorum* (Munich: Körösi Csoma Sándor, 1985), p.107.

15 Peter H. Wilson, *German Armies. War and German Politics, 1648–1806* (London: UCL Press, 1998), p.42.

Count Wolfgang Julius von Hohenlohe-Neuenstein (1622–1698) was archetypal of the small German nobility who entered the military career in the seventeenth century. Educated as a man of letters and soldiers, Hohenlohe had a very turbulent adolescence. He had to end his studies at the University of Tübingen prematurely, because during the Thirty Years' War, the family fled from Hohenlohe to Ohrdruf. In 1637, the 15-year-old was captured having been wounded in the face by a grazing shot. In 1641, he hurried to the Imperial Diet in Regensburg, where his father was dying after suffering a stroke, and Hohenlohe brought the body back to the family home. In 1643, he went on tour to France. In order to earn money, he joined the Régiment Rantzau incognito as a simple trooper. After becoming commander of a squadron, he identified himself as a member of the House of Hohenlohe and was appointed colonel of a regiment of German cavalry by Gaston, Duc d'Orléans. He won the favour of the Duc's daughter, Anne-Marie-Louise of Montpensier, who was commonly known as *La Grande Mademoiselle*. During the French civil war, known as the Fronde, the Duc d'Orléans initially sided with the court party, but then switched to the aristocratic party with the Prince de Condé. Under d'Orléans' leadership, Wolfgang Julius became embroiled in intrigues and finally tried to leave the army without authorisation, which earned him seven months' imprisonment in Antwerp. He was only able to return home in 1657 after the intercession of several German Princes. There he became *Generalleutnant* of the troops of the Rhenish Alliance in 1658 for his knowledge of French affairs. In the same year he was present at the Imperial election in Frankfurt. For his skill as a general, Louis XIV received him in person in 1662 and he met his former patroness, the Duchesse de Montpensier, who awarded him an annual pension for his services to the French Army. However, the pension was only paid to him for eight years. In 1663, he was appointed as commander of the *Deutsche Allianz* for the Hungarian campaign against the Ottoman Porte.

cavalry there was even a squadron from Sweden.[16] The composition of these units appeared to be quite heterogeneous; while the cavalry had squadrons of unequal strength but were still of a uniform nationality. Infantry battalions were assembled by combining the companies of different contingents; such as the infantry regiment *Leyen*, which was mainly composed of soldiers from Münster, amalgamated with companies from Trier and Cologne.[17] Some of these states' contingents, though forming part of the *Reichsarmee*, were split under separate commands. In other circumstances, some princes changed their individual contributions as they wished. Mainz replaced his 300 cavalry by twice the number of foot soldiers, as did the two Landgraves of Hessen. All these troops suffered a great deal from the climate in Hungary and were more than decimated by disease. Most of them manned the border fortresses and only a small percentage actually participated in the field operation of 1664.[18]

Despite the poor performance in the Hungarian campaign, the *Deutsche Allianz* proved capable of assembling a significant military force, especially with the support of France.[19] As a consequence, the Sun King became de facto the actual master of the Alliance being the prince with the most powerful army in Europe. The increasing French influence became clear to all in October 1664, when 6,000 French soldiers joined the Allies for the siege of Mainz's exclave of Erfurt, which had rebelled against the Elector: after the Hungarian campaign, the presence of French troops in the heart of the Empire resounded in Vienna as an outrage.[20] The tension between Schönborn and the Emperor also affected the dealings of the *Rheinbund*, and renewed confessional tensions soon began to undermine the league's solidarity. The Elector of Mainz himself contributed to this when he enlisted the league's forces to suppress the liberties of the Protestant Erfurt, whose forcible 'reduction' outraged many Protestant princes.

However, in the long run the connection with France proved a serious liability. The Rhenish League was rapidly undermined when Louis XIV embarked on a more aggressive foreign policy. This was one of the reasons for the League's collapse by 1668, since it was already clear that the organisation was incapable of serving as a viable alternative to the *Reichstag*. Schönborn had already abandoned this element of his programme by 1662 and joined the others calling for the Imperial Diet to reassemble, and led the League into the treaty providing military support for the Emperor against the Ottomans. The Rhenish League faced another problem as, by 1665, serious tensions were emerging between the Dutch Republic, France, Münster and Brandenburg.

16 Kurt Peball, 'Die Schlacht bei St. Gotthard-Mogersdorf, 1664' in *Militärhistorische Schriftenreihe* (Vienna: 1964), p.28.

17 Georg Tessin, 'Reichsarmee und Allianzkorps im Türkenfeldzug 1663/64', in *Zeitschrift für Heereskunde*, VII, (Hamburg: Deutsche Gesellschaft für Heereskunde, 1983).

18 Galeazzo Gualdo Priorato, *Historia di Leopoldo Cesare* (Vienna, 1670), vol. II, p.322.

19 By the summer of 1664, the French contingent in Hungary comprised 4,000 infantry and 2,000 cavalry, including 300 mounted aristocratic volunteers. See Peball, 'Die Schlacht bei St. Gotthard-Mogersdorf, 1664', pp.6–7.

20 Peter H. Wilson, *German Armies. War and German Politics, 1648–1806* (London: UCL Press, 1998), p.32.

French diplomats manipulated Schönborn's eagerness for peace as a cloak for their own objectives, using him as an unwitting front man in the 1666 Cleves Conference to resolve the Anglo-Dutch-Münster War, and after 1667 in Mainz and Cologne's efforts to end the War of Devolution.[21]

The decline of the Rhenish League favoured the genesis of other alliances formed between its members and other German princes. Pacts of mutual assistance were signed between 1660 and 1667 by the Duke of Brunswick, the Hohenzollerns of Franconia and Brandenburg, and by Electoral Cologne, Pfalz-Neuburg and the Bishopric of Strasbourg. The latter alliance was expressly signed as an 'armed neutrality' to secure the common Rhine border from the French troops marching into Flanders.[22]

The siege of Douai, July 1667, an episode of the opening campaign of the War of Devolution, in a copy of the Gobelin tapestry after van der Meulen. (Public Domain)

When the War of Devolution broke out in 1667, the Imperial Diet was confronted with the question whether the Spanish Low Countries, which formed the Burgundian Circle of the Empire, should be protected. The French Ambassador used all the means at his disposal to prevent such a decision, while the Imperial representative, the Archbishop of Salzburg, tried to counteract his influence. Meanwhile Louis XIV conquered town after town, but the Imperial Diet remained silent. In September, the Electors pronounced in favour of mediation, ignoring the question of whether the Spanish Low Countries formed a part of the Empire. Among the princes, the Salzburg resolution which affirmed the latter point obtained only 30 votes, while 41 were in favour of mediation and 13 without any instructions, abstained.

21 Joachim Whaley, *Germany and the Holy Roman Empire. Vol. 2: from the Peace of Westphalia to the Dissolution of the Reich. 1648–1806* (Oxford-New York, NY: Oxford University Press, 2012), p.33.

22 On this alliance see Oskar Bezzel, *Geschichte des Kurpfälzischen Heeres von Seinen Anfängen bis zur Vereinigung von Kurpfalz und Kurbayern* (Munich: Lindauer LTR-Verl, 1925), band I, p.153.

In 1667, the French assault on the Spanish Low Countries removed the common ground by alarming the Rhenish principalities, who had feared that they might be Louis's next victims, and signalling the start of the new French method of managing German politics after 1668 through bilateral alliances with key princes. The emergence of this pro-French group is an indication that the Schönborn era was drawing to a close. Soon, Louis XIV's increase in predominance in Germany revealed the fragility of the Rhenish League's system, bringing the Alliance to collapse. These difficulties coincided with the failure of Schönborn's efforts at international peace-making, which were related to the Alliance's nominal stance as a neutral 'third party' between the Habsburgs and Bourbons.[23] The French occupation of Lorraine in August 1670 removed one of Schönborn's major supporters and neutralised the army which he thought to exploit as a core of the new military alliance.

In its final version, in early August 1670, the proposed new 'League of Schwalbach' based on a plan that required each member should have one vote in return for providing 1,000 men to the common army. Though Leopold I was offered two votes, the League was to keep its distance from the Emperor's control by maintaining its own permanent directory and war council in Frankfurt. Like the Rhenish League, it was hoped that the new organisation would allow Schönborn to preserve peace by holding the ring in Imperial and international politics.[24] As Schönborn's project faltered and French diplomatic activity increased, many of those who wanted peace moved closer to France through the new bilateral subsidy treaties, as occurred with Bavaria, Pfalz-Neuburg, Electoral Cologne, Münster, Brandenburg, Hannover, and Osnabrück, which became the basis for French attempts to influence German politics in anticipation of the planned invasion of the Dutch Republic. Schönborn's policy had depended on subsuming 'particularist' ambitions in a single alliance, coordinating all efforts towards the twin goals of peace and security, but it proved impossible for him to reassemble the pieces of the Rhenish League after its collapse in 1668.

Between 1669 and 1673 no less than seven different initiatives were launched by princes, all seeking a medium that would enhance their say in Imperial politics while providing security against the risks that this inevitably involved. These initiatives included the revival of the 1650s 'Extensionist League', which included Bavaria, Cologne, Brandenburg, Pfalz-Neuberg and Mecklenburg-Schwerin. They carried the Imperial Diet, which endorsed their

23 'Undaunted by these setbacks, Schönborn tried to link the Peace of Aachen (1668) with his old project of a general guarantee for the Westphalian Settlement to be signed by the Triple Alliance, the Emperor and the German princes. Princely interests were to be safeguarded by a new military alliance to uphold the guarantee which was to extend to both the Burgundian *Kreis* and the territory of his ally, the Hertzog van Lorraine. It is only in retrospect that it is easy to dismiss these ideas as Utopian: to Schönborn and many of his contemporaries, such schemes were the very essence of Imperial politics. However, French opposition and the Elector's own protracted dispute with the Palatinate condemned the plan to failure.' Peter H. Wilson, *German Armies. War and German Politics, 1648–1806* (London: UCL Press, 1998), p.174.

24 Derek McKay, 'Small-power diplomacy in the age of Louis XIV: the foreign policy of the Great Elector during the 1660s and 1670s', in R. Oresko et al. (editors), *Royal and Republican Sovereignty in Early Modern Europe,* (Cambridge: Cambridge University Press, 1997), pp.188–215.

proposals.[25] After this was vetoed by Leopold I in 1671, the members agreed to establish a common force of 20,000 men to crush potential opposition within their territories and reinforce their lobbying of the Emperor.

This was followed by the 'Brunswick Union' of September 1672, signed by the Emperor with the Duke of Brunswick-Wolfenbüttel, Lüneburg-Celle, Brandenburg, Denmark, and in 1674 by Hessen-Kassel. Its short existence, however, was more a demonstration of political solidarity, since the Alliance had little military significance.[26]

Before the end of 1673, another project of common Alliance was discussed by the South German Circles, followed by the northern 'Quedlinburg Association' (1673) and by a series of schemes sponsored by Pfalz-Neuburg.[27] In this period, Schönborn was increasingly looking to the Emperor for leadership. In 1672, he promoted the 'Marienburg Alliance' formed in August after a long negotiation. This included Austria, Mainz, Trier, Saxony, the Imperial Cities of Frankfurt and Cologne, followed by Brandenburg-Bayreuth and Paderborn; even Münster, probably to hide the negotiations with France, entered the alliance. The members discussed assembling a force of 10,205 foot and horse.[28] It was also stipulated that states that did not contribute men or money to the formation of the contingent, had to bear the maintenance of the troops on campaign and in winter quarters. There was no independent directory, and the projected joint army numbered only 8,000 and never actually assembled, particularly as Münster openly joined Cologne and France in April 1672.

Following his alliance with Brandenburg in June 1672, Leopold I made his own treaty with the Dutch Republic on 25 July, placing him in a strong position to control the next princely initiative, which coalesced as the Union of Brunswick on 22 September 1672. Unlike the Marienburg Alliance, which was still attempting to incorporate Imperial Cities and minor principalities, this was an exclusive union of armed princes, pledging mutual assistance in the absence of a viable formal structure for common defence. However, Denmark and Brandenburg refused to cooperate unless their own territories were threatened, while Celle and Wolfenbüttel both made their own subsidy arrangements with the Dutch so that no Union army ever took the field. As a result, the membership was small and attempts to recruit other principalities such as Bavaria, Electoral Cologne and Hannover failed, as these were now secretly allied to France. Nonetheless, Trier did join, creating the possibility that Austria could merge the Brunswick Union and the Marienburg Alliance

---

25 Their members, known as *Extendisten*, focused on the economic issue, and wished to widen the legislation of 1654 and 1658 to remove all restraints on the princely monopoly of taxation.

26 Joachim Whaley, *Germany and the Holy Roman Empire. From the Peace of Westphalia to the Dissolution of the Reich, 1648–1806* (Oxford: Oxford University Press, 2012), pp.34–35.

27 The 'Quedlinburg Association' was promoted by the dukes of Wolfenbüttel and Celle, and joined by the lesser princes of Franconian and Swabian Circles. Later, this association evolved in the 'Laxemburg Allianz'; see also Bruno Mugnai, *Wars and Soldiers in the Early Reign of Louis XIV, volume 2: The Imperial Army 1657–1687* (Warwick: Helion & Company, 2019), pp.121–123.

28 Joachim Whaley, *Germany and the Holy Roman Empire. Vol. 2: from the Peace of Westphalia to the Dissolution of the Reich. 1648–1806* (Oxford-New York, NY: Oxford University Press, 2012), p.177.

under Leopold's leadership. The death of Schönborn and the temporary withdrawal of Brandenburg from the war by the Peace of Vossem on 6 June 1673 removed both the Alliance and the Union as active elements.

By this stage two new initiatives had emerged to challenge Leopold's control over events, both oriented to involve the Imperial Circles. Since 1667, Bavaria had been negotiating with Württemberg for a general pacification of Southern Germany, but turned this scheme to suit French interests after its bilateral alliance with Louis XIV in 1670. At a meeting at Dinkelsbühl in August 1673, Bavarian diplomats proposed an association of their own Circle with Swabia and Franconia to provide a basis for armed neutrality during the Franco-Dutch War. North German princes also moved closer within the Circle structure, building on the ties that had existed before the formal separation of the Upper and Lower Saxony in the sixteenth century. In 1672 both Circles agreed to extend their alliance to include Franconia, where the Saxon rulers shared some territories. The Upper and Lower Saxon Assemblies met in joint session in January 1673, formally establishing a common policy and sanctioning protection for the Bishopric of Hildesheim, which belonged to the pro-French Elector of Cologne.

Austrian diplomacy was able to smooth out vetoes on the Emperor's influence in the Alliance, sustaining the initiative of the Prince-Bishop of Bamberg, Peter Philipp von Dernbach. This latter steered the Franconian Circle into the Quedlinburg group at a meeting in Mühlhausen on 14 August 1673, thus frustrating Bavaria's efforts at Dinkelsbühl and providing a watchful eye on the pro-French Hannover's activities in Lower Saxony. The expanded Quedlinburg Association agreed a joint army of about 11,000 men in addition to the contribution to any *Reichsarmee*.[29] Dernbach pushed for the immediate dispatch of this force to the Rhine, but Swedish and Hannoverian machinations prevented agreement from the two Saxon Circles. However, a bilateral agreement between Leopold and Elector Johann Georg II of Saxony was concluded on 3 August 1673, after the latter's failure to form a firm connection with France.[30] To further strengthen the Alliance, the French occupation of Trier in September 1673 moved the lesser German principalities to join the new Association.

All the negotiations preceding the Empire's entry into the war, which finally declared the *Reichskrieg* against Louis XIV on 31 March 1674, came to a standstill during the following years, when the maintenance of allied soldiers became a serious problem for many of the states involved in the conflict. The principle that soldiers of 'armed states' would receive billets from

29 Richard Fester, *Die Armirten Stände und die Reichskriegsverfassung, 1681–1697* (Frankfurt am Main: Gebrüder Knauer (Druck) 1886), p 28.

30 'Austrian military operations were portrayed simply as efforts to restore the public peace within the *Reich* rather than formal war against France,' Peter H. Wilson, *German Armies. War and German Politics, 1648–1806* (London: UCL Press, 1998), p.46. The success of French diplomacy in manipulating the appeasement lobby amongst the princes ensured there was no prospect of persuading the *Reichstag* to declare war in 1673 even if this had been Leopold's intention. Despite a public show of concern for the areas ravaged by France, the Emperor had no desire to hand the princes another opportunity to extract formal concessions, while the lack of progress on matricular revision left it unlikely that such a move would produce the force required.

the 'unarmed' ones became unsustainable for the latter. The cost sustained for quartering the troops accelerated a political crisis, as the existing mechanism of mobilising collective defence proved incapable of meeting the French challenge.[31]

The political dangers presented by the new alliance had been neutralised, and although the two Saxon Circles ratified their cooperation in 1674 and 1675, the Quedlinburg group ceased to function as an autonomous body when the Saxons failed to respond to Franconia's call for assistance as Turenne appeared on the River Main in 1674.

The billeting crisis of winter 1676–1677 encouraged some princes to seek the cooperation of territories in a similar position, and led to a project for a combination of Mainz, Trier, Würzburg-Bamberg, Hessen-Kassel, Hessen-Darmstadt, the Ernestine Saxon duchies and Pfalz-Neuburg with a common army of 30,000 men, partly funded by Dutch and Spanish subsidies, to achieve collective 'armed states' title and end extortion by other powers. Although Hessen-Kassel and others opposed it, the project got some support from Hessen-Darmstadt and elsewhere, encouraging Duke Philipp Wilhelm of Pfalz-Neuburg to continue with this idea after spring 1678 and to include all the larger territories of Westphalia, Lower Saxony and the Electoral Rhine in an effort to impose peace west of the Rhine. This time he won the support of fellow Westphalian principalities, Friedrich Wilhelm of Brandenburg and Prince-Bishop Christoph Bernard of Münster, who saw it as a means of protecting their gains in Northern Germany from French intervention. It was agreed that the Westphalian Circle would contribute 15,000 men to a common force under Duke Ernst August of Osnabrück (by 1679 Duke of Hannover). Some troops did assemble along the western frontier but were unable to prevent the French threat into Westphalia in 1679 to compel Münster, Brandenburg and Celle to return their conquests to Sweden.

Außführlicher Discurs
Von den
Winterquartieren/
was dabey Gutes oder Böses
vorlauffet/ und wie dieselbe recht
einzurichten.
Gedruckt im Jahr Christi/ 1677.

First page of the *Außführlicher Discurs von den Winterquartieren was Dabey Gutes oder Böses Vorlauffet und wie Dieselbe Recht Einzurichten* (1677) (*Detailed Discourse On Winter Quarters, What is Good Or Bad About These and How to Set These Up Properly*) (Public domain). As was typical in the seventeenth century, troops were given billets providing food and shelter during the winter months. This consisted of beds (of straw), salt, wine (or beer), vinegar and firewood for cooking and candles for light.. Officers and horsemen also received fodder for their horses. All other necessities had to be paid for when they were not distributed by the magazines. Territories could choose to pay in cash rather than in kind. Usually, the choice was given to the commanders, who most often chose to receive cash.

After the Peace of Nijmegen, Leopold I was determined to retain full control over military policy management and peace-making. The Austrian diplomacy concealed the true intentions of the Emperor, who approached the *Reichstag* in October 1679 only for general advice as to how the French threat might be confronted. In December, the Elector of Mainz, Anselm Franz von Ingelheim, was prevented from tabling the question for open discussion on the grounds that the Emperor wished to consult the Electors first. Meanwhile, Vienna negotiated separately with the major princes, ostensibly for bilateral

31 See also Bruno Mugnai, *Wars and Soldiers in the Early Reign of Louis XIV, volume 2: The Imperial Army 1657–1687* (Warwick: Helion & Co. 2019), p.119.

Louis XIV performing the part of the sun in the *Ballet Royal de la Nuit*; illustration by Maurice Leloir for *Le Roi Soleil* by Gustave Toudouze. (Public domain)

The Franco-Dutch War had decreased the political influence of the pro-French princes in Germany, but after the Peace of Nijmegen in 1679, the diplomacy of Louis XIV managed to re-build a strong group of supporters, with Brandenburg among the most notable. As occurred before the war, the scions of the German Princes and nobility in their turn were sent to France to admire the marvel of Versailles and to study French accomplishments and manners at the source. The first performance of the Jean-Baptiste Lully's ballet *Le Triomphe de l'Amour* at Versailles in 1681 was attended by the Margrave of Ansbach, the Duke of Hanover, Holstein and Württemberg, among other princes.

defensive pacts, but really to create an alliance network that could be converted into a new system of collective security. The others princes were simply expected to fall in with whatever was decided.[32] On the other hand, France sought to frustrate this plan by a mixture of bribes and intimidation, hoping also to win the key princes over to a permanent recognition of the *Réunions*. In 1680, with French troops already across their frontiers, the four Rhenish Electors of Mainz, Trier, Cologne and the Palatinate wanted to do nothing that might antagonise Louis, and so rejected Leopold's offers of an alliance.

After Nijmegen, the danger of new wars was still strong. In 1682, after failing to subdue Hamburg in 1679, Denmark invaded Holstein-Gottorf. By the early 1680s large areas of the Lower Saxon, Upper and Electoral Rhenish Circles along with the remainder of Burgundy were occupied by foreign powers who were unlikely to respect their continued integration within The Empire. These developments were compounded by the collapse of collective security and the rise of the armed princes.[33]

Though this was not in line with his plans, Emperor Leopold I was compelled to change tack and consider the lesser princes' demands. One of the most active was Prince Georg Friedrich zu Waldeck, whose lands continued to suffer the depredations of the armed states, notably Münster. Predicting that France would exploit the disaffection of the lesser rulers to prevent unified opposition to the *Réunions*, Waldeck rallied 10 of the worst affected in a mutual assistance pact known as the Wetterau Union on 19 September 1679.[34]

Post-war aftermath saw the emerging of the Circles as subject to the raising permanent corps of troops, especially when Dernbach in Würzburg and Waldeck implemented their project in the Laxenburg Alliance, which included Franconia, Swabia and Upper Rhine principalities in a stronger *Reichsarmee*.[35] This project worked to Leopold's advantage by reducing the likelihood of autonomous princely alliances. Only the major princes, who were reluctant to contribute to the new defence structure, remained open to traditional alliances: who would want to enter into an arrangement obliging them to provide a contingent when they were already required to field one for

---

32 Peter H. Wilson, *German Armies. War and German Politics, 1648–1806* (London: UCL Press, 1998), p.178.

33 Peter H. Wilson, *German Armies. War and German Politics, 1648–1806* (London: UCL Press, 1998), p.59.

34 Whaley, *Germany and the Holy Roman Empire*, p 41: 'William III of Orange's family links with the Wetterau counts (of whom Waldeck was one) were initially instrumental in connecting the various elements of this new set of agreements.'

35 What made the Union significant was its unique military organisation. Instead of relying on the traditional contingent system, each member paid into a central treasury in Frankfurt that maintained a single integrated army with common arms, uniforms and drill under the unified command of Waldeck himself. Cf Bruno Mugnai, *Wars and Soldiers in the Early reign of Louis XIV, volume 2: The Imperial Army 1657–1687* (Warwick: Helion & Co., 2019), pp.108–121, and *Wars and Soldiers in the Early Reign of Louis XIV, volume 7: German Armies 1655–1690, part 1* (Warwick: Helion & C0., 2024), pp.24–25.

the *Reichsarmee*?[36] Leopold now sought to bring them on board by inviting them to field their armies within the overall system of collective security but outside the restrictive structure of the Circles. The Alliance envisaged the formation of three corps to defend the western frontier. The middle Rhine was to be held by the existing 18,000 strong Union and Franconian forces, assisted by 3,000 Imperial cavalry. A further 20,000 Imperialists were to guard the Upper Rhine, with 10,000 more troops to be provided by Electoral Bavaria and the Bavarian Circle, if these could be persuaded to join. Hannover and Saxony were invited to contribute the 20,000 needed to cover the northern sector.

Suspicions and mistrust emerged, but the Laxenburg Alliance managed to join Protestants and Catholics together in the plan; Dernbach, Waldeck and their allies, recognising the collective and important armed status while integrating their cross-regional grouping and the small Saxon principalities into a permanent organisation under the control of the *Reichstag* and Vienna too. Their plan received a new impulse in 1683, when the Ottoman offensive against Austria revealed the lack of cohesion among the major powers. Brandenburg was asked to participate but, mindful of its still valid treaty with France, set such an outrageous price, of 600,000 thaler for 12,000 men plus a whole series of territorial concessions for itself and religious guarantees for the Hungarian Calvinists, that a deal was impossible. Brandenburg's recalcitrance and loyalty to France also induced the Brunswick Dukes at Hannover, Celle, and Wolfenbüttel to remain passive.[37]

Throughout the years Bavaria, Hannover, Saxony and Brandenburg all signed separate treaties with the Emperor. With his objective achieved, Leopold had little interest in extending the group further, as this would diminish the pool of potential winter quarters for the Alliance troops. Despite the failure to renew the Alliance when it expired in 1685, the League of Augsburg signed on 9 July 1686 duplicated its structure and allowed Leopold I to retain enough control.[38] Intended to provide 58,000 men to defend South Germany against potential French aggression, the figure was soon revised to 41,000, of which 25,000 were to be provided by the German states.[39] Sweden joined, promising an unspecified number on behalf of its German territories, while separate treaties with Saxony and Brandenburg ensured some protection for the north. The Burgundian Circle had at last

36 Peter H. Wilson, *German Armies. War and German Politics, 1648–1806* (London: UCL Press, 1998), p.180.

37 Joachim Whaley, *Germany and the Holy Roman Empire. From the Peace of Westphalia to the Dissolution of the Reich, 1648–1806* (Oxford: Oxford University Press, 2012), p.42.

38 Richard Fester, *Die Augsburger Allianz von 1686* (Munich: Rieger, 1893), pp.23–24. 'The formation of the League of Augsburg seemed to confirm Leopold's growing hold over the Empire and prompted intensified French efforts to win over the key princes during 1687–1688. Despite renewing offers of diplomatic and financial support for princely ambitions, negotiations in Bavaria, Brandenburg, Hannover, Württemberg and elsewhere failed to secure firm support. Louis continued to underestimate the resentment aroused by the *Réunions*, which had deprived several potential allies of parts of their territory.' Peter H. Wilson, *German Armies. War and German Politics, 1648–1806* (London: UCL Press, 1998), p.87:

39 Richard Fester, *Die Armirten Stände und die Reichskriegsverfassung, 1681–1697* (Frankfurt am Main: Gebrüder Knauer (Druck) 1886), p.70.

been included, extending collective security westward across the Rhine. Although commanders were appointed, no troops took position, but the League's importance remained politically. The defence plans remained only partially implemented, while Vienna's control over the armed princes hung precariously on its ability to manipulate their conflicting ambitions. These underlying weaknesses were exposed when French armies invaded the Rhineland late in 1688.

The crisis merely vindicated what the armed states had been arguing all along; the small principalities were clearly unable to defend themselves and should pay those whose economies of scale enabled them to field effective fighting forces. The immediate consequence was the Magdeburg Concert, formed in October 1688 by the northern and central German armed princes for securing the Rhine. While Brandenburg assisted the Dutch Republic to defend the Lower Rhine, a second army would be sent to clear the French from the middle Rhine. Arrangements were made to quarter the latter force on the line of the Main-Tauber rivers at the expense of the local inhabitants until the start of offensive operations in the spring. The armies would comprise troops from Brandenburg, Saxony, Hessen-Kassel, Hannover, Münster, and the Saxon Ernestine duchies, for a total of 50,900 men in all, of which 18,400 were Brandenburgers under Dutch subsidy on the Lower Rhine.[40] These arrangements were made unilaterally without reference to the Emperor, who was powerless to prevent them.

In the autumn of 1688, the Saxon troops under *General* Flemming arrived in the theatre of war and joined the Franconian and Swabian troops, which were desperately needed to expel the French raiding parties. Unable to pay the subsidies the Princes demanded, Leopold I was compelled to acknowledge their division of South and West Germany into zones of extraction by sanctioning the distribution of quarters through assignations. A treaty was signed with Franconian Circle's states on 6 January 1689, assigning monthly billets until June to Saxony, which was also permitted to draw money from the unarmed Upper Saxon principalities as well as from districts belonging to Mainz.[41] Meanwhile, the pre-war situation in the north was consolidated by the Hannover Compromise between Duke of Ernst August and Friedrich III of Brandenburg, who on 30 January 1689, agreed a bilateral division of Westphalia and Lower Saxony to extract provision and billets.[42] Even the armed princes could not abide by their own agreement.

The Hannover Compromise broke up over who should draw money from East Frisia, while both Hannover and Brandenburg were opposed elsewhere

---

40 Peter H. Wilson, *German Armies. War and German Politics, 1648–1806* (London: UCL Press, 1998), p.183.

41 Oskar Schuster & Friedrich August Francke, *Die Geschichte der Sächsische Armee von der Errichtung bis in die Neueste Zeit: Unter Benutzung Handschriftlicher und Urkundlicher Quellen*, (Leipzig, Verlag von Duncker & Humblot 1885), bande I, p.120.

42 That evening, Duke Ernst August of Hannover entertained the Elector of Brandenburg in his new opera house with a performance of Agostino Steffani's *Enrico Leone*, a clear reference to his pretensions to the vast north German territory of the medieval Guelph monarch, Henry the Lion.

in Westphalia by Münster.[43] The Hannoverian contingent with the Concert's second army behaved so badly in their quarters in Hessen-Darmstadt, Fulda and Gelnhausen that many inhabitants fled over the frontier. The rivalry over resources began to affect strategy, as the Hannoverians refused to cooperate with a Hessian plan to start blockading the French in Mainz in April 1689 for fear that they would lose their present billets to the advancing Austrians. In the end, the arrival of his own troops enabled Leopold to evict the Hannoverians, but only after they had extorted money in addition to free food and quartering.

Resentment grew amongst the Franconian and Swabian states, which had fielded their contingents continuously since 1683 and were angry at the additional burdens placed on them without their consent. The Franconians were particularly incensed, since they had negotiated renewed promises of exemption in return for providing extra troops: Würzburg agreed to send two of its own infantry regiments after December 1688, while Franconia promised another three on 5 July 1689 to obtain three years' freedom from further billeting. Neither of these agreements had been respected by Leopold, who continued to assign the area to the Saxons.[44] Both Circles were determined not to surrender the initiative and withdrew into helpless neutrality as in 1677. In the 1690s, all these difficulties reverberated in the Diet and prevented the Elector of Mainz and the German Arch-Chancellor Lothar Franz von Schönberg from exploiting the groundswell of opinion among the smaller territories in areas that remained outside the original Franconian-Swabian Association. Small principalities in the Upper Rhine had grown progressively dissatisfied with Hessen-Kassel's leadership, while Hessen-Darmstadt broke away and was recognised as an armed state by Leopold in return for it fielding about 1,600 soldiers in addition to its 510 *Reichs* troops.

Despite the difficulties, Waldeck-Dernbach's initiative turned out to be the most suitable one to reconcile the supremacy of the large armed states with the aspiration of the smaller states for a common defence. The effectiveness of this new organisation was confirmed after 1701, when the Rhine front was almost entirely manned by contingents from the Western Circles.

43 Peter H. Wilson, *German Armies. War and German Politics, 1648–1806* (London: UCL Press, 1998), p.184. Hannover began hinting at possible negotiations with France to force Leopold I to sanction his increasingly extravagant demands, which now overlapped with areas claimed by Hessen-Kassel and Saxony.

44 Peter H. Wilson, *German Armies. War and German Politics, 1648–1806* (London: UCL Press, 1998), p.59.

3

The Electoral Prince-Archbishoprics

Although the three ecclesiastical Electorates did not represent particularly large territorial entities, their rulers were important political actors in Germany, not only because of their function as Electors of the Emperor, but especially because of their influence in the *Reichstag* (the Diet) they held the direction of Empire when the Emperorship was vacant and held the *Reich*'s Chancelleries: Mainz dealt with the affairs of Germany; Cologne the ones of Italy; Trier the ones of France.[1] In addition, the territories under their rule occupied strategically important positions, which increased considerably after the Peace of Westphalia, because all three were wedged between Germany, France and the Low Countries on the Rhine and Main areas, and their domains were part of the three Western Circles of the Empire.[2] Meanwhile, they could be elected as the ruler of other ecclesiastical principalities, and consequently this increased their influence in the Empire. A further relevance derived from the dynastic dynamics, since the election of the Prince-Bishop-Elector by the respective cathedral chapter represented a political variable of great importance, especially when an exponent of a first-ranking German family was elected, as occurred in Cologne between 1650 and 1688 during the mandate of the Bavarian Prince Maximilian Heinrich von Wittelsbach.

1 In the second half of the century, the latter functions were nominal, only the Mainz *Reichserzkanzler* actually functioned in practice, and 'nothing could be done in the Empire without him', Galeazzo Gualdo Priorato, *Relatione delle Corti e Stati .... dell'Arcivescovato e Principato di Magonza* (Leyden: 1668), p.37.

2 Peter H. Wilson, *German Armies. War and German Politics, 1648–1806* (London: UCL Press, 1998), p.11: 'The three most prestigious Electorates (Mainz, Cologne, Trier) were ruled by prince archbishops elected by their cathedral chapter, which was dominated by aristocratic canons who controlled considerable wealth within and outside the territory as well as many of the chief offices of state.'

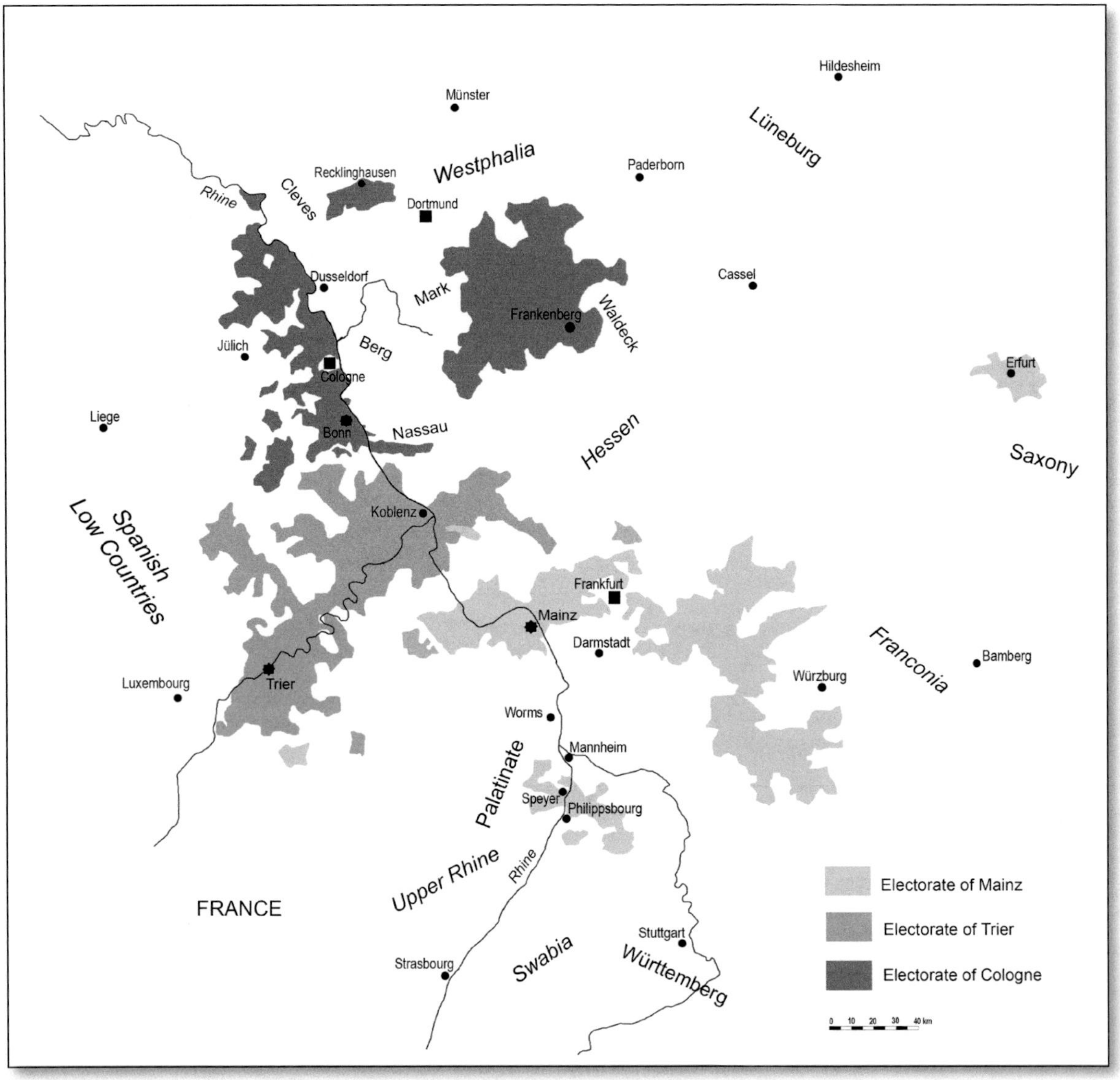

The Territories of The Ecclesiastical Electorates After 1648

To the left, the Arms of the three Ecclesiastical Electors, in a print by Caspar Merian (*Beschreibung und Abbildung Aller Königl. und Churfürstl. Ein-Züge, Wahl und Crönungs Acta*, 1658) (Public domain).
Although they ruled only small to medium principalities, each Elector Prince-Bishop held prestigious positions in the Empire and with their dynastic links managed to achieve a prominent status.

After 1648, a common feature of the three Electorates was their foreign policy. The common desire of autonomy from the Emperor marked their action until the 1670s. At the same time, the need for security saw them as promoters of regional alliances that were anti-Habsburg in their core tendency.[3] Chief among these three Electorates was Mainz, which, as the premier Electorate strategically situated on the middle Rhine, already provided an alternative to the Emperor's traditional leadership of the weaker territories. This represented a source of further problems, because the action of the Catholic Electors was soon countered by the formation of a broad

3 Jeroen Duindam, 'The Habsburg Court in Vienna. Kaiserhof or Reichshof?' in R. J. W. Evans and P. H. Wilson (eds), *The Holy Roman Empire, 1495–1806. A European Perspective* (Leiden and Boston: Brill, 2012), vol. I, p.101.

coalition of Protestant princes. In both cases, Imperial mediation proved ineffective, and the crisis was only defused by French intervention.[4]

As for concerns about the geostrategic scenario, the three Electorates were particularly vulnerable. The Electorate of Cologne, was at no point more than 20km wide, which made real control of the territory virtually impossible. Similar problems in Mainz and Trier led to early cooperation between the Electors in the matter of defence.[5] In addition to these concerns, some principalities shared common frontiers and enclaves with Protestant states, as the Duchy of Westphalia and the enclave of Recklinghausen belonging to Electoral Cologne lay detached from the principality by the secular Duchy of Mark ruled by Brandenburg.

To strengthen their position, in the spring of 1651, the three ecclesiastical Electorates adhered to the League of Frankfurt,[6] and in contrast to their later image as unmilitarised backwaters, the ecclesiastical Electorates were at the forefront of these developments, with Cologne and Mainz emerging as the two maintaining the most powerful forces. Both Electorates were linked by personal rule to other bishoprics, expanding their resource base and permitting the maintenance of several thousand soldiers by the 1670s as well as the construction of modern fortifications.[7]

Mainz

The Elector of Mainz, as Arch-Chancellor of Germany, was the foremost prince of the Empire, since no act could be discussed in the *Reichstag* without him. Additionally, along with the Emperor, the Elector relied on the Catholic ecclesiastical princes of the *Reichskirche* and the Catholic secular princes of Germany.[8] Exploiting such rights, the Prince-Bishop Elector Johann Philipp von Schönborn (r. 1647–1673) strongly influenced the geopolitical trajectory of Mainz and of Germany. In the debates of the early 1650s, some leading princes, with the Elector of Mainz among the foremost, argued that the continued existence of a group of nobles directly subject to the crown outside the *Reichstag* provided too much scope for direct Imperial intervention in

4 Joachim Whaley, *Germany and the Holy Roman Empire. Vol. 2: from the Peace of Westphalia to the Dissolution of the Reich. 1648–1806* (Oxford & New York: Oxford University Press, 2012), p.27.

5 Whaley, *Germany and the Holy Roman Empire*, p.261: '…systems for providing the deserving poor with passes or badges and jointly organised transports of condemned gypsies and vagrants to the galleys in Venice in the early eighteenth century.'

6 Peter H. Wilson, *German Armies. War and German Politics, 1648–1806* (London: UCL Press, 1998), p.169.

7 Peter H. Wilson, *German Armies. War and German Politics, 1648–1806* (London: UCL Press, 1998), p.30.

8 The order of precedence started with the Imperial Arch-Chancellor of the Reich (Mainz), followed by the Arch-Chancellors for Italy (Cologne) and Burgundy (Trier), the Arch-Marshal (Saxony), the Arch-Chamberlain (Brandenburg), the Arch-Cupbearer (Bohemia), the Arch-High Steward (the Palatinate, then Bavaria from 1623), and the Arch-Treasurer (created in 1648 for the Palatinate). See also Bruno Mugnai, *Wars and Soldiers in the Early Reign of Louis XIV, Volume 2: The Imperial Army 1657–1687* (Warwick: Helion & Company, 2019), pp.39–40.

Germany.[9] Soon, the Elector of Mainz became the most important opponent of the Emperor and Imperial policy, such as the offer of mediation which challenged the Austrian influence in the *Reich*. During the First Northern War of 1655–60, Schönborn managed to open the talks, taking advantage of Poland and Denmark who wanted peace. Emperor Leopold I and the Elector Friedrich Wilhelm of Brandenburg were obliged to acquiesce to the agreements brokered by France at the monastery of Oliva in May 1660.

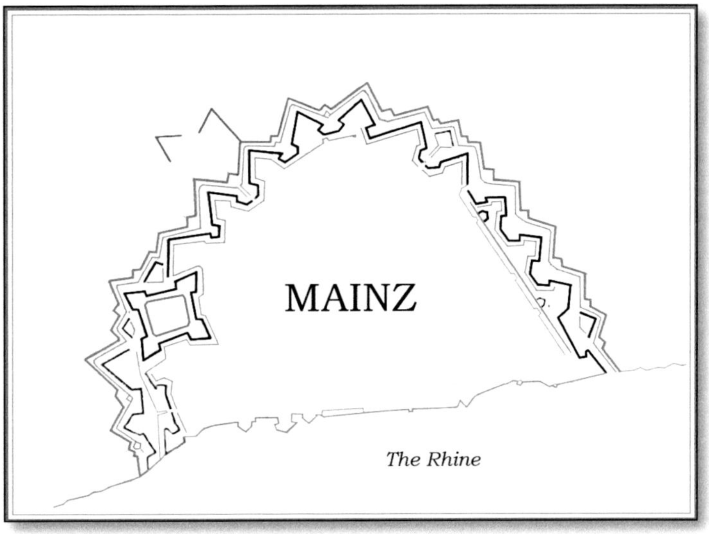

Plan of the fortifications of Mainz, from the *Livre des Plans des Places de l'Alsace et des Batailles qui le Roi Gagné en ces Quartiers là*, *c.* 1690. (Author's artwork)

Under Schönborn the Electorate comprised 39 territories with the rank of 'city' scattered in modern day Nordrhein-Westphalen and Rheinland-Pfalz *Länder*, as well as in more remote locations such as Erfurt, in Thüringen, 260km from Mainz. Since 1642, the Elector and Archbishop also ruled the Bishopric of Würzburg, and by 1663 he added Worms. According to the contemporaries Mainz had a population of 30,000, and the city enjoyed an excellent location straddling the Rhine and Main rivers and both favoured the trade.[10] As with the other ecclesiastical territories of western Germany, Mainz was often able to considerably enhance its income by means of canonicates and other ecclesiastical benefices. By the 1650s, the Electorate of Mainz also offered openings to Protestants, just as the Habsburgs' court and administration offered numerous opportunities to both Catholic *and* Protestant nobles and officials.

Elector Johan Philipp von Schönborn was also instrumental in creating a permanent military establishment. After the Imperialists left Mainz in October 1648, he established a secretary of war and raised his own professional troops to garrison the capital and other strategic locations, and then organised the territorial militia, the *Ausschuss*, of both horse and foot. This little standing force was not increased until 1657, when the Elector put the infantry companies together into one field regiment to join the troops of Christoph Bernard von Galen who were besieging Münster.[11] Schönborn managed to maximise the potential of his states by coordinating their policies. An 'Union and Alliance' between Mainz and Würzburg was

9 Joachim Whaley, *Germany and the Holy Roman Empire. From the Peace of Westphalia to the Dissolution of the Reich, 1648–1806* (Oxford: Oxford University Press, 2012), p.203.

10 Galeazzo Gualdo Priorato, *Relatione delle Corti e Stati .... dell'Arcivescovato e Principato di Magonza (*Leyden: 1668), p.23.

11 Georg Tessin, *Die Regimenter der Europäischen Staaten im Ancien Régime des XVI bis XVIII Jahrhunderts* (Osnabrück: Biblio Verlag, 1986), Teil 1, p.213.

established on 3 November 1656 to resolve mutual disagreements peacefully and facilitate political and military cooperation; this was supplemented on 26 January 1663 by a further agreement to collaborate on religious issues.[12] Despite reluctance from the two cathedral chapters, Schönborn attempted to harmonise civil and military administration and introduced common regulations for both armies in 1655. Weapons and personnel were exchanged, including the Mainz *Obrist* Kuno von der Leyen, who later transferred to command the Würzburg troops.

In 1658, the meeting of the *Rheinbund*'s members discussed the formation of a permanent force, and Mainz agreed to provide 300 cavalry and 600 infantry.[13] In 1661, Schönborn recruited mercenaries both in his states and outside of them in order to raise two infantry regiments – one from Mainz and another from Würzburg – to join the Imperialists in Transylvania.[14] In 1662, a regiment size unit of foot was established under *Obrist* Köth (KmI-3), which comprised the garrisons of the Electorate, with its headquarters based in the Castle of Schweikkardtsburg. A year later, Schönborn's troops failed in their first attempt to seize the Protestant enclave of Erfurt, which had claimed its autonomy from Mainz, but military action was accompanied by concerted campaigns to sway public opinion and win diplomatic backing. Imperial support proved an essential prerequisite in all of these cases.[15] Despite his full support to the *Deutsche Allianz*, Schönborn also held the office of *Kreisdirektor* of the Electoral Rhenish Circle, even though he did not provide soldiers for the contingent. Before the end of the year, a mixed Mainz-Würzburg regiment of foot was raised and marched alongside the *Deutsche Allianz* contingent to Hungary under Kuno von der Leyen, while two companies joined the infantry regiment of *Obrist* Johann Gottfried von Uffeln, raised by the Westphalian Circle.[16] At the Battle of Szentgotthárd, 1 August 1664, *Leyen zu Fuss* (KmI-4) fielded a single battalion,[17] as did *Uffeln zu Fuss*; both regiments suffered heavy casualties.[18]

Schönborn also called on *Deutsche Allianz* support in his second attempt to deprive Erfurt of its autonomy, and exploited the *Reichsexekution* to receive

12 Peter H. Wilson, *German Armies. War and German Politics, 1648–1806* (London: UCL Press, 1998), p.152: 'A relatively high degree of military integration was achieved with the two forces cooperating against Erfurt in 1663–4 and sending a combined regiment to fight the Turks in 1663.'

13 Peter H. Wilson, *German Armies. War and German Politics, 1648–1806* (London: UCL Press, 1998), p.172

14 The regiment of Mainz, *Post zu Fuss*, was ceded to Austria and merged into the regiment *Jung-Wolframsdorf*, cf Bruno Mugnai, *Wars and Soldiers in the Early Reign of Louis XIV, volume 2: The Imperial Army 1657–1687* (Warwick: Helion & Co. 2019), p.267.

15 Peter H. Wilson, *German Armies. War and German Politics, 1648–1806* (London: UCL Press, 1998), p.32.

16 Georg Tessin, 'Beiträge zur Formationsgeschichte des Münsterischen Militärs', *in Westfälische Forschungen. Mitteilungen des Provinzialinstituts für westfälische Landes und Volksforschung des Landschaftsverband Westfalen-Lippe*, vol. 32 (Münster: Aschendorffsche Verlagsbuchhandlung, 1982), p.89.

17 Kurt Peball, 'Die Schlacht bei St. Gotthard-Mogersdorf 1664', in *Militärhistorische Schriftenreihe*, III 1964.

18 Bruno Mugnai, *Wars and Soldiers in the Early Reign of Louis XIV, volume 2 The Imperial Army 1657–1687* (Warwick: Helion & Co. 2019), pp.158–159.

assistance from the Empire.[19] In October, 600 infantry, plus 800 mercenaries hired from Lorraine, joined the 15,000 German troops sent by the Emperor, France, Münster and other German princes, to besiege Erfurt. After the campaign against the rebel city, the Elector dismissed most of the troops, reducing the standing force to less than 1,000 men, but the tension with the Palatinate in 1665 forced the Elector to increase his troop numbers again. In 1666, about 300 horse and 600 foot from Mainz joined the allied troops of Cologne, Trier and Lorraine, but their involvement in the war remained limited, since the conflict soon turned into a struggle between the Elector Carl Ludwig and the Prince Charles IV of Lorraine.

Linstock, dating to the end of the seventeenth century, with the Arms of Schönborn engraved on the blade. (Private Collection)

In February 1667, French emissaries met the Elector's brother in Mainz in sight of the invasion of the Spanish Low Countries. Both sides agreed to raise, in Mainz, a force of 3,500 men with subsidy from France and join them to a field army of the German princes to face an enemy moving towards the Rhine. The agreement included the maintenance of 300 horse and 2,000 foot as permanent troops.[20] The treaty had a duration of three years and was to be protected by the most strict secrecy. The Elector, however, did not sign the agreement because it infringed on the terms of the Rhenish League, and this caused irritation to the Paris cabinet, which excluded Mainz from the peace talks in Aachen (Aix-La-Chapelle). The margins for manoeuvre were about to become very tight despite the fact that the previous year the Elector had been the main supporter of non-intervention.[21]

At the end of the 1660s, Mainz had a permanent garrison of 400 foot, including those in the castle of Aschaffenburg, the Elector's residence, and a further two companies were distributed between Königstein and Egersheim.[22] By 1671, the Elector established further garrisons at Erfurt, Bingen, and Starkenburg provided by the standing regiment, as well as other minor places using independent companies of foot. However, the permanent troops never exceeded 1,200 men and unlike other German princes, Schönborn did not engage in the mercenary trade with the foreign European powers.

The 1670s marked a turning point for Mainz, since the aggressive French foreign policy caused the loss of the support of many German princes,

19 The *Reichsexekution* (Empire's execution) was an intervention voted by the Imperial Diet against a member state – using military force if necessary.

20 Gottschalk Eduard Guhrauer, *Kur-Mainz in der Epoche von 1672* (Hamburg: Perthes, 1839), band I, p.95. The field force was established at 500 horse and 3,000 foot.

21 Whaley, *Germany and the Holy Roman Empire*, p.33. At the beginning of the War of Devolution, the Upper Rhine Circle's *Kreisdirector*, and Prince-Elector of Mainz, refused to call the Diet despite the presence of French troops near the border of the states comprised in the circle.

22 Gualdo Priorato, *Relatione delle Corti e Stati*, p.32.

Johann Philipp von Schönborn included. The Elector, fearful of a French invasion if a new war broke out, aimed to form an alliance dedicated not only to neutrality but also to brokering a peace. Schönborn's first attempt at such a large alliance in 1670 was prompted by a desire to restore the Prince of Lorraine, with a view to making his army the core of a new *Rheinbund*. The league itself was to be commanded by the Elector of Mainz and the Austrian Habsburg role was largely restricted to defence of the Empire against the Porte. The scheme was elegantly outlined by the young Gottfried Wilhelm Leibniz, who served the Electors of Mainz between 1668 and 1676, but it was impractical. By 1672, all that Leibniz could offer his employers was his *Concilium Aegyptiacum*: the suggestion that Germany might be spared and peace preserved in Europe if Louis XIV diverted his aggression to the conquest of Egypt.[23]

Filing these improbable plans, Schönborn turned to Vienna, promoting the Emperor for his leadership of the Marienburg Alliance. The Elector agreed to assemble 150 horse and 1,000 foot as a part of a field force of 10,205 men.[24] The practical and military significance of this defensive league was minimal; the fact that Schönborn now agreed to accept Emperor Leopold I as its leader was, however, indicative of the Elector's re-approach to Vienna. This change modified the military policy of the Electorate and favoured the meeting of the Electoral Rhenish diets, which by 1666 had remained paralysed by the struggle between Mainz and the Palatinate, and by common fear of French retaliation.[25]

This policy did not change in 1673, when Lothar Friedrich von Metternich-Burscheid (r. 1673–75) succeeded Schönborn. During his short mandate, Mainz sided with the Emperor and supported the party which voted in favour of the declaration of the *Reichskrieg* against Louis XIV. In August 1673, about 2,000 Mainz infantry marched to Trier to join the Allied army in the siege of the city.[26] In 1674, the Electoral infantry guarded the Upper Rhine. Two years later, Mainz organised its 2,000 infantry into four battalions under the Count of Lippe and they joined the allied army under Ottone Enrico Del Carretto, fighting in the Battle of Conzerbrücke.[27] In the following years, Mainz's military effort was conditioned by a succession of Electors. Damian Hartard von der Leyen took office in February 1676, during the chaotic assignments of the winter quarter for the Allied troops. Mainz supported this burden paying a high cost in both billets and provisions. Von der Leyen died in December 1678, and was succeeded by Carl Heinrich von

23 Martin Wrede, *Das Reich und seine Feinde: Politische Feindbilder in der reichspatriotischen Publizistik zwischen Westfälischem Frieden und Siebenjährigem Krieg* (Mainz: Vandenhoeck & Ruprecht, 2004), p.337

24 Peter H. Wilson, *German Armies. War and German Politics, 1648–1806* (London: UCL Press, 1998), p.177.

25 Peter H. Wilson, *German Armies. War and German Politics, 1648–1806* (London: UCL Press, 1998), p.66.

26 Arthur Janke, *Die Belagerungen der Stadt Trier in den Jahren 1673 bis 1675 und die Schlacht an der Conzer Brücke am 11. August 1675* (Trier: Lintz, 1890), p.17.

27 Anton Marr, 'Der Feldzüg im Jahre 1675 in Deutschland', in *Österreichische Militärische Zeitschrift* (Vienna: Kaiserl. Koenigli und Hof und Staatsdruckerei 1839), band III, p.121.

The Allied siege of Mainz from June to September 1689 is shown here in a contemporary print. (Author's collection) The city was the main goal of the French Army on the Rhine, but the prompt reaction of the German principalities thwarted the plans of Versailles.

Metternich-Winneburg, who held the Electorship for less than a year, from January to September 1679.

After Schönborn, the new establishment of Mainz resulted in the separation from Würzburg and the loss of prestige in Germany. Subsequent ties with Worms (1673–1675), Speyer (1673–1675) and Bamberg (1695–1729) did not compensate Mainz for the loss of Würzburg's resources.[28] The new Elector Anselm Franz von Ingelheim (r. 1680–95) took office on 7 November 1680, and immediately faced the post-war policy. However, Mainz was losing its prominence in the Empire. The poor action of Ingelheim in foreign policy was decisive, since this inaction deprived the smaller territories of the traditional alternative to Habsburg leadership.[29] In some respects, the choice proved to be wise, since Louis XIV's foreign policy was becoming less conciliatory towards the German Princes. In early September 1679, French troops occupied territories on the left bank of the Rhine culminating in the seizure of Strasbourg on 30 September 1681. Thereafter, attention switched to the north, where incursions into Luxembourg escalated into a full war

28 Peter H. Wilson, *German Armies. War and German Politics, 1648–1806* (London: UCL Press, 1998), p.152.

29 Peter H. Wilson, *German Armies. War and German Politics, 1648–1806* (London: UCL Press, 1998), p.62.

Lothar Franz von Schönborn (1655–1729), Elector Prince-Bishop of Mainz from 1694. The connection with Würzburg, the largest (after Salzburg) and most heavily militarised South German Bishopric, was a major factor in raising Mainz's, and Schönborn's, political profile but this did not survive his death. His nephew, Lothar Franz, tried to revive it, standing as a candidate for coadjutor, and later Bishop, in Würzburg in 1697–1699 but without success.

with Spain in 1683–1684, leading to the absorption of the Duchy by France.

The impression of French aggression was magnified by Louis's policies elsewhere. As a result, the attention of Mainz was focused on its western border. By 1683, Louis XIV resorted to violence to redress the setbacks, calculating that a limited strike in the Rhineland would stiffen Ottoman resolve in Hungary as well as intimidate the German states into giving way to his demands over the Rhine territories and the *Réunions*. Crossing the frontier on 24 September 1688, French troops rapidly overran Electoral Cologne and the Palatinate, taking Philippsburg, Mainz and other key fortified posts. However, they failed to seize the city of Cologne. Mainz was occupied by the French until 1689 and then re-taken by the Allies, who entered the city after a three-month siege.

In the same year, with recruits drawn from the militia, two infantry regiments and one dragoon regiment were raised. They formed the core of the growing military effort of Mainz, which in the 1690s increased the army to 3,000 to 4,000 men.[30]

30 Peter H. Wilson, *German Armies. War and German Politics, 1648–1806* (London: UCL Press, 1998), p.91.

Cologne

Being the westernmost of the ecclesiastical Electoral principalities, Cologne remained for a long time exposed to external influence. After 1648, France always sought friendly relations with its ruler, and even when the nomination fell on a prince less close to France, Louis XIV's diplomacy skilfully succeeded in securing his friendship. The events favoured the French plans, because the Archbishopric was effectively a secundogeniture of the Bavarian Wittelsbachs.[31]

The Electorate possessed a very fragmented territorial continuity with the presence of enclaves of other principalities, especially the Duchy of Pfalz-Neuburg and of the Palatinate. Together with Cologne's domains, since 1581 the Electors had held the government of the Bishopric of Liège, and by 1612 also that of Hildesheim, which increased their political weight, but this influence was counterbalanced by the two other ecclesiastical principalities, and the fact that Mainz had an exclusive monopoly of executive authority, because of the post of Arch-Chancellery of Germany. The Rhenish domains were divided into two sectors, the Upper and the Lower Electorate, most of them lying on the left bank of the river. To the east, separated by the territories of Cleves, Berg and Mark, the Duchy of Westphalia constituted the third main domain of the Electorate. This made Electoral Cologne the largest ecclesiastical principality, but this did not correspond to the number of inhabitants, which was the smallest of the three.

Bonn, the Electoral capital, had a population of about 4,000 in the 1660s.[32]

In these years, the city was building modern curtains and bastions, but only a few places were protected by updated defences; one of these, Rheinberg, in 1668 was still manned by a Dutch garrison, which had replaced the Spanish one in 1648.[33] Other strategic places were Neuss, and Kaiserswerth, both guarding the routes on the Rhine. Before 1672, the Elector had already tried to counter the Dutch predominance in the region by both political and religious acts, as occurred in Bentheim in 1668, encouraging the conversion of the

The fortification of Bonn, from the *Livre des Plans des Places de l'Alsace et des Batailles qui le Roi Gagné en ces Quartiers là*, c. 1690. (Author's artwork)

31 In the second half of the seventeenth century, Cologne's Elector, Maximilian Heinrich von Wittelsbach (r. 1650–1688), was a first cousin of Ferdinand Maria, Prince-Elector of Bavaria. He was succeeded by Joseph Clemens (r. 1688–1723), a brother of Maximilian II Emanuel, who would receive the Imperial ban for siding with France in the War of the Spanish Succession.

32 Gualdo Priorato, *Relatione delle Corti e Stati*, p.48.

33 Gualdo Priorato, *Relatione delle Corti e Stati*, p.48. As for Bonn, the Italian historian refers to the construction of modern curtain and bastions, five of which were completed in 1668, and the final project included the construction of further three.

Elector Prince-Bishop Maximilian Heinrich von Wittelsbach (r. 1650–1688). Print after an engraving of Matthäus Merian the Elder in *Beschreibung und Abbildung Aller Königl. und Churfürstl. Ein-Züge, Wahl und Crönungs Acta ...* (Frankfurt am Main, 1658).
Under Maximilian Heinrich, Electoral Cologne became one of the leading partners of France, but Bishop Bernhard von Galen's more forceful personality prevailed over Maximilian Heinrich, particularly as Münster developed into one of the most heavily armed German territories by the 1670s. Galen took the lead in reorienting cooperation towards external aggression, beginning with his attack on the Dutch Republic in 1665. Although Maximilian Heinrich was supportive at first, he refused to provide any concrete assistance, but later concern at possible Dutch retaliation led to an agreement in 1670 to collaborate on strengthening Cologne's fortress of Dorsten, near Recklinghausen.

ruling House to Catholicism.[34] Additionally, France supported the Elector's efforts to control the Imperial Free City of Cologne, which was surrounded by his territory, but to balance French influence, the Republic backed the City of Cologne. Just as in 1661 the States General had tried to save the city of Münster from the encroaching absolutism of the Prince-Bishop, so now they sought to defend Cologne's autonomy against the Elector. In the same years, Louis XIV encouraged the Elector of Cologne to demand Dutch evacuation of Rheinberg and the transfer of part of the Overmaas to the Bishopric of Liège.

Since the previous century, the Electors of Cologne had also ruled as Prince-Bishops of Liège and Hildesheim. Both domains gave to the Elector a relevant political importance in Germany because they provided significant resources and political advantages. Liège was a rich territory, and because of its position in the middle of the Spanish Low Countries could exploit the rivalry between Spain and France to receive support from one or the other as the situation suited. Liège and Hildesheim were also good recruitment pools for mercenaries. In the Bishopric of Liège, Huy and Dinant were the main fortresses in the central and southern territories, while Liège itself and Verviers guarded the north-eastern border. The fortress of Maastricht also *formally* belonged to the Bishopric of Liège, but was firmly held by the Dutch, who did not intend to return it, nor did the French in 1673.[35] On the other hand, the Bishopric of Hildesheim did not have modern fortresses, and was almost surrounded by the territories of the Brunswick principalities and by Brandenburg, and was a Catholic enclave amidst the Protestant states of the Lower Saxon Circle.

The first standing troops of the Electorate were recruited by Prince Ernst von Wittelsbach in 1583, and formed the core of a professional army which increased in size over subsequent years. In the Thirty Years' War, the Electorate sided with the Catholic League, and like other German territories, was repeatedly invaded by foreign armies, such as between January and

34 Exploiting dissension in the Calvinist county of Bentheim, the Elector persuaded the Count, previously a client of the Dutch, to convert to Catholicism. See also Jonathan Israel, *The Dutch Republic, Its Rise, Greatness and Fall, 1477–1806* (Oxford: Clarendon Press, 1995), p.735.

35 In July 1673, the Prince-Bishop Elector asked Louis XIV for the return of Maastricht, but the King replied that from now on the city would be French. See John B. Wolf, *Louis XIV.* (Italian edition Turin: Garzanti, 1983), p.264.

September 1642, when the Franco-Weimarian and Hessian troops crossed the border to loot the country with devastating effects. After the Peace of Westphalia, Elector Maximilian Heinrich von Wittelsbach (r. 1650–1688) raised three companies of foot which manned the garrisons on the Rhine. In 1654, Electoral Cologne did not send troops to support Christoph Bernard von Galen to besiege the rebel city of Münster, but allowed the Prince-Bishop to enlist mercenaries in the Electorate, and through cardinal and state secretary Wilhelm Egon von Fürstenberg, favoured the hire of infantry from other German princes.

In 1657, the Elector formed a field infantry regiment by combining the companies quartered in the garrisons, and in 1660, a regiment of cavalry was also raised. Before the end of the year, 500 infantry with artillery joined Galen's troops for the third siege of Münster. The Electorate also granted permission for soldiers to be recruited in its territory. In March 1659, the Elector agreed to the recruitment of 15 infantry companies for the Imperial Army. However, the recruiting raised just 500 men who were destined for a newly formed Imperial cuirassier regiment.[36]

As a member of the Electoral Rhenish, Westphalian and Lower Saxony Circles, the Prince-Elector had to provide troops for the *Reichsarmee.* In 1661, eight infantry companies formed a two battalion regiment under colonel Roist (KkI-2) which took part on the campaign against the Ottomans in Upper Hungary and Transylvania. In 1663, the Elector raised infantry regiment Waldeck (KkI-3) as a part of the *Deutsche Allianz*, while an entire cavalry regiment was recruited in France, Cologne provided 420 horse and

Wilhelm Egon von Fürstenberg (1629-1704) (Collection of the Château ducal de Cadillac, Public Domain)
In 1672 the Emperor joined the Franco-Dutch War as an ally of the Dutch, finding himself opposed by the bishops in the northwest part of the Empire. The Fürstenberg brothers being regarded by the Emperor as the main cause of this disaster, Wilhelm Egon was arrested for treason on 14 February 1674 by Imperial cavalry after they had chased his carriage through Cologne. He was hurried off to Vienna and was tried for his life. He was saved by the intervention of the Papal nuncio at Cologne, but was kept in prison until the signature of the Treaty of Nijmwegen in 1679. As a reward for his services, in 1682 Louis XIV appointed Wilhelm Egon Bishop of Strasbourg in succession to his brother Franz, and in 1686 obtained for him the cardinal's hat from Pope Innocent XI, and in 1688 succeeded in obtaining his election as Coadjutor-Archbishop of Cologne and successor to Maximilian. At the insistence of the Emperor, however, the Pope imposed his veto on 26 August 1688 and the canons followed the papal lead. In the same year, Louis XIV attacked the Empire, citing this action as well as his sister-in-law's claim to the inheritance of the Palatinate as pretexts. However, the progress of the Allies against Louis XIV in the Nine Years' War deprived Fürstenberg of all prospect of success forcing him to retire to France. He spent the rest of his life in the Abbey of St-Germain-des-Prés near Paris, where he died on 10 April 1704.

36 Alphons von Wrede, *Geschichte der K. und K. Wehrmacht on 1618 bis zum Ende des XIX Jahrhunderts* (Vienna, 1898–1905), band II, p.136.

800 foot according to the agreement of 1658.[37] In March 1666 France, then an ally of the Dutch Republic, moved reinforcements through Liège with the blessing of Elector Maximilian Heinrich, and in the following summer, Electoral troops participated in the relief of Bremen, which was besieged by the Swedes.

In 1668, the number of soldiers had been reduced to a few hundred. Bonn quartered no professional troops, and this duty of garrisoning was entrusted to the city's militia, which numbered two companies.[38] The Elector also had a personal mounted escort of 100 'light cavalrymen', while 30 *Trabanten* served as palace guards in his residence.[39] As for the troops of Liège, the Elector had garrisons of single infantry companies in the main fortresses, to which a militia could be added in case of need, Hildesheim had no regular troops of a strength higher than a company. Only in 1670 did Liège raise a dragoon regiment, which entered the service of Celle in the following year.[40]

The military policy of the Electorate registered a significant change with the treaty signed with France on 4 January 1672. Not only did French troops infringe the Empire's neutrality by using the Bishopric of Liège as an invasion route, but Electoral Cologne, with Münster, actively assisted Louis XIV against the Dutch Republic in return for subsidies and political support. The architects of the Franco-Cologne agreement were the brothers Wilhelm, Franz and Hermann Egon von Fürstenberg.

They secured the support of Elector's brother Ferdinand Maria of Bavaria and assisted Maximilian Heinrich in the negotiations with Louis XIV. In 1672, the Elector pledged to raise 1,700 cavalry and 400 dragoons and 16,000 infantry for the war against the Dutch Republic. The list of troops raised by the Elector, and which also included one infantry regiment and two companies of dragoons from Bavaria, comprised eight cavalry regiments, one dragoon regiments and six infantry regiments. Before the end of 1672, another infantry regiment came from Lorraine, and one from Mecklenburg.[41] The field army totalled approximately 10,000 men when in April 1672 the Elector joined the Prince-Bishop of Münster for the upcoming campaign against the Dutch Republic, while further troops were still to be assembled.[42]

The successful outcome of the campaign had outdated the original plans, and soon divergences emerged between the allies for the continued conduct of the war. Elector Maximilian Heinrich aimed to consolidate the conquests in Drenthe and Overijssel, while Christoph Bernhard von Galen insisted on a further advance into Friesland and Groningen to meet the English fleet on

37 Georg Tessin *Die Regimenter der Europäischen Staaten im Ancien Régime des XVI bis XVIII Jahrhunderts* (Osnabrück: Biblio Verlag, 1986), Teil 1, p.189.

38 Galeazzo Gualdo Priorato, *Relationi delle Città Imperiali & Anseatiche di Colonia, Lubecca, Bremen, & Amburgo, ... delle Corti e Stati de' Serenissimi Elettor di Baviera, e de' Langravi d'Hassia in Kassel e Darmstadt* (Bologna, 1674), p.49.

39 Gualdo Priorato, *Relatione delle Corti e Stati*, p.51.

40 Georg Tessin, *Die Regimenter der Europäischen Staaten im Ancien Régime des XVI bis XVIII Jahrhunderts* (Osnabrück: Biblio Verlag, 1986), Teil 1, p.209.

41 Georg Tessin, *Die Regimenter der Europäischen Staaten im Ancien Régime des XVI bis XVIII Jahrhunderts* (Osnabrück: Biblio Verlag, 1986), Teil 1, pp.191 and 221.

42 Georges Bernard Depping, *Geschichte des Krieges der Münsterer und Cölner im Bundnisse mit Frankreich gegen Holland in den Jahren 1672, 1673 und 1674* (Münster: Theissing,1840), p.107.

Franz Egon von Fürstenberg (1626–1683), an engraving by Anselmus van Hulle in *Les Hommes Illustres qui ont Vecu dans le XVII Siècle* (Amsterdam, 1717). A French party, orchestrated by the Grand Chamberlain Hermann Egon von Fürstenberg prevailed in Bavaria and secretly envisaged the marriage of the Elector's daughter to the Dauphin and, in the event of Leopold's death, the election of Louis XIV as Holy Roman Emperor, and Elector Ferdinand Maria as King of the Romans. Fürstenberg's brother, Franz Egon, the chief minister in Cologne, ensured that the Wittelsbach Elector Maximilian Heinrich entered into an offensive alliance with France, as did Bishop Christoph Bernhard of Galen in Münster. Pfalz-Neuburg, Württemberg, Hanover, and Osnabrück committed themselves to varying degrees of neutrality or tacit support for France.

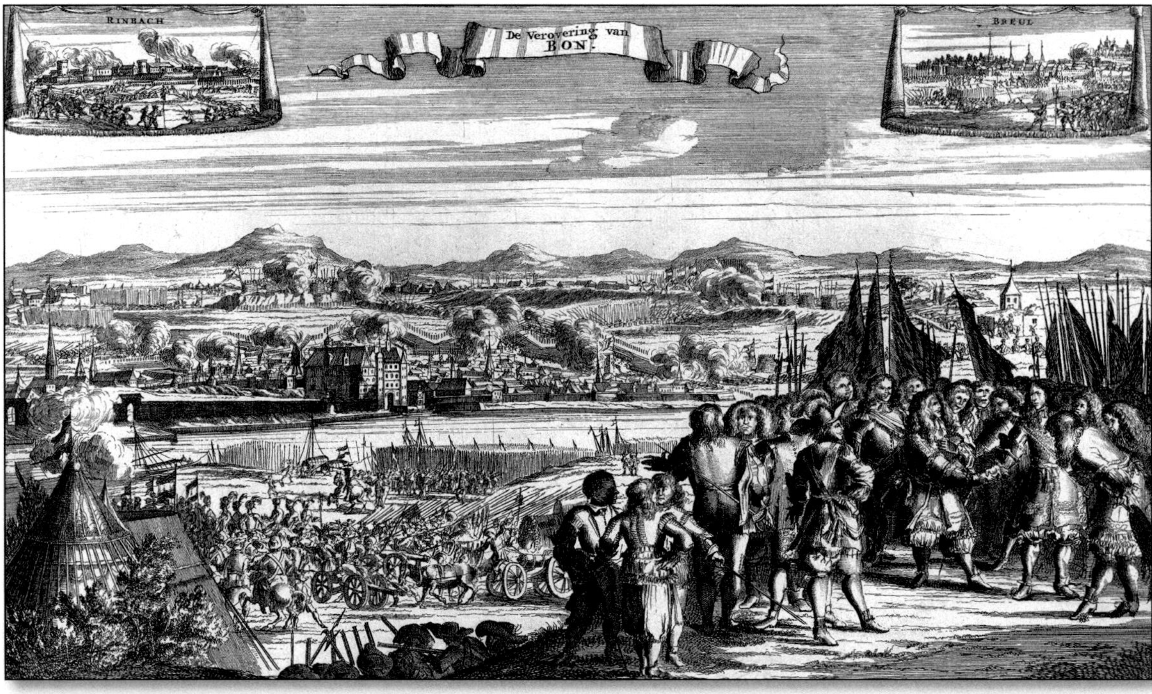

Bonn besieged by the Allies under Prince William of Orange and Raimondo Montecuccoli from 3 to 12 November 1673, in a contemporary Dutch print. (Collection of the Rijksmuseum, Amsterdam)
The loss of the Electoral capital forced the Elector to sign a truce with the Dutch Republic and the Emperor in May 1674.

the northern coast. In September, after the bitter retreat from Groningen, the Cologne troops numbered 6,300 men in all.[43] The army entered winter quarters between Deventer, Zwolle and other minor posts, where it remained on the defensive without participating in further field operations. In November 1673, Bonn, defended by 2,000 regular soldiers and militia under *Generalmajor* Landsberg, was seized by Montecuccoli and William III of Orange.

This loss took Electoral Cologne out of the war, forcing Maximilian Heinrich to sign a truce with the Allies on 15 November 1673, which was followed by a peace treaty with the Emperor and the Dutch Republic in May 1674.

The following summer, the Electoral Army was disbanded and some of the troops entered Imperial or French service; the *Leibregiment* of foot, which deserted under its colonel, a nephew of the Fürstenberg brothers, entered French service.[44] The Electorate paid a huge cost for the maintenance of the Allies, while Bonn remained under Imperial-Dutch control until 1678. The war put a pause in the military policy of the Electorate, which retained only a small corps of regular troops for garrison duties, but which were organised as a regiment sized unit under *Obrist* Frens for administrative purposes (Kki-8).

43 Georges Bernard Depping, *Geschichte des Krieges der Münsterer und Cölner im Bundnisse mit Frankreich gegen Holland in den Jahren 1672, 1673 und 1674* (Münster: Theissing,1840), p.118.

44 The regiment became *Fürstenberg Allemand* in the French Army.

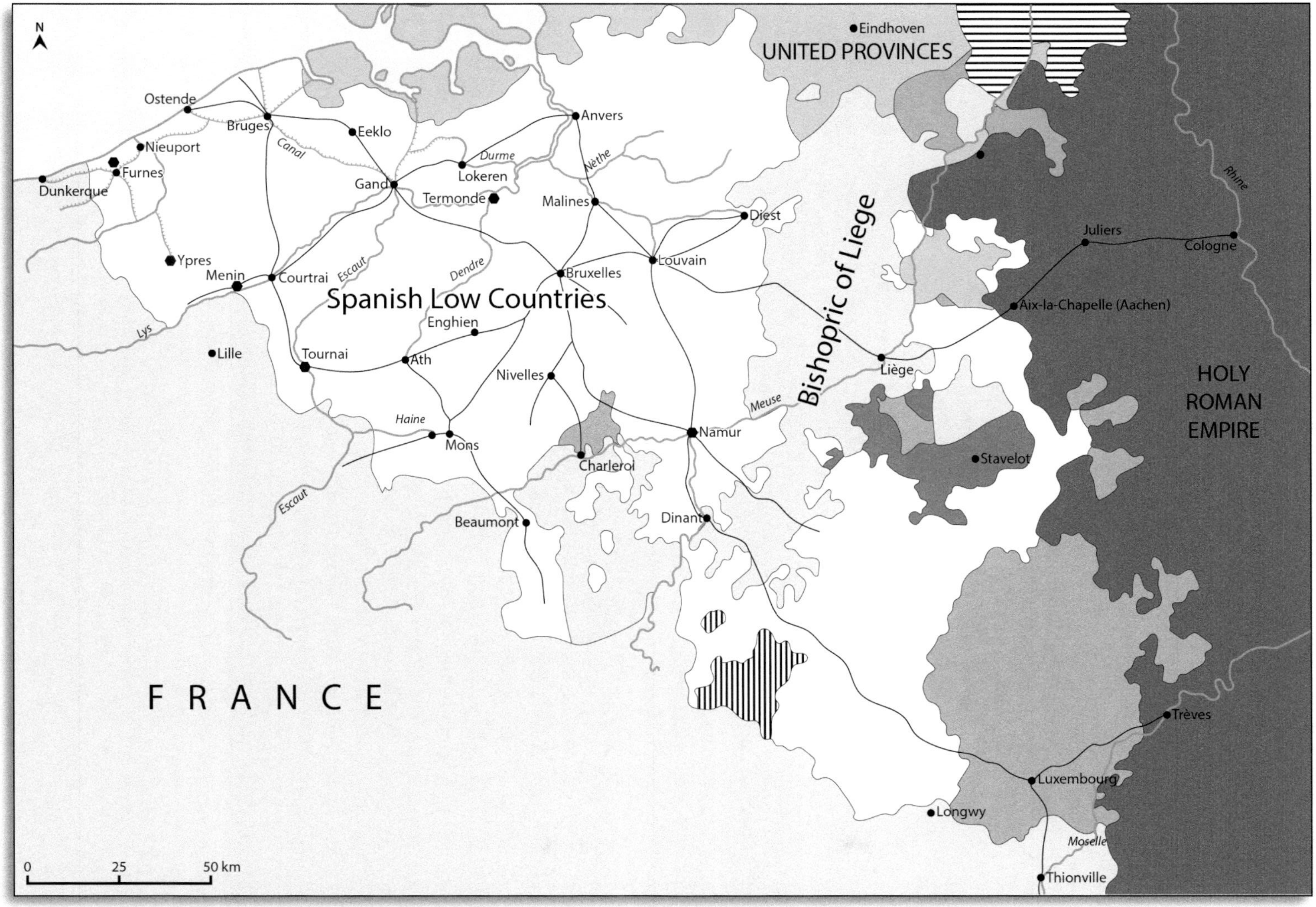

The Bishopric of Liège. (Map by George Anderson ©Helion & Co. 2024)

The strategic relevance of the Bishopric of Liège is apparent from its territory bordering with the Spanish Low Countries. After being the bridge for the invasion of the Dutch Republic in 1672, in 1679 Liège lost the territory of Bouillon to the family of la Tour d'Auvergne, and the fortress of Maastricht, which was annexed by the Dutch Republic. In the 1680s, Liège remained involved in the French Réunions and in the campaign of 1684 in Luxembourg. Then, in 1688, Huy was occupied by the French who retained it until 1697.

After the surrender of Bonn, the Imperialists entered the territory of Liège and occupied the eastern part. The heavy contribution extorted and the bad behaviour of the Imperial soldiers caused a reaction by the local authorities. In September 1674, the Governor of Dinant expelled the Imperial troops, and in retaliation, *General der Cavallerie* Johann von Sporck occupied Huy, which had also rebelled. After he had blockaded Dinant with the cavalry, Sporck turned to the citadel of Huy which was still held by troops of Liège. The resistance lasted until December, when artillery fire forced the besieged garrison to surrender; in violation of the terms the Imperial general ordered the sacking of the city.[45] Dinant followed the same fate in June 1675. In April 1676, the French evacuated all the towns of the Bishopric of Liège after destroying the fortifications. Spanish and Dutch troops occupied the northern territories, and refused to re-establish the neutrality of Liège. The capital was occupied by the Spaniards, who looted and fired the suburbs. In 1678, the Dutch-Spanish returned to being in possession of Maastricht, and other locations in the Bishoprics, and the Peace of Nijmegen of 1678–1679, confirmed the definitive succession of Maastricht to the Dutch Republic.

The events of the first half of the 1680s threatened the Electorate again, but this time Maximilian Heinrich maintained a low profile. In August 1684, an Electoral Cologne corps of 1,500 cavalry and 5,000 infantry served under special arrangement with Vienna against the Ottomans, and before the end of the year, one infantry regiment was passed to the Emperor, who joined it to the army in Hungary.[46] In 1685, the Elector raised one regiment of dragoons, of six companies, and two infantry regiments for the auxiliary corps gathered by Münster and Paderborn for the campaign in Hungary. This contingent served under Imperial command until 1688.

After the death of Maximilian Heinrich in June 1688, the coadjutor and Regent Wilhelm Egon von Fürstenberg tried to take the Electoral throne with French help. At the insistence of the Emperor, however, the Pope imposed his veto on 26 August; the Cologne chapter followed the papal lead and Joseph Clemens of Wittelsbach became the new Elector. Regardless of whether he was ruling them or not, Joseph Clemens hired Münster units to garrison Dorsten and Recklinghausen during the disputed election of 1688.[47]

When Louis XIV invaded the Rhineland in autumn 1688, Bonn was occupied by French troops, but they evacuated the city on 12 October 1689 after the Allied siege, frustrating Fürstenberg's plans. The soldiers took the oath to Joseph Clemens, who reorganised the troops and in the following years increased the strength to 8,000 to 10,000 men.[48] Regimental sized units were also raised in Liège in 1687, and Hildesheim between 1685 and 1689. In 1685, the latter territory contributed one cavalry and one infantry

45 Jean-Pierre Rorive, *Les Miseres de la Guerre sous le Roi Soleil* (Liège: Perron, 1991), p.18.

46 Georg Tessin *Die Regimenter der Europäischen Staaten im Ancien Régime des XVI bis XVIII Jahrhunderts* (Osnabrück: Biblio Verlag, 1986), Teil 1, p.191.

47 Peter H. Wilson, *German Armies. War and German Politics, 1648–1806* (London: UCL Press, 1998), p.153.

48 Heinrich Ludwig Gude, *Staat der Fünff Teutschen Erb Bischöffe als des Erb Bischöffen und Chur-Fürsten zu Mainz, Trier und Köln, dann der Erb Bischöffen zu Salzburg und Besançon. Ingleichen des Hoch Meisters Teutschen Ordens* (Halle, before 1708), p.39.

regiment for the campaign in Hungary. These comprised 435 cavalry in six companies, and 836 foot in eight companies, who joined the Cologne, Münster and Paderborn contingent in Imperial service.[49] Both regiments served for only two years. Liège also contributed to the war against the Ottomans, but in another theatre. In 1687, the Republic of Venice signed an agreement for the recruitment in Liège of eight companies of foot for a regiment entrusted to *Obrist* Leonard Cleuter of a family of mercenaries who had already served the Pope against the Ottomans. Cleuter took the command of the regiment in March 1687 and headed for Venice, from where he and his soldiers sailed to Greece before the summer. Disease and war attritions caused the disbanding of the regiment in 1688 after the bitter siege of Negroponte.[50]

Trier

Highly exposed to foreign invasions similar to Mainz and Cologne, in the second half of the seventeenth century the Electorate of Trier occupied a minor political role compared to the two other ecclesiastical Electorates. Due to dynastic dynamics, the ruling princes did not benefit from relations with the most important Houses of the Empire, nor did they hold the government of other German principalities. Trier was only connected to relatively unimportant bishoprics, a factor that made its position the weakest among the Rhenish Electorates.[51] Prince-Archbishop Philipp Christoph von Sötern (r. 1623–1652), who also held the Prince-Bishopric of Speyer, succeeded Carl Caspar von der Leyen-Hohengeroldseck, who ruled until 1676 only in Trier, and then Johann Hugo von Orsbeck, already Prince-Bishop of Speyer, held the Electorate until 1711.

Elector and Prince-Bishop Johann Hugo von Orsbeck, who ruled Trier, along with the Bishopric of Speyer, from 1676 to 1711, contemporary engraving. (Art Collection of the Veste Coburg).
Under Orsbeck, Trier had to face the French who repeatedly invaded the Electorate. After the French occupation of 1674 to 1675, Louis XIV succeeded in depriving Trier of some border territories, which prompted Johann Hugo to protest to the Imperial Diet on 22 June 1680. In June-July 1684, the Electorate was occupied again by the French troops coming via Luxembourg. After these events, in 1686 Orsbeck was able to obtain from the Estates 150,000 thalers to maintain a professional force.

49 Georg Tessin *Die Regimenter der Europäischen Staaten im Ancien Régime des XVI bis XVIII Jahrhunderts* (Osnabrück: Biblio Verlag, 1986), Teil 1, p.182.

50 Bruno Mugnai, *Wars and Soldiers in the Early Reign of Louis XIV, volume 1: Armies of the Italian States, 1660–90, Part 1* (Warwick: Helion & Company, 2023), p.184.

51 Peter H. Wilson, *German Armies. War and German Politics, 1648–1806* (London: UCL Press, 1998), p.153.

During the Thirty Years' War, Elector Philipp Christoph von Sötern supported France against the Habsburgs, but in 1630 Trier opened its gates to Spanish troops to defend its rights against the Elector. French troops seized the city in 1632 to help Sötern, and in return, they were allowed to install garrisons there and in the fortress of Ehrenbreitstein. In 1635 the Spaniards seized Trier and imprisoned Sötern. In 1637 the Imperialists expelled the French garrisons and occupied the Electorate until the end of the war. The archbishop was released from captivity in 1645 because of French demands. After 1648, the Electorate did not lose its integrity and still comprised a series of homogeneous territories along the river Moselle between Trier, near the French border, and Koblenz on the Rhine. However, the war had halved the population, and the economy was also in a very poor state. The Archbishops and Electors made an honest effort to fulfil their promise to restore everything to its former glory. In the seventeenth century, they relocated their residence to Philippsburg Castle, in Ehrenbreitstein near Coblenz. This latter place and Trier were updated with modern defences between the 1660s and 1670s.[52]

Trier was a member of the Rhenish Electoral Circle, but like Mainz and Cologne, did not cooperate in the mustering of a common contingent, and in 1658 adhered to the *Rheinbund* agreeing to provide 580 soldiers in all. In 1660, about 500 foot from Trier formed a field regiment under *Obrist* Wolframsdorf to support Prince-Bishop Christoph Bernard von Galen in the siege of Münster. By 1661, the maintaining of these troops represented a burden for the state's treasury, but the Elector did not disband the regiment but instead sold it the Emperor, who transferred Wolframsdorf and his men to Transylvania.[53] This was the first significant 'trade' of soldiers by Trier. In 1662, an infantry regiment of six companies was raised by the Elector's relative *Obrist* von der Leyen. From this regiment, three companies, numbering 380 men, headed to Hungary with the *Deutsche Allianz* and fought at Szentgotthárd on 1 August 1664.[54] Before the end of the year, the regiment marched to Erfurt, which was besieged by the Rhenish League's troops. Shortage of resources forced the Elector to disband some troops, but the infantry regiment formally survived throughout the next decades. The regular troops also carried out police duties, for example: on 3 June 1672, in order to combat robberies, state officials were instructed to have the streets and roads in their districts patrolled with sufficient soldiers and to have all suspicious persons checked who did not have a certified passport. Those

52 Gottfried Kentenich, *Geschichte der Stadt Trier: von ihrer Gründung bis zur Gegenwart; Denkschrift zum 100 Jährigen Jubiläum der Zugehörigkeit der Stadt zum preussischen Staat* (Trier: Interbook, 1915), p.516.

53 Georg Tessin *Die Regimenter der Europäischen Staaten im Ancien Régime des XVI bis XVIII Jahrhunderts* (Osnabrück: Biblio Verlag, 1986), Teil 1, p.316. Alphons von Wrede, *Geschichte der K.u.K. Wehrmacht von 1618 bis zum Ende des XIX Jahrhunderts* (Vienna, 1898–1905), band II, p.140, attributes the regiment *Wolframsdorf zu Fuss* to Münster.

54 Georg Tessin *Die Regimenter der Europäischen Staaten im Ancien Régime des XVI bis XVIII Jahrhunderts* (Osnabrück: Biblio Verlag, 1986), Teil 1, p.316

who did not meet these requirements were to be deported across the border or arrested.'[55]

In 1652, the Elector reorganised the Trier City Militia. All adult males aged between 18 to 50 were divided into five *Fendellein* (companies), half musketeers and half pikemen, and attached to the two companies of the regular garrison. Officers were appointed from among the citizens who were experienced in military matters, and, together with their men, guarded the *Dhumb* (cathedral) and other places in the city. 22 *Gefreite* were also appointed, together with six officers 'well-dressed and armed with their swords and *Bartisanen*.'[56]

Trier remained neutral during the War of Devolution (1667–1668), confirming the address of the Rhenish League, but soon the events turned in another direction. In 1671, the Electorate entered the Marienburg Alliance with 75 horse and 500 foot,[57] but hopes to maintain the Electorate safe from foreign invasions were dashed during the Franco-Dutch War. Louis XIV began his campaign against The Netherlands from the Lower Rhine in 1672, but French troops had already crossed the Trier territory before the end of 1671. From May 1672 onwards, the transport of French troops and supplies along the Moselle River continued unabated. In the summer, the French entered the Electorate to exact contributions, then in late autumn Turenne quartered a part of his army near Trier. In 1673, the Imperial Austrian involvement in the Franco-Dutch War increased the tension, as Louis XIV intensified his requests to pro-French German princes to declare the neutrality of the Empire, in order to secure the flank of his armies in The Netherlands from the Imperial-Brandenburg army moving from the east. From April to August 1673, one convoy of French boats after another sailed down the rivers with soldiers and supplies – over 200 ships were recorded. Elector Carl Caspar von der Leyen rightly believed that he was not breaking neutrality, but continued to allow the passage of French troops.[58]

The conquest of Maastricht on 1 July 1673 confronted the Rhine principalities with a serious choice, and the Elector of Trier had to declare himself first. By the spring, the Elector had raised additional companies of infantry to protect the principal places and had complained about the behaviour of the Turenne's troops to the Diet of Regensburg. For the protection of his state, Leyen also called on the Emperor for the quartering of regular troops in Trier. In a misguided attempt to deter such interference, Louis XIV deliberately spread the war to the right bank of the Rhine, and ordered

55 Gottfried Kentenich, *Geschichte der Stadt Trier: von ihrer Gründung bis zur Gegenwart; Denkschrift zum 100 Jährigen Jubiläum der Zugehörigkeit der Stadt zum preussischen Staat* (Trier: Interbook, 1915), p.516.

56 Gottfried Kentenich, *Geschichte der Stadt Trier: von ihrer Gründung bis zur Gegenwart; Denkschrift zum 100 Jährigen Jubiläum der Zugehörigkeit der Stadt zum preussischen Staat* (Trier: Interbook, 1915), p.514.

57 Peter H. Wilson, *German Armies. War and German Politics, 1648–1806* (London: UCL Press, 1998), p.177.

58 Gottfried Kentenich, *Geschichte der Stadt Trier: von ihrer Gründung bis zur Gegenwart; Denkschrift zum 100 Jährigen Jubiläum der Zugehörigkeit der Stadt zum preussischen Staat* (Trier: Interbook, 1915), p.523.

his generals to consider the Electorate of Trier as enemy territory: 'The French diplomats declared that these complaints were an embarrassing matter and that the King of France should punish the German princes who opposed his plans. The storm approached over Trier.'[59] On 31 July 1673, the French besieged Trier; the garrison of 400 infantry and 1,000 militia resisted until 7 September before surrendering – the defenders claimed to have lost only 10 men.[60]

In the spring of 1674, as the Diet declared the *Reichskrieg* against France on 31 March; the Elector raised about 2,000 infantrymen with subsidies from the The Netherlands, and mustered them into the existing infantry regiment. The Electorate was disastrously involved in the war, and Trier remained under French occupation until 1675. However, the Elector managed to increase his troops to 3,000 men, and joined the Allies for the campaign on the middle Rhine.[61] On 11 August 1675, about 2,000 infantrymen fought under *Generalwachtmeister* von der Leyen at the Battle of Conzer Brücke, and in the course of the campaign the Allies seized Trier on 4 September.[62]

The move to the Dutch-Spanish-Imperial side brought no other benefits, on the contrary, the Electorate was forced

268 Anderer Periodus. I. Capitel.

XVII. durch des Crequi Concept (der sonst/ als weit schwächer/ aus seinem vortheilhafften Posten nicht würde heraus gegangen seyn / und sich in eine Bataille eingelassen haben) verruckt worden. Crequy defendirte sich zwar in der Stadt tapffer / weil aber die Guarnison von fünff tausend Mann bis auf 1500. abgenommen / und nechstens einen General-Sturm zu erwarten hatte / wollten diese länger nicht fechten / sondern machten ihre Capitulation vor sich / Krafft dessen der Marechal de Crequy, der Intendant und einige Commissarii als Kriegs-Gefangene verbleiben / die übrige Guarnison aber mit ihrem Unter-Gewehr frey abziehen sollte; Wiewohl ihnen der Accord schlecht gehalten worden / dann weiln ein Teutscher Soldat auf einem Posten / aus Unvorsichtigkeit einen Lunten auf einen Hauffen Granaten fallen lassen / welche darüber loß giengen / und zimlichen Schaden thaten / meynten die Teutschen Soldaten / es wäre eine heimlich-angelegte Mine / (wie dann etliche noch der Meynung sind / Crequy habe es vorsetzlich also angestellt / umb unter währender Unordnung durchzukommen) wurden deßhalben über die ausziehende Guarnison erbittert / und ver-

The Allied reconquest of Trier in 1675 from the chronicle *Trier Erobert*, in *Neueröffneten Historischen Bilder-Saals* (Nuremberg, 1701). Engraving by Andreas Lazarus von Imhof and Conrad Schönleben. (Author's collection).
Immediately after their arrival in front of the city on 4 August 1675, the Allied army, including 2,000 infantrymen from Trier, set up the camp on the Markusberg and opened the approaches to the city. Before the actual siege work began, the Allies learned that the French under Créqui were coming to relieve the city. The French plan failed at the Battle of Conzer Brücke on 11 August 1675. The siege of Trier resumed after the battle and lasted until 4 September.

59 Arthur Janke, *Die Belagerungen der Stadt Trier in den Jahren 1673 bis 1675 und die Schlacht an der Conzer Brücke am 11. August 1675* (Trier: Lintz, 1890), p.5.

60 Arthur Janke, *Die Belagerungen der Stadt Trier in den Jahren 1673 bis 1675 und die Schlacht an der Conzer Brücke am 11. August 1675* (Trier: Lintz, 1890), p.6.

61 Arthur Janke, *Die Belagerungen der Stadt Trier in den Jahren 1673 bis 1675 und die Schlacht an der Conzer Brücke am 11. August 1675* (Trier: Lintz, 1890), p.16.

62 Marr, 'Der Feldzüg 1675 in Deutschland…', p.121, while Janke, *Die Belagerungen der Stadt Trier in den Jahren 1673 bis 1675*, pp.16–17, says this number was 3,000 infantry.

to supply billets and to provision the Imperial troops. The Elector kept his militia ready to march, carefully avoided active intervention, and protested to the Diet when Imperial troops crossed his lands in October 1675 and June 1676. In 1679, after the Peace of Nijmegen, the Electorate resumed its stand of neutrality, but the new French threats in the early 1680s forced the Elector to pursue an active military policy.

In June and July of 1684, after the conquest of Luxembourg, Trier was also occupied by French troops and the fortifications were torn down. In the following years, in order to control the Moselle region, France began building the Mont Royal Fortress in the Electoral territory of Sponheim. Facing these new threats from France, in 1686 Elector Johann Hugo von Orsbeck summoned the Estates to ask the payment of 150,000 thalers to maintain the garrisons and the infantry regiment at full strength. By 1688, around 2,000 men guarded the middle Rhine forts.[63] After the French invasion of the Palatinate in 1688, the French almost completely occupied the Bishoprics of Speyer and Trier. Electoral troops was only able to save Koblenz and Ehrenbreitstein from occupation. Speyer was completely destroyed, the towns of Cochem, Mayen, Wittlich and many other places north of Mont Royal went up in flames, and the left bank of the Rhine remained in French hands until 1694; with the Peace of Rijswijk, France finally returned all the territories of Trier and Speyer, withdrew its remaining troops and destroyed the fortress of Mont Royal, which was still under construction.[64] In the 1690s, the Elector tried to support his military policy by hiring troops to foreign powers, notably the Dutch Republic, and in the next century, even England.[65]

63 Peter H. Wilson, *German Armies. War and German Politics, 1648–1806* (London: UCL Press, 1998), p.91.

64 Max Braubach, 'Johann Hugo von Orsbeck' in *Neue Deutsche Biographie*, vol. 10 (Berlin: Duncker & Humblot, 1974), pp.540–542.

65 Peter H. Wilson, *German Armies. War and German Politics, 1648–1806* (London: UCL Press, 1998), p.109.

4

The Three Brunswicks

Since the Middle Age, the history of the duchy and its principalities was characterised by numerous divisions and reunifications. In order not to disperse the common heritage, the domains belonging to the different dynastic lines could be inherited by a side line when a particular family line died out.[1] Consequently, the states that were created, and which had the legal status of immediate principalities of the Empire, were generally named after the residence of their rulers.

The ruling Houses of Brunswick-Wolfenbüttel and Brunswick-Lüneburg were also known by the inclusive term of *Welfen* (the Guelphs). The hierarchical relations between the princely branches were regulated by mutual agreements. With sole rights to their duchies, the line of Celle provided a conditional sub-lease of the Principality of Lüneburg to the new line of Calenberg, together with the recognition to the Wolfenbüttel heirs – as chiefs of the House – that guaranteed that only his descendants would inherit this senior principality. In 1635, the Guelph domains had split into states of unequal size but each inhabited by between 150,000 and 200,000 people in the late seventeenth century.[2] These parts were ruled by the line of Wolfenbüttel (3,828km^2), Calenberg-Hannover (3,850km^2), and Celle (13,470km^2). Additionally, about a dozen subdivisions still existed, but some were only dynastic and not recognised as immediate states of the Empire. In 1663, only four Guelph principalities had their own place in the *Reichstag*: Brunswick-Wolfenbüttel, Lüneburg-Celle, Lüneburg Hannover, and Grübenhagen.[3]

During the Thirty Years' War, the duchies were the scene of military conflict and suffered from the temporary occupation and the quartering of

---

1 Over the course of the centuries there were the Old, Middle and New Houses – or Lines – of Brunswick, and the Old, Middle and New Houses of Lüneburg. During the second half of the seventeenth century there were three simultaneously reigning dynastic lines represented by immediate Princes of the Empire.

2 Peter H. Wilson, *German Armies. War and German Politics, 1648–1806* (London: UCL Press, 1998), p.21.

3 The Duchy of Grübenhagen was ruled in *Condominium* between Celle and other branches. Among the branches that did not have full sovereignty, were the lordships of Dannenberg, Harburg, Gifhorn, Bevern, Osterode, Herzberg, Salzderhelden, and Einbeck.

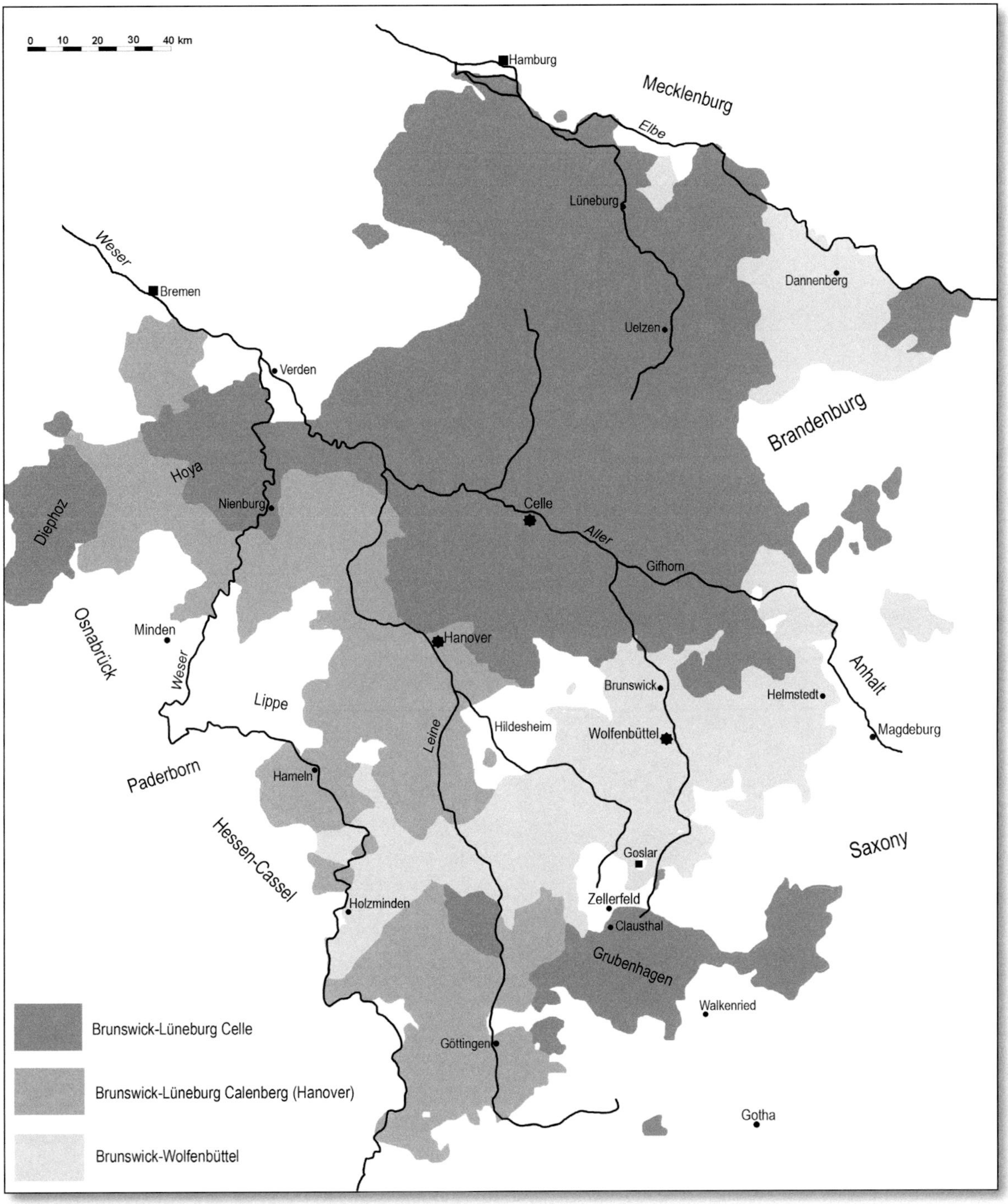

In the seventeenth century, Brandenburg's expansion had been considerable and had alarmed the Guelph Dukes, whose substantial holdings were fragmented by frequent dynastic partitions. Though they had collaborated during the Thirty Years' War, they had not matched Brandenburg's gains, obtaining only partial control of the Lower Saxon Bishopric of Osnabrück, assigned by the Westphalian Settlement to a junior Guelph branch in alternation with Catholic bishops elected by the cathedral chapter. They also exercised a protectorate over the territory of Hildesheim, where they protected the Protestant citizens from their Catholic bishop, but they failed in their efforts to convert this into full secularisation and annexation. Nonetheless, they remained the dominant force within the Lower Saxony Circle, where the senior branch of the family always held one of the executive posts.

Swedish troops. For a long time, the Dukes had attempted a policy of armed neutrality and to this end, the three Houses concluded a treaty of military cooperation. In 1636 it was decided to raise an army for the entire House of Brunswick-Lüneburg. In the following year, the Guelph troops entered Lüneburg, which had been occupied by the Swedes for a year. From 1641, the policy of neutrality was increasingly abandoned and an understanding was sought with the Imperial side, which led to the Peace of Goslar in 1642. At the urging of Emperor Ferdinand III, Duke Friedrich IV began to disband the Brunswick-Lüneburg troops in the same year, thereby considerably weakening his negotiating position at the peace talks in Münster. The territory of the Principality of Lüneburg was not directly affected by the results of the Peace of Westphalia, but the Celle line lost some rights on the Lower Saxony's bishoprics. Though the principalities had sided with Sweden, they had not received any considerable gains, obtaining only partial control of the Bishopric of Osnabrück (2,750km^2), assigned by the Treaty of Westphalia to a junior branch in alternation with Catholic bishops. Furthermore, the line of Celle continued to exercise a protectorate over the town of Hildesheim, where they protected the Protestant citizens from their Catholic bishop, but they failed in their efforts to convert this into full secularisation and annexation. Nonetheless, the principalities became the dominant force within the Lower Saxony Circle, where the senior branch always held one of the executive posts.[4] Certainly, Brandenburg's expansion alarmed the Guelphs, whose substantial holdings were fragmented by dynastic partitions, but, increasingly, the line of Wolfenbüttel as well as Celle and Calenberg were to see the *Kreis* as a convenient mechanism to extend their regional influence and as a bulwark against the Great Elector, as well as against Sweden and Denmark.

Duke Rudolph August of Brunswick-Wolfenbüttel portrayed by Hans Heinrich Rundt. (Herzog August Bibliotek, Wolfenbüttel. Public domain)

Despite the dynastic link between the three Houses, the destinies of the Guelph princes were definitively separate in the first half of the seventeenth century. By 1635, in Brunswick, Duke August the Younger (1579–1666), of the branch of Lüneburg-Dannenberg, took over the power in the principality of Wolfenbüttel and founded a new line. After his long reign, his eldest son Rudolph August (1627–1704) succeeded as the new Duke. In the other Guelph territories, the dynastic events took a less linear trajectory.

4 The other post was exercised by the Bishop of Magdeburg until 1666, who was, however, in no position to oppose the Guelph princes, while the only other substantial territory, the combined Duchies of Mecklenburg, was too weak and was still recovering from the devastation of the war. Peter H. Wilson, *German Armies. War and German Politics, 1648–1806* (London: UCL Press, 1998), p.21.

In 1610, the line of Lüneburg-Celle agreed that the Duchy with all its dependencies should be held by Duke Ernst II and by his brothers as an indivisible whole. Ernst's reign was initially limited to eight years by the Estates, but this arrangement was later cancelled and a 'Family Treaty' was concluded under him in 1610, which agreed the inheritance to the Duke Ernst's descendants. The next of the Ernst's brothers, Georg, held the rule as Duke of Lüneburg Calenberg (Hannover), while Duke Ernst ruled in Celle until his death in 1611, and was succeeded by his brother Christian. After Christian's death in 1633, August Friedrich, the last of the Ernst's brothers, became the ruler from 1636 to 1648. At that date, none of the male heirs of Lüneburg-Celle was alive, and thus Prince Christian Ludwig (r.1648–1665), son of Georg of Calenberg, who in the meantime had transferred the residence to Hannover, inherited the Duchy of Celle. In the same year, he passed Calenberg to his brother Georg Wilhelm in appanage. In 1665, Christian Ludwig died childless, and in turn, Georg Wilhelm inherited Celle settling for the larger duchy of Celle in a settlement brokered by Prince Georg Friedrich of Waldeck, ruling until 1705. Georg Wilhelm then ceded Calenberg to his next brother, Johann Friedrich (r.1665–1679), after a short family struggle for the succession.

Duke Georg Wilhelm of Braunschweig-Lüneburg (1624–1705) in his youth, portrait by Anselmus van Hulle from *Les hommes Illustres* (Amsterdam, 1717).
Georg Wilhelm, often referred to as the *Heideherzog* (Heath Duke), succeeded in leading the court through a considerable flourishing. Under the influence of his wife Eleonore, Georg Wilhelm issued an edict on 7 August 1684 promising to respect the rights of the reformed religious refugees from France and welcome and support them in the Principality. The Celle Court thus became a large Huguenot community, whose members, mostly from Poitou, quickly rose to leading positions at court.

The scenario became complicated again a few years later. Georg Wilhelm's failure to produce an heir left the way for his elder brother, Ernst August, to succeed as Duke of Celle after Georg's death. In 1662, Ernst August was elected as Lutheran Prince-Bishop of Osnabrück and in 1679 added to this title that of Duke of Calenberg in succession to Johann Friedrich. In 1692, Duke Ernst August was appointed by the Emperor as the eighth Prince-Elector, an event that strongly favoured the ascent of the House of Lüneburg in the German arena, sealed in 1705 when Celle and Hannover were reunited into a single state.

Left: Johann Friedrich (1625–1679), who succeeded his brother Georg Wilhelm as Duke of Hannover, and Ernst August (1629–1698), who in turn held Hannover from 1679. After the death of Christian Ludwig of Celle in 1665, Georg Wilhelm took over the Principality, while he passed Calenberg-Hannover to his next younger brother Johann Friedrich. The ascent to the throne was, however, very troubled: in terms of Imperial law, the principalities all remained part of the Duchy of Brunswick-Lüneburg. The changing internal divisions of this territory by the dynasty into *Fürstentümer* did not affect the undivided Imperial fiefdom however. This is why Georg Wilhelm, like his brothers, always bore the title Duke of Brunswick und Lüneburg. In 1656, at the urging of the estates, he became engaged to Sophia of the Palatinate, who he and his youngest brother Ernst August (1629–1698) met in autumn 1656. The brothers had then travelled to the carnival in Venice, as they did every winter. On their return, however, Georg Wilhelm postponed the planned wedding indefinitely. In 1658, his renunciation of the claim to Celle had happened in exchange for being freed from the obligation to marry Princess Sophia. In the same year, Georg Wilhelm ceded his claim on inheriting Calenberg to his youngest brother Ernst August, settling for the Duchy of Celle, and promising to remain unmarried so that he would produce no legitimate heir who might pose a challenge to his brother's claim. The absence of heirs would also mean that Celle would lapse back into Calenberg, since Celle was only supposed to give Georg Wilhelm an income for his lifetime. The reason for this was that Georg Wilhelm had contracted a venereal infection in Venice. He tried to save the honour of the House by persuading his brother Ernst August to take the bride, who was now a somewhat elderly – for the time – 28-year-old, in his place. After reaching this agreement, Ernst August was elected Prince-Bishop of Osnabrück in 1662 and in 1665, after the death of Duke Christian Ludwig von Celle, Georg Wilhelm finally moved there as the new ruler. However, the succession was hindered by his other brother, Johann Friedrich, who installed himself as the new ruler in Celle for a few weeks. Another negotiation was then necessary, which eventually granted Johann Friedrich the Duchy of Hanover together with the territorial compensation of the principality of Grübenhagen.

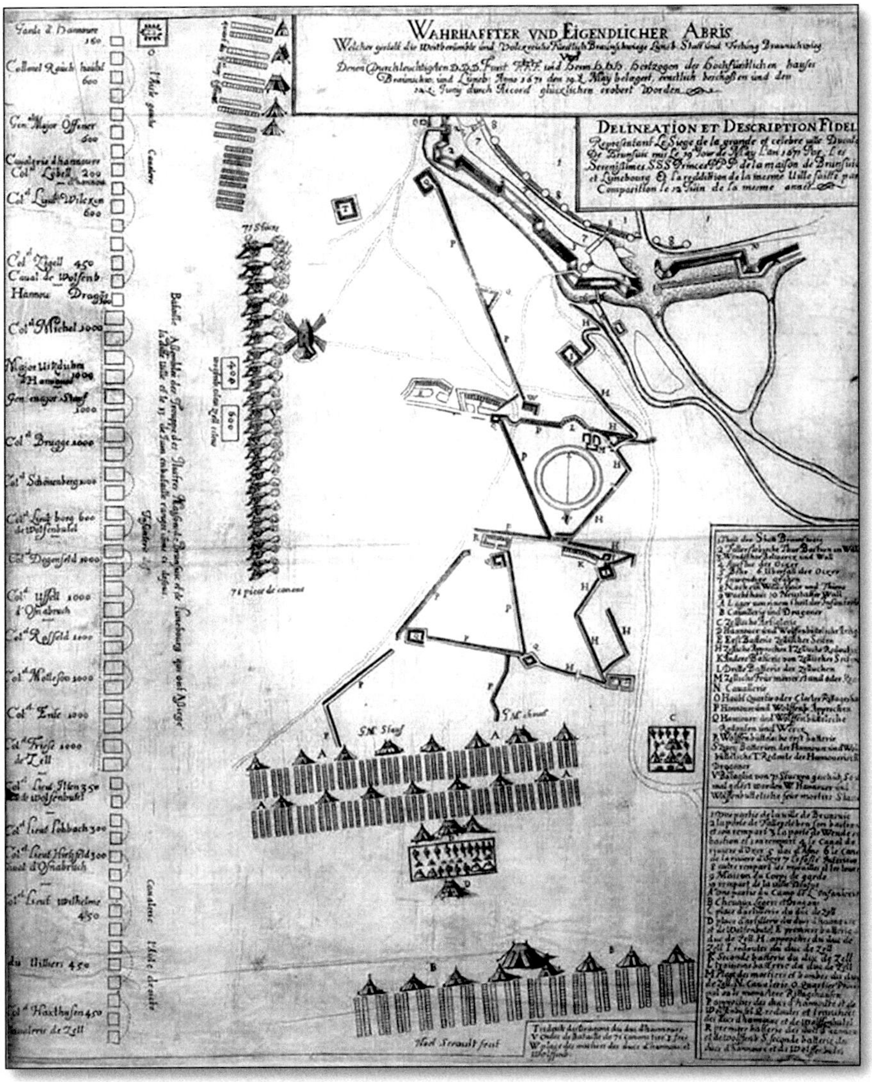

The city of Brunswick besieged in June 1671, contemporary print (Author's collection). The old pipe dreams of the House came true when the joint armies of the different dynastic lines were able to seize the rebel town and return it to the Wolfenbüttel House.

Although the difference in military strength was sometime substantial between one duchy and the other, the three Brunswick emerged alongside the major German states as a territory capable of fielding 18,000–20,000 men, though their armed forces' average peacetime strength was closer to 5,000.[5] Between the 1660s and 1680s, the foreign policy of the Dukes of Brunswick had been fluctuating between neutrality and rapprochements with France or the Emperor depending on the rulers of the duchies. However, the Princes of Lüneburg especially, exploited the military forces to gain reputation,

5 Peter H. Wilson, *German Armies. War and German Politics, 1648–1806* (London: UCL Press, 1998), p.29.

and incomes, lending their troops to other powers. In June 1671, the three Guelph principalities assembled no less than 20,000 men and 100 cannon to besiege the town of Brunswick, which had refused to submit to the authority of Wolfenbüttel.[6]

In early 1675, the war between Brandenburg and Sweden caused great concern among the Lower Saxon territories, to the point that a contingent to face the French on the Rhine was formed. The next assembly of the Circle was convened in March 1677, and saw the members sharply divided between the Swedish and Danish parties. Despite this, a force of 4,615 horse and 15,115 foot was agreed, to form an 'observation corps' on the border with the Swedish territory of Verden-Bremen. Expectations were not realised and this force was never actually assembled, mainly because of conflicting interests and also because many states abused it to obtain more subsidies.[7]

Historians have often considered the military history of the Guelph duchies in a unified perspective. This is most apparent with regard to the two duchies of Lüneburg that were subject to frequent changes of government. With these changes not only individual officers and men, but even companies and sometimes regimental staffs were transferred from one service to another.[8]

Brunswick-Lüneburg-Celle

Being the largest and most populated of the Guelph duchies, Celle was always able to deploy a considerable military contingent. However, the rulers had to face the opposition of the Estates every time they dealt with military matters. In October 1650, Duke Christian Ludwig discussed with the Estates the reduction of the professional troops. He agreed to retain 10 companies of infantry, his own *Leibgarde zu Ross*, and two free companies of cavalry, approximately 500 horse and 2,000 foot.[9] In exchange, the Estates authorised him to improve the fortifications of the state. The next year, Christian Ludwig returned to the matter of the military to reform the militia, which was divided into three district: Celle, Gifhorn and Lüneburg. In each district, he appointed a captain and a lieutenant entrusted to organise and drill able-bodied subjects who could carry weapons. In 1657, a further diminution

6 Rainer Jakobs, 'Braunschweigisches Militärwesen 1641–1714. Heeresorganization in Spannungsfeld von landständischer Verfassung und Fürstlichem Absolutismus', in *Braunschweigisches Jahrbuch für Landesgesichte* 81 (Wolfenbüttel: Braunschweigischer Geschichtsverein, 2000), p.55.

7 Georg Tessin, 'Mecklenburgisches Militär in Türken und Franzosenkriegen 1648–1718' in *Mitteldeutsche Forschungen*, band 42 (Cologne: Böhlau, 1966), p.83.

8 As a result, German historians outline the complex and confused military history of the two Lüneburg duchies. According to Felix Schütz von Brandis, *Übersicht der Geschichte der Hannoversche Armee von 1617 bis 1866* (Hannover & Leipzig: Hahn, 1903), p.45, the military relationships in the two principalities, which were already subject to constant changes during the period of development of the standing armies, became confused, and it is extremely difficult to clarify the numerous apparent contradictions and to analyse the history of the Celle and Hannoverian troops under the various dukes.

9 Robert Wilhelm Georg von Sichart, *Geschichte der Königlich-Hannoverschen Armee* (Hannover, (Hannover, Hahn'sche Hofbuchhandlung, 1866), band 1, pp.119–120.

of the professional troops was arranged and the foot's strength was halved to just 5 companies, while the cavalry increased by an agreement with the Count of Nassau-Saarbrück to provide two companies of 50 *Einspänninge* each[10], increased to 100 in 1659 forming a field regiment.

In 1663, Celle met the request of the Rhenish League for raising a contingent to Hungary. Duke Christian Ludwig personally dealt with the formation of the contingent. On 2 September, he mustered the troops and, according to the chroniclers, urged them to behave honourably by promising 'to care for those who become sick from the battle wounds and to ransom anyone who falls into slavery with the Turks,' as well as to provide officers who did not have the money the necessary field equipment with the necessary wagons and horses.[11] The troops formed a joint contingent of Celle, Hannover and Wolfenbüttel under General Count Wolfgang Julius von Hohenlohe, and comprising one regiment of cavalry of 420 men, one regiment of foot with 810 men, and 9 field guns.[12] The foot regiment consisted of 6 companies of 135 men each, to which Wolfenbüttel, Celle and Hannover each contributed with two companies. As for the cavalry, Celle provided two companies of 105 horsemen, and one each came from the other duchies. Despite Celle and the other Guelph princes being members of the Rhenish League, the contingent served alongside the troops of the Lower Saxony Circle. The harshness of the campaign reduced the contingent to less than half, and when the survivors returned from Hungary in November 1664, the whole contingent passed into the Army of Celle.

While the troops served against the Ottomans in Hungary, the Duke continued to take care of his soldiers. In 1663, the infantry companies formed three battalions which were the origins of the regiments raised in 1665 by Duke Georg Wilhelm as one of his first acts of government, after he succeeded his elder brother. The new Duke swiftly demonstrated his readiness to support the Dutch Republic in the struggle against England and the warlike Prince-Bishop of Münster, Bernhard von Galen. Alongside his brother Ernst August of Osnabrück, Georg Wilhelm offered to raise 4,000 cavalry and 8,000 infantry and to immediately make half of these available to the Republic – followed by the remainder a month later – 'provided that the States General form with them a league of mutual defence and promptly furnish the money for the levying of half of these troops.'[13] One year later, another contingent, joined by troops from Hannover and Osnabrück, supported Bremen against Sweden.

---

10 *Einspänninge* was a synonym for 'horseman', and was widely used in seventeenth century Germany and Austria.

11 Robert Sichart, *Geschichte der Königlich-Hannoverschen Armee* (Hannover, Hahn'sche Hofbuchhandlung, 1866), band 1, pp.124–125.

12 These were regiments *Rauchhaupt zu Pferd* and *Mücheln zu Fuss*; each duchy provided three 3 field guns. See also Bruno Mugnia, *Wars and Soldiers in the Early Reign of Louis XIV, volume 2, The Imperial Army 1657–1687* (Warwick: Helion & Company, 2019), pp.287–288. Each duchy provided 3 field guns.

13 Olaf van Nimwegen, *The Dutch Army and the Military Revolutions, 1588-1688* (Woodbridge: Boydel Press, 2010), p.417. At the end of July 1665, Den Haag sent colonel Aarent Jurren van Haersolte to Celle to negotiate the terms of the hiring of auxiliary troops in Celle and Osnabrück.

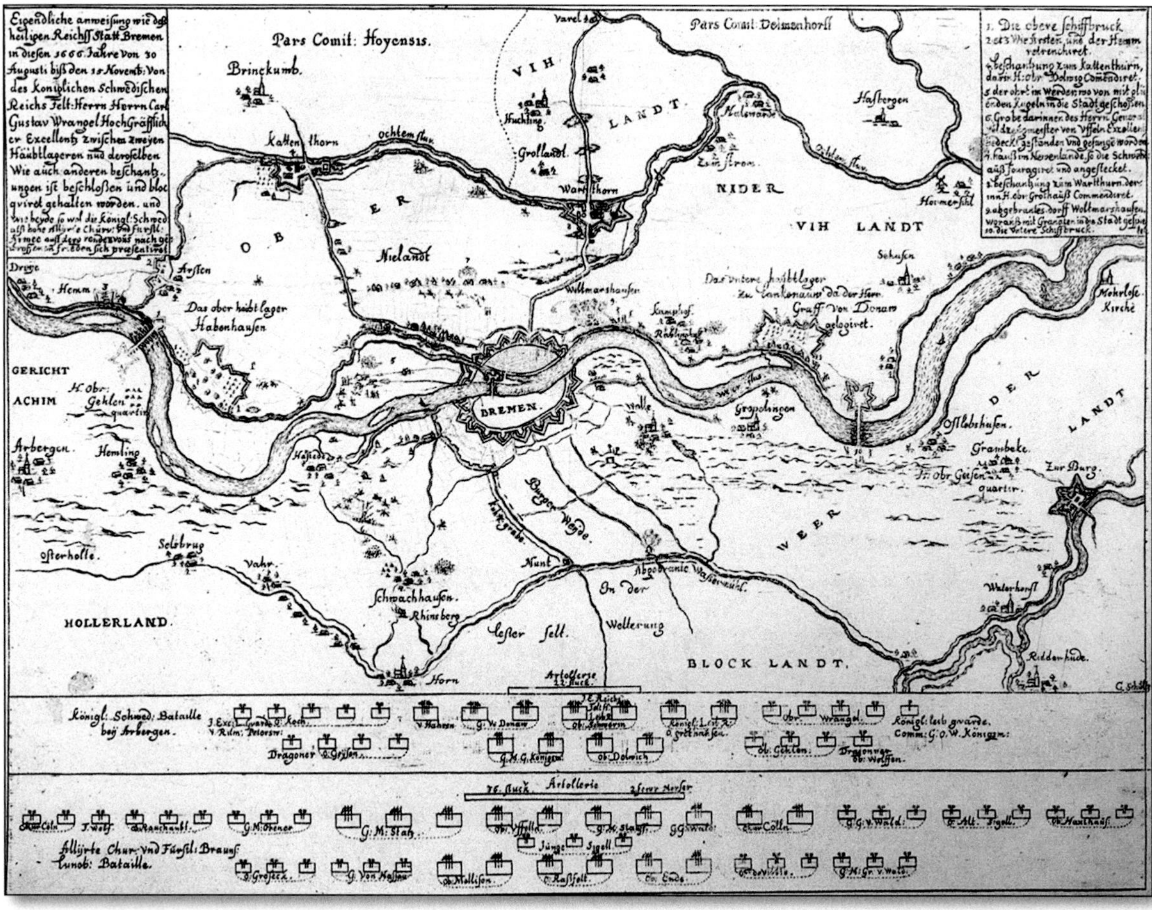

The Swedish siege of Bremen in 1666, contemporary print (Author's collection).
Celle contributed to the relief army with 1,680 cavalry and 4,000 infantry supported by field artillery.

In 1665, the Duke transferred to Celle some of the officers who had served him in Hannover, including *Generalmajor* Goertz, who became Commander-in-Chief.[14] He expelled from Celle some of the officers who had served under Christian Ludwig, causing the irritation of Georg Wilhelm.[15] After this, Goertz was replaced by Count Josias von Waldeck who became the actual organiser of the permanent army, which in 1665 numbered approximately 1,000 cavalry and 1,600 infantry, the former increased to about 1,200 before the end of the year with the newly raised regiment *Villiers zu Pferd* (BcB-4). This field force included the company of the foot guards, three regiments of infantry each with 10 companies and 600 men, and three free companies. The cavalry comprised the *Trabanten Garde*, and four

14 Robert Sichart, *Geschichte der Königlich-Hannoverschen Armee* (Hannover, Hahn'sche Hofbuchhandlung, 1866), band 1, p.126.

15 Incidentally, both dukes kept the troops they had recruited during the dispute after it had been settled.

Count Josias of Waldeck-Wildungen (1636–1669), portrait by an unknown artist (Collection of the Bergheim Castle, *Kreis* of Waldeck).
Von Waldeck was the second son of Count Philipp VII, and cousin of Prince Georg Friedrich. Like the latter, he started his military career in the Army of Brandenburg in 1655 as a colonel of infantry. In 1669, he held the command of the Celle contingent in Venetian service during the last phase of the Cretan War. During the defence of Candia, after having previously been wounded in the arm, on 16 July he suffered another serious wound, this time in the leg. The prevailing heat and his state of mind, resulting from quarrels with the Venetian Captain General Francesco Morosini, aggravated his condition, and on 8 August, he died to the great consternation of his officers and soldiers.

regiments of horse. The standing troops also included an artillery section.[16] This was entrusted to Captain Christoph von Bobart, who later was promoted to *major* and finally *obristlieutenant* in 1671.[17]

Among the 'foreign' advisers who entered Georg Wilhelm's service, Prince Georg Friedrich of Waldeck proved fundamental in revitalising the territories and boosting the prestige of Celle. Through his relative, Josias, in the seven years of his employment Waldeck raised the strength of the professional force from less than 3,000 men in 1665 to over 7,000 in 1671. The growth was not only numerical, but also qualitative, contributing to increasing the reputation of Celle's soldiers abroad, while Waldeck's influence in Germany led to Georg Wilhelm becoming a major supplier of auxiliaries. On Waldeck's recommendation, several foreign veteran officers entered Celle's service, such as the Scottish *Obristleutnants* Mollesson and Melleville (or Melvill), who had served as soldiers of fortune in the Army of Sweden. With them, came other officers from German states. The *Obristlieutenant* Krosigk, previously in Brandenburg service, entered the Celle army in 1665 receiving the patent for the recruitment of a cavalry regiment of 4 companies, later increased to 6, becoming colonel proprietor before the end of the year.

16 Robert Sichart, *Geschichte der Königlich-Hannoverschen Armee* (Hannover, Hahn'sche Hofbuchhandlung, 1866), band 1, pp.127–128.
17 Robert Sichart, *Geschichte der Königlich-Hannoverschen Armee* (Hannover, Hahn'sche Hofbuchhandlung, 1866), band 1, p.144.

In 1666, the regiment passed to *Obristwachtmeister* Wilm, and in 1667 was hired to the Dutch Republic, which returned it the next year.[18] In the same period, the militia was reformed gathering the able subjects in four *Auschuss Kompagnien* of different strength: two companies of 400 men, one of 200 and another of 170, each under a captain and a commander with the rank of *Obrist*.

In late 1667, Duke Georg Wilhelm discussed with the Estates the maintenance of the professional troops, but only modest adjustments were granted. However, foreign policy offered an opportunity to achieve this goal. In December, Georg Wilhelm discussed an agreement with the Governor of the Spanish Low Countries for the provision of 2,000 horse and 4,000 foot in exchange for a subsidy. The agreement did not materialise however, since the Treaty of Aix-la-Chapelle put an end to the emergency. Pressed by the economic shortage, and stimulated in his vanity by the prospects that an involvement in the war against the Porte could offer, the Duke discussed with the Republic of Venice the hiring of troops to be employed in Crete.

Horseman and infantryman in a plate (XIV / 47) from Richard Knötel's *Die Grosse Uniformenkunde* (Stephen Ede-Borrett collection). The artist reconstructed these figures from the monumental gravestone of Josias von Waldeck built in 1674, when the body of the commander was returned home from Crete (see also in the colour plates commentaries).

18 Robert Sichart, *Geschichte der Königlich-Hannoverschen Armee* (Hannover, Hahn'sche Hofbuchhandlung, 1866), band 1, p.144. In 1671, a regiment with the same name marched to Brunswick to join the Guelph cousin of Wolfenbüttel for the submission of the rebel city.

After the approach of the Venetian government to Georg Wilhelm, who was in the city for the carnival season of 1668, the Duke agreed to supply three regiments of infantry. The contingent, 3,300 men, sailed to Crete with the experienced Josias von Waldeck as field commander. He served until 16 July 1669, the day he was seriously wounded in action during the defence of Candia. As well as von Waldeck, 1,680 officers and rank and file died in the 14 months of fighting. The survivors returned to Celle in 1670 after spending a painful quarantine on the Ionian islands.[19]

The period of peace after 1668 led to a reduction in the strength of the army. The most significant act was the disbanding of three cavalry regiments between 1669 and 1671, retaining only the life companies, one of which became the *Garde zu Pferd* in 1672. The disbanding of the regiments also caused some changes in the posts of the colonel-proprietors. One of them, *Obrist* Jeremias de Chauvet entered Celle's service in 1670 as *obrist* of the former regiment *Haxthausen zu Pferd* (BcC-1). Chauvet came from the French army, but had previously served for Portugal until 1668. He had performed with distinction during the occupation of Lorraine; but his arrival in Celle caused great unease among the officers. However, the reduction of the mounted force was short-lived, as in 1671 Georg Wilhelm took over the permission from the Elector of Cologne to raise a regiment of dragoons in Liège mounted on horses purchased in Poland. It consisted of four companies and was entrusted to Obrist Franke (BcD-1).[20]

Cover page of the *Novissima Praxis Militaris* by Johann Scheiter (Braunschweig: Zilliger & Gruber, 1672). (Author's collection) An artillery officer in the Celle contingent on Crete, Scheiter participated in the defence of Candia from March until the surrender on 9 September 1669. He left an interesting account of the dramatic fighting, which he published in an appendix to his military treaty in 1672. Thanks to the experience gained during the Cretan War, Celle developed siege warfare and other technical improvements in the infantry equipment.

After the French invasion of the Dutch Republic in 1672, and exploiting the insecurity arising from Hannover's siding with France, the Duke negotiated with the Estates for a considerable increase in professional troops, while further subsidies were discussed with Den Haag. With these resources, Georg Wilhelm increased the cavalry regiments to 9 companies, forming

19 Wilhelm Kohlaas, *Candia 1645–1669. Die Tragödie einer abendländischen Verteidigung mit dem Nachspiel Athen 1687* (Osnabrück: Biblio Verlag, 1978), p.234.

20 Robert Sichart, *Geschichte der Königlich-Hannoverschen Armee* (Hannover, Hahn'sche Hofbuchhandlung, 1866), band 1, p.147.

three field squadrons. The *Garde zu Pferd* was also increased to the strength of one squadron. An independent company quartered at Celle became the *Dragonergarde*, the Walloon *Kapitän* Chevalier du Bocage was appointed as commander. Another free-company of dragoons was raised under *Kapitän* Henning. In 1673, *Obrist* Melleville received command of the former militia infantry regiment, which had been transformed into a unit of regular soldiers in 1671.[21] The same year the independent companies of militia were also formed into a regiment of 2 battalions and 10 companies under *Obrist* Friesen, however, the regiment remained *ohnmondirt* (without uniform). In 1673, the strategic scenario played directly into the hands of Georg Wilhelm, who wanted to displace both Brandenburg and Münster as the dominant power in Northern Germany. With Hannover neutral and the other two Guelph rulers in Wolfenbüttel and Osnabrück following his lead, Georg Wilhelm exploited his influence in the Lower Saxon Circle (*Kreis*) to buttress his ambitions. Already elected *Kreisoberst* in 1671, he exploited his mobilisation powers to make policy without reference to the other members of the Circle. The 3,000 *Kreistruppen* sanctioned by the Diet in 1674 in response to the call for assistance against France were in fact entirely provided by Celle and Wolfenbüttel at the other States' expense.[22]

Duke Johann Adolph of Holstein-Ploen (1634–1704) Imperial *Feldmarschall* and Commander-in-Chief of the Celle-Wolfenbüttel-Osnabrück auxiliary corps in Alsace for the campaigns of 1674–1675 (*Theatrum Europeum*, Frankfurt am Main, 1680. Public domain)

In spring 1674, with subsidies from the Dutch Republic, Austria and Spain, Celle gathered the troops to join the allied army on the Rhine. According to the treaty, signed on 20 June, the troops of Celle were united into a single corps with those of Wolfenbüttel to a total of 13,000 men with 26 field guns. Duke Johann Adolph of Holstein-Ploen held the rank of Commander-in-Chief. He was the brother-in-law of Duke Rudolph August of Wolfenbüttel, whom both dukes had jointly appointed as *Feldmarschall*.

The troops of Celle comprised 1,896 horse, 125 dragoons, 3,500 foot, 23 field and 2 siege guns.[23] One company of the *Garde zu Pferd* and some reinforcements escorted Georg Wilhelm while he accompanied Holstein-Ploen during the march to the border. A further newly raised infantry regiment joined the corps before the autumn, increasing the number of the infantry to approximately 6,500 men, although still lower than the establishment number of 7,520.

21 Robert Sichart, *Geschichte der Königlich-Hannoverschen Armee* (Hannover, Hahn'sche Hofbuchhandlung, 1866), band 1, p.148.

22 Peter H. Wilson, *German Armies. War and German Politics, 1648–1806* (London: UCL Press, 1998), p.52.

23 Robert Sichart, *Geschichte der Königlich-Hannoverschen Armee* (Hannover, Hahn'sche Hofbuchhandlung, 1866), band 1, pp.149–150.

Holstein-Ploen joined the allied army under Bournonville in Alsace, and with his men was involved in the unfortunate winter campaign of 1674–1675. Celle soldiers fought at Entzheim on 4 October, Muhlouse on 29 December, and Türkheim on 5 January. The casualties suffered by the Celle troops are known. At Entzheim, the contingent lost: in the cavalry 10 officers, 8 NCOs, 120 troopers and 119 horses, and in the infantry 8 Officers, 44 NCOs and 198 privates;[24] while a contemporary witness refers to 394 dead including 2 field officers.[25] At the end of the campaign, the casualties must have

Melleville *Ausschuss* regiment of Celle clashes with French infantry at Entzheim, 4 October 1674, in a drawing by Rothgaengel published in the magazine *Die Mölkerbastei*, in the 1970s. (Public domain)
Although the fight was not actually at such close quarters, the battle did result in a bloody action. An eyewitness relates that 'the smoke obscured even the sun and the sky wept, for the continuous deluge of blood that the Christians were shedding among them. After four hours of fighting, the two armies stopped within musket-shot of each other and no more shots were heard from the enemy. Our troops, however, thundered with such vigour that at times whole enemy companies fell to the ground dead, that one could not believe it.'[26] In his drawing, Rothgaengel depicts the militiamen wearing their civilian dress, as referred to in the accounts, which mention the regiment as *Ohnnmondierte* (without uniform). However, reports say that after the battle, the militiamen retrieved coats and headwear from the fallen infantrymen and cavalrymen and wore them despite the multiple variations in colour. Duke Georg Wilhelm, upon seeing them, was greatly amused.

24 Robert Sichart, *Geschichte der Königlich-Hannoverschen Armee* (Hannover, Hahn'sche Hofbuchhandlung, 1866), band 1, p.377.

25 Friedrich Schirmer, 'Die Schlacht bei Entzheim, 24. 9. 1674', in *Alte und Neue Zinnfiguren* – 1971 – Heft 9, p.176. Schirmer quotes the report of Berkemeyer: 'We too were not saved in the battle and lost many men, including two colonels, 44 other high and low officers and 348 privates'.

26 Report of Berkemeyer, quoted by Friedrich Schirmer, 'Die Schlacht bei Entzheim, 24. 9. 1674', in *Alte und Neue Zinnfiguren*, 1971 Heft 9, p.176.

been considerable, since on 3 March 1675, regiment Linstrow (BcI-5) was disbanded during the winter quarters in Swabia; about 500 men were merged into to the regiments Ende (BcI-1), Malortie (BcI-3) and Melleville (BcI-4); the rest returned to Celle with the regiment Mollesson (BcI-2).[27] The lack of professional troops was filled by one battalion of the *ausschuss* militia under *Major* Grübenhagen, which marched to the Rhine in the spring.

The campaign of 1675 was memorable for the House of Celle, despite its unfavourable start marked by strong internal disagreements. In the spring, Duke Georg Wilhelm had joined the army, in open disagreement with his cousins from Wolfenbüttel, with the firm intention of replacing Holstein-Ploen. The political-dynastic problems were increased by the simultaneous presence of four Princes of the Empire: Johann Adolph of Holstein-Ploen, Charles IV of Lorraine, Ernst August of Osnabrück, and Georg Wilhelm of Celle. Eventually, field command was given to Marchese Grana del Carretto, an Italian general in the service of the Emperor, and Duke Charles IV of Lorraine. On 11 August, the troops of Celle comprised 11 squadrons and 1 company of cavalry, 6 squadrons and 1 company of dragoons and 3 battalions of infantry. The composite army comprised Imperial, Spanish, Lorrainer and further German troops from Trier, Mainz, and Cologne, which had been given the task of protecting the main army while it was besieging Trier, from the attempt to relieve the French garrison led by *Maréchal* Créqui.

The successful outcome of the battle generated great enthusiasm throughout pro-Allied Germany. Duke Georg Wilhem wrote a letter to his pro-French brother Johann Friedrich, remarking on the size of the victory.[28] At Celle, the enthusiasm involved the entire court and festive celebrations took place throughout the duchy. On 26 August, in gratitude for his action in the battle, Duke Georg Wilhelm promoted his favourite, Jeremias de Chauvet, to the rank of *generalleutnant* and privy war councillor. This appointment not only gave Chauvet advantages in terms of rank and income, but he also acquired a considerable influence over the ducal army, to the great annoyance of the German officers. However, the complaints passed into second place when the Swedish invasion of Pomerania turned the attention of the Lower Saxony Circle to the northern territories.

The new strategic scenario diminished the involvement of Celle on the Rhine. With a Dutch subsidy an expeditionary force of 4,000 infantry was gathered to face the new threat, while the cavalry and dragoons remained in the Spanish Low Countries. Such measures played directly into the hands of Georg Wilhelm, who still wanted to displace both Brandenburg and

27 Robert Sichart, *Geschichte der Königlich-Hannoverschen Armee* (Hannover, Hahn'sche Hofbuchhandlung, 1866), band 1, p.151.

28 Georg Wilhelm stated that the number of flags and standards captured amounted to 40–50, the number of cannon to 10, and mentions that 'the enemy had abandoned all ammunition and the entire baggage with horses, wagons, carriages, mules, ... and he had lost many people both in the flight and in the gathering place, so that many distinguished officers were killed or taken prisoner.' Robert Sichart, *Geschichte der Königlich-Hannoverschen Armee* (Hannover, Hahn'sche Hofbuchhandlung, 1866), band 1, p.394.

Münster as the dominant power in Northern Germany.[29] The campaign in Verden-Bremen, conducted together with the Allies achieved a considerable series of conquests, but was also marked by quarrels and mutual discourtesy, especially with Münster and Brandenburg.[30] Celle troops participated in the major actions, included the sieges of Stade, where *Obrist* Mollesson was killed; he was replaced by *Obrist* Jäger. In 1677, 3,000 men were sent to Swedish Pomerania to face the Swedes. In July, before Stettin, Jäger was also killed, leaving the regiment to the *Obristlieutenant* Carmaillon, a client of Chauvet.[31]

Celle's ensigns captured by the French at Neerwinden, 29 July 1693, from *Les Triomphes de Louis XIV Représentés par Les Drapeaux pris sur Les Ennemis de S. M.* (Author's artwork).
There is little information about the Standards and Colours of the Celle regiments before 1693, but both the regiments already existed in the previous decades under the same colonel-proprietors. Left, regiment *La Motte zu Fuss* (BcI-2): scarlet red background, white shells, golden lion head and arrow, blue tongue. Right, regiment *Franke Dragoner* (BcD-1): carmine red background, white horse, golden laurels and crown, white pearls and scroll, black letters. The guidons of the *Franke Dragoner*, as well as *De Carles zu Fuss* (former *Dalberg*, BcI-1) carried the ducal motto *QUO FAS ET GLORIA DUCUNT* and the white horse as emblem. While not really a representative selection, it suggests that all Celle flags and standards had similar decoration. NB the colour of the field was not necessarily the same as that of the facings.

29 Peter H. Wilson, *German Armies. War and German Politics, 1648–1806* (London: UCL Press, 1998). Conflict with Brandenburg emerged already in April 1677, when the Great Elector was enraged that Celle proceeded to close off Lower Saxony to his troops, where he hoped to extort contributions, p.54.

30 See also in *Wars and Soldiers in the Early Reign of Louis XIV, volume 7, German Armies 1655–1669, Part 1* (Warwick: Helion & Company, 2024), pp.270–278.

31 Robert Sichart, *Geschichte der Königlich-Hannoverschen Armee* (Hannover, Hahn'sche Hofbuchhandlung, 1866), band 1, p.152.

The Peace of Nijmegen ended the war against France, but the campaigns against Sweden lasted until 1679. In the winter of 1678–1679, Celle troops took their quarters between the Elbe and Weser River extorting billets and contributions, but the negotiation for the partitioning of the conquests brought little gains to Georg Wilhelm, who had to share them with Hannover, now ruled by Duke Ernst August.[32] Further disputes involving Celle were within the Empire.[33] In summer 1679, the troops returned home. The economic situation required an immediate reduction of the army not only in the number of regiments, but also in the overall strength. In October, there were 13 horse, 6 dragoon and 21 foot companies, some of which were joined into regiments for administrative purposes.[34] Except for the Life Guards, the size of the companies was halved, and the overall strength fell by approximately 5,000 men.[35]

International concerns soon turned attention to the military again. In summer 1679, Denmark renewed its ambitions to impose its rule over the city-port of Hamburg, forcing Duke Georg Wilhelm to intervene to support the city. In October, the settlement of Pinneberg settled the conflict.[36] In the early 1680s, Brandenburg's resistance to Austria and loyalty to Louis XIV, who resumed the pressure on the Rhine, persuaded Celle not to remain passive. In 1682–1683, the professional troops increased to 8,562 men in response to the changing strategic situation.[37] In the next years, the Army's strength varied – it climbed to 8,964 men in 1684, falling to 7,914 in 1685 and 5,060 in 1688.[38]

---

32 Peter H. Wilson, *German Armies. War and German Politics, 1648–1806* (London: UCL Press, 1998), p.57. The French intervention in Westphalia early in 1679 compelled the Allies to return their conquests, leaving the pre-war situation unchanged. However, it remained to be seen which principality would profit from Sweden's weakness, but there were already signs that it would be the Protestant powers of Hannover, Celle and Brandenburg provided that they could defeat Danish ambitions. The Dutch Republic was already showing less interest in the region, because of the more immediate threat to their southern frontier from France, while Münster's inability to make any permanent gains ensured its belligerence did not survive the death of its energetic Bishop Bernard von Galen in 1678.

33 Joachim Whaley, *Germany and the Holy Roman Empire. Vol. 2: from the Peace of Westphalia to the Dissolution of the Reich. 1648–1806* (Oxford & New York: Oxford University Press, 2012), p.57: In 1678, the Imperial Diet was paralysed for months by the 'legitimation controversy', which arose because a new representative from Celle sent his credentials to the directorate office of the Elector of Mainz via one of his officials, who refused to accept them on the grounds that only the representatives of a new Elector could present their credentials in this way; the envoys of Princes were required to attend in person.'

34 Robert Sichart, *Geschichte der Königlich-Hannoverschen Armee* (Hannover, Hahn'sche Hofbuchhandlung, 1866), band 1, pp.152–153.

35 Peter H. Wilson, *German Armies. War and German Politics, 1648–1806* (London: UCL Press, 1998), p.162.

36 Under the Treaty of Pinneberg, Denmark agreed to receive from Hamburg a sum of money, but the main matter was suspended until a legal discussion.

37 Robert Sichart, *Geschichte der Königlich-Hannoverschen Armee* (Hannover, Hahn'sche Hofbuchhandlung, 1866), band 1, pp.258–260.

38 Peter H. Wilson, *German Armies. War and German Politics, 1648–1806* (London: UCL Press, 1998), p.162.

In 1683, Georg Wilhelm discussed with Vienna the hiring of auxiliary troops for Hungary.[39] After the agreement signed in September 1684 at Linz, Celle mustered its contingent together with Hannover and Wolfenbüttel. In early 1685, two cavalry and one dragoon regiment, each of 6 companies, and 4 infantry regiments, each of 7 companies, were assembled and mustered by *Generals* Chauvet and Boisdavid to whom the duke had entrusted his troops. The overall strength was 4,900 men.[40] The harshness of the Hungarian theatre severely affected the troops. In the end, the cost in men and money was considerable and no prince made a profit on the arrangements even if they considered the political benefits worthwhile. Together with Hannover and Wolfenbüttel, the corps lost 400 killed and 1,500 wounded, nearly a fifth of its strength.[41] In 1686, the agreement halved the participation of Celle in the war against the Ottomans, which lasted until 1687.

In January 1686, to resolve the internal struggle in Hamburg, Georg Wilhelm sent 2,000 men to the Elbe, consisting of the dragoon regiment Franke (BcD-1) and the infantry regiment Linstrow (BcI-4). This force remained in the Hamburg territory until October 1686, to counter the Danish intervention.[42]

Celle was among the first German states to deal with aged, invalid and infirm soldiers. By the end of the 1680s, Duke Georg Wilhelm endowed the St Wilhelm Hospital in Celle with funds for this purpose. Elderly and wounded NCOs and soldiers were admitted to the hospital and fed, clothed and their wounds tended for the rest of their lives. Since the hospital could only accommodate a small number of invalids, and was restricted only to those who were unmarried, the other invalids in the village were granted a pension. However, to prevent these expenses from burdening the state's finance, the money for invalids was deducted from the wages of serving soldiers. A similar initiative was also introduced in Hannover from 1692.[43]

Despite the renewed cooperation of the Guelph Dukes to raise common contingents for Hungary and Germany, strong differences would emerge with Denmark in the following years for the succession of Saxe-Lauenburg, and the rise of Hannover to the rank of Electoral Principality; problems which lasted until 1705.

39 According to some sources, the *Lebgarde zu Pferd* and the cavalry regiment Chauvet took part in the campaign of 1684. However, as neither the documents of the archives nor the available news about the campaign confirm this statement, the participation of Celle remains doubtful. Nevertheless, it is not impossible that, even if a subsidy treaty has not yet been concluded, Duke Georg Wilhelm would have provided his contingent to the *Reichsarmee*. See Sichart, *Geschichte der Königlich-Hannoverschen Armee* (Hannover, Hahn'sche Hofbuchhandlung, 1866), band 1, p.448.

40 Robert Sichart, *Geschichte der Königlich-Hannoverschen Armee* (Hannover, Hahn'sche Hofbuchhandlung, 1866), band 1, pp.450–451. These were: infantry regiment Nettelhorst (BcI-1), Boisdavid (BcI-3), La Motte (BcI-2), Linstrow (BcI-4); cavalry regiments Chauvet (BcC-1), Beauregard (BcC-5), and Franke Dragoner (BcD-1)

41 Peter H. Wilson, *German Armies. War and German Politics, 1648–1806* (London: UCL Press, 1998), p.76.

42 Robert Sichart, *Geschichte der Königlich-Hannoverschen Armee* (Hannover, Hahn'sche Hofbuchhandlung, 1866), band 1, p.405.

43 Robert Sichart, *Geschichte der Königlich-Hannoverschen Armee* (Hannover, Hahn'sche Hofbuchhandlung, 1866), band 1, p.342.

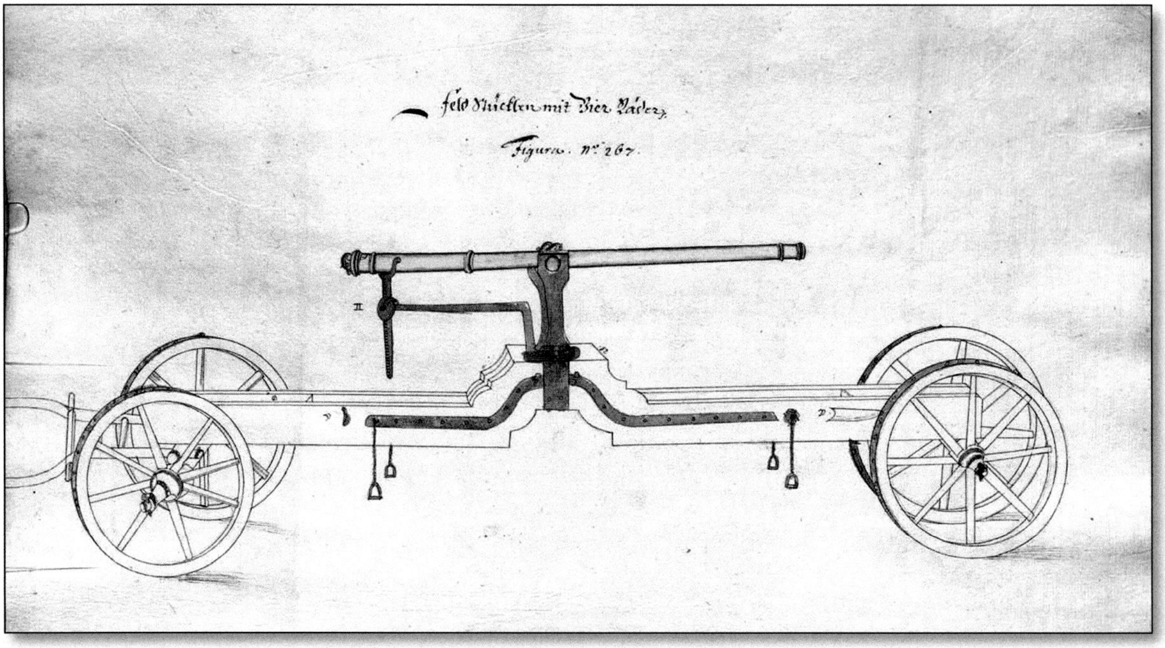

Light field gun on four wheels, from the Anton Faulhaber's *Artilleriekunst*, written and illustrated by the author between 1680 and 1702 (Bayerischer Staatsbibliothek, Munich).
Little, although accurate, documentation exists on Celle artillery thanks to the Brückmanns *Artilleriebuch* and to the writings of Christoph von Bobart, who was *oberstleutnant* of the artillery from 1671. The constable depicted in the original illustration wears a pale grey uniform with red facings, but on another illustration in the same book, he is wearing a red coat. The painting in the Bomann Museum in Celle was made after this drawing. It shows Bobart in full uniform of a full red *Rock* with a single row of eight yellow metal (brass?) buttons on the front. The cuffs are turquoise with three yellow metal (brass?) buttons. A white neckcloth, brown leather breeches, and greenish blue stockings complete his appearance. On the side of his black headwear he has a yellow cockade. Cuffs, hat and buttonholes are embroidered with a narrow yellow lace. The men serving the light cannon are shown with buttonholes down the whole front of the coat but without lace.

Brunswick-Lüneburg Hannover

Less extensive and less populated than the Duchy of Celle, Calenberg-Hannover was economically on a par with its neighbouring state. This allowed the principality to raise a significant standing army. In 1665, just before leaving Hannover for Celle, Georg Wilhelm had 1,434 horse and dragoons and 3,024 foot.[44]

A year before, the Duke had provided one-third of the contingent of the three Guelph principalities for the *Deutsche Allianz* in Hungary, 140 horse and 300 foot. In May 1665, Georg Wilhelm signed an agreement with the Palatinate to hire mercenaries for the *Wildfang* Dispute against Mainz and its allies. These were four companies of cavalry and 100 dragoons, joined to the contingent of Osnabrück, under *Obrist* Hilten.[45] In 1666, Duke

44 Robert Sichart, *Geschichte der Königlich-Hannoverschen Armee* (Hannover, Hahn'sche Hofbuchhandlung, 1866), band 1, pp.127–128.

45 Karl Brunner, *Der Pfälzische Wildfangstreit unter Kurfürft Karl Ludwig (1664–1667)* (Innsbruck: Wagner´schen Universität-Buchhandlung, 1896), p.28.

Johann Friedrich agreed to join the relief corps 'in warding off unwelcome Swedish encroachments on the city of Bremen.'[46] Two years later, Hannover met the call of Duke Georg Wilhelm of Celle to raise troops for Venice. Johann Friedrich provided four infantry companies that formed a battalion of 400 men under *Obristlieutenant* Pallandt. They sailed to Crete alongside the regiments assembled by Celle, and in 1670 returned home, reduced to 3 officers, 37 NCOs and drummers, and 50 private soldiers.[47] In 1671, responding to the appeal of his cousin of Wolfenbüttel, Johann Friedrich sent a contingent of his troops to besiege the rebellious city of Brunswick.

However, by the winter 1670–71, Johann Friedrich was turning decisively to an autonomous foreign policy, separating his territory from the Guelph common ground. In early 1671, the Duke signed a secret treaty with Louis XIV to support the French policy in the Empire. The alliance with France also brought one with Sweden forming the basis for the future military project of both powers. Probably, this new course did not remain unnoticed, because signals also reverberated into the army. In July 1671, on the recommendation of Louis XIV and Turenne, Johann Friedrich took *General* Heinrich von Podewils from the French army into his service, appointing him *Generalleutnant* and Commander-in-Chief. Podewils also became colonel proprietor of an infantry regiment replacing the late *Generalmajor* Goertz.[48] French taste also influenced the nomenclature of some units, like the *Leibgarde zu Ross* that assumed the name *Garde du Corps*. The Duke also established

Musketeer, regiment *Mücheln zu Fuss*, or *Das Blauen Regiment*, 1665–1666 (Author's illustration). In 1668, the Hanoverian infantry formed four regiments, each identified by the colour of their coat: red, blue, yellow or grey. This had been usual in several German armies since the Thirty Years' War, but the colour more often referred to that of the regiment's ensigns. In Hannover, the denomination of the infantry regiments actually came from the clothing colour.

46 Peter H. Wilson, *German Armies. War and German Politics, 1648–1806* (London: UCL Press, 1998), p.162.

47 Robert Sichart, *Geschichte der Königlich-Hannoverschen Armee* (Hannover, Hahn'sche Hofbuchhandlung, 1866), band 1, pp.360–361.

48 Robert Sichart, *Geschichte der Königlich-Hannoverschen Armee* (Hannover, Hahn'sche Hofbuchhandlung, 1866), band 1, p.128.

a *Kriegsrat* (war council) with *Generals* Podewils, Flemming and Öffener as councillors, and also established his own *Generalstab* comprising two adjutants, technical personnel and assistants.

By the treaty signed on 10 December 1672, Johann Friedrich, who had also converted to Catholicism, promised to provide Louis XIV with 10,000 soldiers 'drilled on the French model.' In detail, these were to be 3,000 cavalry, 1,000 dragoons and 6,000 foot.[49] France paid the costs for the recruitment in Hannover in order to maintain the secrecy. With this subsidy, the army increased to a figure even greater, and in 1673 the professional troops numbered 15,000 men. According to a report of 23 May 1673, issued by the war council in Hannover, Johann Friedrich gave the specifications regarding the formation of the infantry, distributing the men in the units without forgetting any detail. Each regiment was to have 12 companies of 125 men; the 9 free companies still out of the regimental organisation resulted in a surplus of 416 rank and file to be organised into a further 3 companies of 125 men each, leaving 41 privates as 'supernumeraries' waiting for further orders.[50] In 1673, after French recommendations, further foreign officers entered the service of Hannover, among them, the Prince Rinaldo d'Este from Modena, who became colonel proprietor of the infantry *Gelbes Regiment* (BhI-3), and after him, some of his Italian clients followed to become officers in the regiment: the *Obristlieutenant* Scandiani, and the *Kapitäns* Pietro Dragoni, and Teodoro Volo; among the other *kapitäns* there was also the Frenchman La Chapelle, and a Conte Volalto became colonel proprietor of the *Weiss Regiment zu Fuss* (BhI-6).[51]

Company Colours, regiment *Bernholz zu Fuss* (former *Modena*, BhI-3, former *Gelbe Regiment*). (Author's collection) Yellow field, grey cannon barrel, red and yellow flames, gold letters. Friedrich Schirmer describes eight ensigns for this regiment in 1680; seven of yellow and one of white – all with mottos in gold as shown in the illustration. The latter ensign, possibly the life colour, has a gold watch at one o'clock in Roman numbers, with the motto O LA DICIOSA O LA POSTRERA. The others are: two green laurels forming a circle tied below by a golden ribbon, with the motto HINC LABOR, HINC MERCES; a silver arrow, with the motto Y MARTI Y SERVE AMORE; two laurels forming a circle above a fire in red and gold, with the motto ARDER Y CAILLAR; a green Medusa head, with the motto VINCIT QUEM RESPICIT HOSTEM; the Roman *Mutio Scevola* and an Etruscan, natural, with a flaming brazier, with the motto AGERE ET PATI FORTIA HEROICUM EST.

49 Robert Sichart, *Geschichte der Königlich-Hannoverschen Armee* (Hannover, Hahn'sche Hofbuchhandlung, 1866), band 1, p.136.

50 Robert Sichart, *Geschichte der Königlich-Hannoverschen Armee* (Hannover, Hahn'sche Hofbuchhandlung, 1866), band 1, p.129.

51 Robert Sichart, *Geschichte der Königlich-Hannoverschen Armee* (Hannover, Hahn'sche Hofbuchhandlung, 1866), band 1, pp.131–132.

Following the invasion of the United Provinces in April 1672, adherence to the French party could no longer be hidden, if it was not already known. In 1673, Johann Friedrich proclaimed the neutrality of Hannover, but he increasingly refrained from interfering in the trade of soldiers of his brothers of Celle and Osnabrück with the Dutch Republic and Spain. Tensions mounted through mutual recriminations over the failure to emerge from the war with permanent gains. Johann Friedrich remained firmly on the French side even when the Imperial Diet proclaimed the *Reichskrieg* against Louis XIV on 31 March 1674.

However, after the defeat of Electoral Cologne and Münster in 1673–1674, Johann Friedrich had to face the growing isolation and the progressive hostility of his neighbouring states. The situation worsened further when the Swedish invasion of Pomerania in December 1674 brought the armies of Brandenburg, Celle, Münster and Denmark dangerously close to the territories of Hannover. Now, the risk of a new war between German states became real, and to avert the danger, Brandenburg and Denmark negotiated the neutrality of Johann Friedrich by offering compensations. On 21 September 1675, the Allies agreed to Hannoverian billeting in Hildesheim and other parts of Lower Saxony as the price of the Duke's non-intervention on behalf of Sweden.[52] Others among the Allies were less willing to negotiate with Johann Friedrich, so tensions remained high. In October 1676, Hannover mobilised its army to block the Brandenburg Army's approach, deploying regular troops and militia to protect the territory from forced contributions. At the cost of a heavy economic effort, Johann Friedrich managed to retain a considerable army sparing his domains from the negative collateral effect of the war. This was a necessary choice, since the Duchy was almost bereft of modern fortresses except for Hannover and Göttingen.

Johann Friedrich's death in 1679 without male heirs removed the tension. The Duchy passed to Ernst August, already Protestant Bishop of Osnabrück, who sided with the Allies. The new Prince combined the troops of Hannover with those of the Bishopric, intending to take part in the partition of Swedish territories in Germany.[53] However, peace negotiations proceeded, and then Ernst August was forced to reduce the strength of his army. Between summer and autumn 1679, the 'peace strength' still numbered 120 horsemen of the *Garde du Corps*; two regiments of cavalry, each of four companies; the *Leib-Schloss Compagnie* with 196 infantry; 4 infantry regiments, each with 6 companies of 100 men; 3 free companies of foot, and a company of artillery, in all 960 cavalry, 1,096 infantry and 50 artillerymen.[54]

52 Peter H. Wilson, *German Armies. War and German Politics, 1648–1806* (London: UCL Press, 1998), p.51.

53 Peter H. Wilson, *German Armies. War and German Politics, 1648–1806* (London: UCL Press, 1998), p.59: 'It's certainly no coincidence that it was precisely Denmark, Brandenburg, and Hannover – all equally disappointed with the settlement of Nijmegen – that conspired with France in 1679–1684 to restart the war in Northern Germany and counselled appeasement rather than resistance to French *Réunions* in the Rhineland.'

54 Robert Sichart, *Geschichte der Königlich-Hannoverschen Armee* (Hannover, Hahn'sche Hofbuchhandlung, 1866), band 1, p.140.

Gravestone of the palace guardsman Christoph Münster (1632–1676), who served in Hannover from 1668 to 1676 in the *Leib-Schloss Compagnie* (Author's photograph).
Münster was an exceptionally tall man measuring 8 feet, 1½ inches, which gave him the nickname of the 'Giant of Hanover.' On the gravestone, Münster is portrayed wearing an old-fashioned *Rock* with long sleeves and Swedish style cuffs without buttons. Twenty-four buttons are visible down the front but there were probably a couple more beneath the waist and others on both the sides of the coat. This ends above the knee, showing the breeches with small ribbons hanging down over the tops of the stockings: a decorative item usual at the time. The shoes also have lace ribbons. Münster has a short cravat hanging on the breast and holds a partisan with a fringe below the blade. Based on the guardsman recorded height, this partisan must have been about 2.4m long. The uniform of the Hanoverian palace guards in the last quarter of the seventeenth century was completely red with golden lace; however, the latter is not recognisable from the gravestone.

In the following years, the Duke continued to devote his time to the reorganisation of the army. In 1683, the war council submitted to him a detailed *Reglement* divided into 14 chapters, dealing with the ranks of the senior officers and a regiment's officers, battle order, marches, detachments, sentinels, parades, quarters and encampments, justice, artillery, tactical organisation of infantry and cavalry. This document, signed by the Duke on 12 June, is an important source that shows characteristics and usages of the north German armies, which developed differently compared to other states. Among these, the decision regarding the rank of the regiments in order was important. The Duke decided that regiments entrusted to *generals* should be given preference over the ones commanded by simple *obrists*, even if these regiments were older. The *generals*, however, were to rank each other according to the quality of the post, based on the date of their commission. The same principle was applied among all officers, whether cavalry, infantry, dragoons or artillery.

As for the tactical instructions, the infantry companies were deployed on the field in 6 ranks divided into 14 *Rott*, each in turn divided into 3 *Pelotons*. The platoons on the right wing and in the centre consisted of 5 *Rott* and the one on the left wing of 4 *Rott*. The platoons on the wing were musketeers, while the platoons in the centre consisted of pikemen. The squadron was the tactical unit of the cavalry and theoretically consisted of 2 companies, although not infrequently it was of 3. As in almost all German armies, the cavalry was deployed in 3 ranks. Regarding the command of the troops, the *Reglement* prescribed that, if the Duke was not present in person, the command would fall on his *generalleutnant*or, or in his absence or infirmity, on the most senior *generalmajor*.[55]

55 Robert Sichart, *Geschichte der Königlich-Hannoverschen Armee* (Hannover, Hahn'sche Hofbuchhandlung, 1866), band 1, p.292.

As for foreign relations, in 1681, Ernst August agreed to contribute with his own troops for the *Reichskontingent*, and in 1683, he signed an agreement with Count Friedrich Christian of Schaumburg-Lippe to create a network of relationships and military assistance in the Lower Saxon Circle.[56] This and other involvements diverted attention from south-eastern Europe. France's threats on the Rhine and Spanish Low Countries caused an increase of military expenditure. An agreement with the Dutch Republic enabled Ernst August to increase the army to 12,748 men in 1682–1683.[57] However, in 1683 Ernst August met the request of the Emperor for auxiliary troops. The matter was negotiated by *Obrist* Pallandt in Vienna, who also held the command of the battalion raised for the Lower Saxony Circle. The talks started in March, but no agreement was reached due to the distance between request and offer, and the 10,000 horse and foot mobilised and gathered between Nienburg and Leese, returned to their quarters.[58] Nevertheless, the two sons of Duke Ernst August, Georg Ludwig and Friedrich August, hurried east to take part in the relief of Vienna.[59] With them, the *Kreis-Bataillon* was also involved in the campaign and in the ensuing events until October 1683, losing, in all, 3 officers, including Pallandt, and 138 rank and file.[60]

As well as negotiating with the Emperor, Ernst August also opened negotiations for another involvement in the struggle against the Porte. During his stay in Venice in May 1684, he pledged to provide the Republic with three infantry regiments of 900 men each 'all formed by veteran soldiers, well-dressed and armed with muskets and swords, each with its companies of grenadiers.'[61] The Duke asked the Senate that his third son Maximilian Wilhelm, who was barely 18 years old, be appointed as commander. The young prince and the troops marched through Imperial and Bavarian territories with the agreement of the local rulers. Maximilian Wilhelm was assisted by *General* Herman Philipp von Ohr. In mid-April, the Hannoverian regiments arrived at the Lido. These were the regiments *Podewils* (BhI-1), *Ohr* (BhI-8), and *Prinz Maximilian Wilhelm* (BhI-12), with 870, 860, and 868 men respectively, and an overall strength of 2,598 men.[62] Each regiment had 9 companies of musketeers and 1 of grenadiers. On 1 May 1685, the regiments sailed to Greece on a convoy led by Ambrosio Bembo. There was

56 Peter H. Wilson, *German Armies. War and German Politics, 1648–1806* (London: UCL Press, 1998), p.21: 'Increasingly, Hannover and the other Guelph princes were to see the *Kreis* as a convenient mechanism to extend their regional influence and as a bulwark against Brandenburg, Sweden and Denmark.'

57 Peter H. Wilson, *German Armies. War and German Politics, 1648–1806* (London: UCL Press, 1998), p.162.

58 Robert Sichart, *Geschichte der Königlich-Hannoverschen Armee* (Hannover, Hahn'sche Hofbuchhandlung, 1866), band 1, p.446.

59 Friedrich August arrived in Vienna on 7 September and the Kronpriz on 11 September, just in time to be present at the battle of 12 September.

60 Felix Schütz von Brandis, *Übersicht der Geschichte der Hannoversche Armee von 1617 bis 1866* (Hannover & Leipzig: Hahn, 1903), p.84.

61 Biblioteca Nazionale Marciana, Venice, ms. 'It VII' 167–168, f. 259.

62 Alexander Schwenke, *Geschichte der Hannoverischen Truppen in Griechenland, 1685–1689 Zugleich als Beitrag zur Geschichte der Türkenkriege. Nach Archivalischen Quellen* (Hannover Hahn, 1854), pp.7–8.

Hanoverian infantry in 1686 depicted by Ignazio Manfroni during the siege of Modone (Methoni) in Greece, copy after the Rossi-Cassigoli Collection (Biblioteca Nazionale Centrale, Florence).
In the centre, NCO, drummer and private (grenadier?) are wearing a full red coat with yellow stockings. Note drummer and private, the latter with a red soft hat, with a large baldric, while the NCO has his sword on a waist belt.

not enough time to acclimatise the troops to the Greek theatre, and soon the soldiers were ravaged by disease rather than enemy action; as a result, the effective strength rapidly fell below the establishment.

A year later, the arrival of reinforcements along with a fourth regiment, the regiment *Raugraf zu Fuss* (BhI-13), brought the contingent to 3,219 men of which 312 sick.[63] It took only four months of campaigning to bring the number down to 1,150 men still fit to serve, while 1,240 lay in the Greek 'hospitals'.[64] The officer corps was not spared, suffering a loss of 140.[65] In

63 Alexander Schwenke, *Geschichte der Hannoverischen Truppen in Griechenland, 1685–1689 Zugleich als Beitrag zur Geschichte der Türkenkriege. Nach Archivalischen Quellen* (Hannover Hahn, 1854), p.418; muster carried out on 10 May 1686.

64 Alexander Schwenke, *Geschichte der Hannoverischen Truppen in Griechenland, 1685–1689 Zugleich als Beitrag zur Geschichte der Türkenkriege. Nach Archivalischen Quellen* (Hannover Hahn, 1854), p.182. In September 1686, the contingent recorded the following numbers: regiment *Prinz Maximilian Wilhelm* 498 men; *Podewils* 574 men; *Ohr* 650 men; *Raugraf* 586 men; an overall strength for the contingent of 2,308 men.

65 'Altogether such losses far exceeded those suffered in the better-known campaigns in colonial America in the next century', Peter H. Wilson, *German Armies. War and German Politics, 1648–1806* (London: UCL Press, 1998), p.78:

September 1686, a new capitulation was concluded between the *Serenissima* and the representatives of Duke Ernst August to reinforce the contingent with 1,400 new recruits,[66] and for this task, *General* Ohr returned to Hannover. On 1 March 1687, the muster recorded only 1,468 fit soldiers awaiting the arrival of the reinforcements. The lack of officers forced the field officers to reform each regiment into 6 companies.

On 12 June, the recruits from Hannover led by Ohr crossed the Republic's border at Borghetto, where the Venetian *inquisitori* recorded 1,234 men,[67] and they joined the regiments in August, during the siege of Athens. At the conclusion of the campaign, the Hannover contingent recorded the loss of 470 men, and only 2,328 able soldiers; only the regiment *Prinz Maximilian Wilhelm*, could deploy a field force close to the established strength with 938 men, while *Podewils*, *Ohr* and *Raugraf* had only 448 men, 479 men, and 463 men respectively.[68]

This dramatically insanitary scenario persuaded the Venetian commanders to transfer the whole contingent to Italy and the Ionian Greek islands for winter quarters and quarantine. However, the treatment received must have been bad, since on 17 April 1688, the Hannoverian soldiers were involved in serious disorders while they were still quartered at the Lido of Venice, enough for the Senate to be concerned and to open an investigation.[69] It was decided that the best solution was to send the regiments back to Hannover. In May, about 1,400 survivors crossed the border and marched for home. As a replacement, *Obrist* Bremer arrived with the newly raised *Prinz Maximilian Wilhelm zu Fuss* (BhI-14), formed of 8 companies from the regiments in Hannover, two free companies, and two of new recruits. The regiment formed two battalions tactically, which would increase to three with a further 457 men recruited through an agent, 'Colonel' Pape, who used the unfair method of lying to the soldiers about their destination.[70] The final strength of the regiment was

Fresco depicting an NCO of the regiment Podewils zu Fuss in 1687 (Bomann Museum, Celle. Author's photograph). This Romantic illustration shows the NCO wearing a red Rock with brass buttons, a short medium blue waistcoat, pale coloured breeches and gloves, light grey stockings, and brown shoes. The black broad-brimmed hat has white edging and a green ribbon on the left side. This regiment was already known as the das alte Rothe Regiment by the 1670s, and although the size of waistcoat is wrongly represented, the reconstruction is reliable.

66 Robert Sichart, *Geschichte der Königlich-Hannoverschen Armee* (Hannover, Hahn'sche Hofbuchhandlung, 1866), band 1, p.428.
67 Robert Sichart, *Geschichte der Königlich-Hannoverschen Armee* (Hannover, Hahn'sche Hofbuchhandlung, 1866), band 1, p.431.
68 Robert Sichart, *Geschichte der Königlich-Hannoverschen Armee* (Hannover, Hahn'sche Hofbuchhandlung, 1866), band 1, p.436.
69 Archivio di Stato di Venezia, *Senato da Mar*, r.154 (1688), f. 114.
70 Robert Sichart, *Geschichte der Königlich-Hannoverschen Armee* (Hannover, Hahn'sche Hofbuchhandlung, 1866), band 1, p.195.

1,234 rank and file.[71] They sailed for the incoming siege of Negroponte and once again, casualties and disease severely affected the contingent in the bloodiest campaign of the Venetian army in Greece. In a muster carried out on 26 January 1689 for the regiment *Prinz Maximilian Wilhelm*, it numbered 2 *majors*, 3 *kapitäns*, 6 *leutnants*, 6 *fähnrich*, 51 *unteroffiziers*, and 127 drummers and other ranks. In four years of campaigning, the loss of soldiers had been considerable, and even among the officers the casualties were heavy, resulting in 146 dead, of whom 8 had served as volunteers.[72] In early 1688, concerns for an involvement against the French on the Rhine forced Duke Ernst August to reject the Venetian request for new troops. In February 1689, under a *major*, the survivors marched through the Tyrol, via Donauwerth, Ansbach and finally arrived in Hannover in late April.[73]

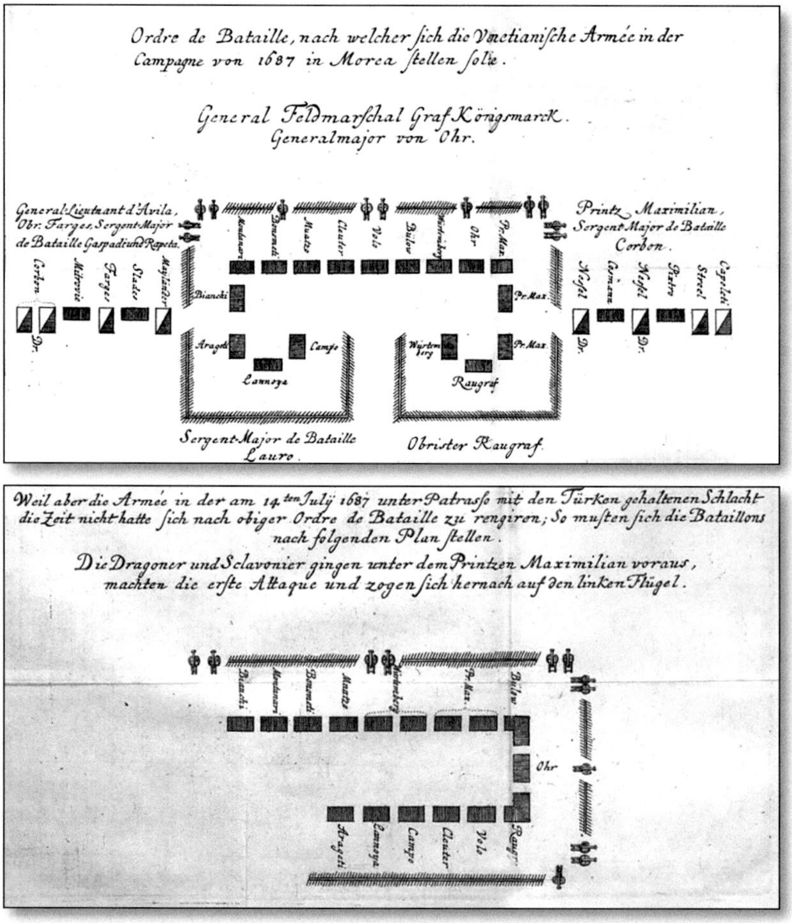

Sketches showing the order of battle of the Venetian field army in 1687, and the right wing's deployment at the Battle of Patras on 14 July, including the Hanoverian infantry regiments, after Georg von Wissel's *Geschichte der Errichtung Sämmtlicher Chur-Braunschweig-Lüneburgischen Truppen* (Celle, 1786). Note the Frisian horse deployed to the front, flank and rear of the infantry.

71 Robert Sichart, *Geschichte der Königlich-Hannoverschen Armee* (Hannover, Hahn'sche Hofbuchhandlung, 1866), band 1, p.195.

72 Robert Sichart, *Geschichte der Königlich-Hannoverschen Armee* (Hannover, Hahn'sche Hofbuchhandlung, 1866), band 1, pp.440–441.

73 Robert Sichart, *Geschichte der Königlich-Hannoverschen Armee* (Hannover, Hahn'sche Hofbuchhandlung, 1866), band 1, p.440.

As for the Austrian subsidies, new talks were opened by Hannover in 1684. This time the Emperor offered Duke Ernst August the right to collect funds from the unarmed territories of the Lower Saxon Circle plus an initial payment from Austria. In September, the *Subsidien* Treaty was signed in Linz in association with Celle and Wolfenbüttel. The Hannoverian contingent was composed of 28 cavalry companies, 8 dragoon companies, and 32 infantry companies, a total of 5,405 men in all, and was under the command of *Generalmajore* Öffener and Du Mont.[74] The cavalry regiments were *Erbrinz* (BhC-8), *Öffener* (BhC-1), *Offen* (BhC-6), *Gordon* (BhC-7) and *Raugraf* (BhC-9); dragoon regiment *Vitry* (BhD-2), and infantry regiments *Marteaux* (BhI-3), *Röbbig* (BhC-10), *Siegelberg* (BhC-9) and *Du Mont* (BhC-2).[75] In detail the force was 1,679 cavalry, 458 dragoons and 3,268 infantry.[76] The treaty clauses entrusted the command of the whole auxiliary corps to the Crown Prince Georg Ludwig.

The first troops from Hannover marched to Hungary before the signing of the agreement. They were the *Leibgarde zu Pferd* (bhc-1) that joined the Lower Saxony Circle's battalion at Komárom in late 1684. In March 1685, the contingent was mustered by the Crown Prince at Göttingen and on the Herzberge and finally headed to Hungary. Some regiments had been raised just for the war, but Ernst August issued the instructions to his officers that the performance of the troops on campaign would have influence on the disbanding of the regiments.[77] The march encountered some problems when the troops arrived near to the border of Saxony. Elector Johann Georg III, who had broken with Vienna, did not give permission for foreign soldiers to cross his lands. However, Ernst August did not listen to the rumours of Saxon troops being ready to block the way and ordered his officers to cross the border without delay: the idea of engaging in an encounter in his own state forced Johann Georg to back down.[78] The contingent marched through Bohemia without further problems and finally joined the Imperial Army on campaign. The Hannoverians participated in all the major actions of 1685, and when they entered winter quarters in late September, the original strength had fallen to 1,294 cavalry and dragoons, and 2,416 infantry.[79] The

74 Robert Sichart, *Geschichte der Königlich-Hannoverschen Armee* (Hannover, Hahn'sche Hofbuchhandlung, 1866), band 1, p.451.

75 Robert Sichart, *Geschichte der Königlich-Hannoverschen Armee* (Hannover, Hahn'sche Hofbuchhandlung, 1866), band 1, p.464.

76 Robert Sichart, *Geschichte der Königlich-Hannoverschen Armee* (Hannover, Hahn'sche Hofbuchhandlung, 1866), band 1, p.191. Each infantry regiment numbered 817 men; three cavalry regiments had a strength of 359 men, and the fourth, *Offen zu Pferd*, 243 men.

77 Robert Sichart, *Geschichte der Königlich-Hannoverschen Armee* (Hannover, Hahn'sche Hofbuchhandlung, 1866), band 1, p.452. This act was probably less than wise, because with regard to regiment Röbbig *zu Fuss*, it is stated that Duke Ernst August wanted to disband it after its return from Hungary, which the colonel, it is said, took so much to heart that he died as a result.

78 Martin Schröder, 'Die bewegte Bellona Die Kursächsische Durchzug-und Marschorganisation am Beispiel eines Braunschweig-Lüneburgischen Durchzugs von 1685', in *Militärgeschichtliche Zeitschrift*; 77 (2018), 1, pp.10–11.

79 Robert Sichart, *Geschichte der Königlich-Hannoverschen Armee* (Hannover, Hahn'sche Hofbuchhandlung, 1866), band 1, p.464. The figure did not include 235 cavalry and dragoons and 677 infantry sick.

economic result was dramatic. Hannoverian officials reckoned the cost of a soldier in the Hungarian theatre to be two to three times the expense of one serving on the Rhine, and the provision of the auxiliary contingent in 1685 cost much more than the sum which the duke had received from Vienna.[80]

In the spring of 1686, the Hannoverian contingent joined the army of Duke Charles of Lorraine in preparation for the campaign targeting Buda. Now this comprised the *Leibgarde zu Pferd*, cavalry regiments *Erbprinz*, and *Breidenbach* (former *Gordon*); the *Garde zu Fuss* (bhi-i), and infantry regiments, *Sommerfeld* (former *Röbbig*) and *Du Mont*.[81] The overall strength had decreased to 2,700 men in all. The contingent served in Hungary until 1687. In 1688, the French invasion of the Palatinate forced the Duke to renounce participation in the war against the Porte.

The war against France opened new agreements and soon Hannover replaced Wolfenbüttel as Celle's partner in the provision of auxiliaries to the Dutch during the War of The League of Augsburg.[82] Although Hannover received large Dutch subsidies, Duke Ernst August initially did not receive these and he experienced cash flow problems during mobilisation. Despite this, in 1689, the standing force numbered 12,308 men, increased to 14,300 two years after.[83] In the following decades, Hannover retained the rank of a major armed state of Lower Saxony, and a contemporary praised the quality of its army, describing it as *formidable*.[84]

In the opening phase of the war, the Hannoverian troops behaved so badly in their quarters in Hessen-Darmstadt, Fulda and Gelnhausen that many inhabitants fled over the frontier. Yet again, the rivalry over resources began to affect strategy, as the Hannoverians refused to cooperate with a Hessian plan to start blockading the French in Mainz in April 1689 for fear that they would lose their present billets to the advancing Imperial troops. In the end, the arrival of his own soldiers enabled Leopold to evict the Hannoverians, but only after they had extorted money in addition to free food and lodging.[85]

Brunswick-Wolfenbüttel

In 1657, Duke August the Younger managed a little standing force comprising 8 companies of cavalry and 5 companies of infantry, numbering

80 Peter H. Wilson, *German Armies. War and German Politics, 1648–1806* (London: UCL Press, 1998), p.76.

81 Robert Sichart, *Geschichte der Königlich-Hannoverschen Armee* (Hannover, Hahn'sche Hofbuchhandlung, 1866), band 1, p.469.

82 The initial French invasion had been countered by the formation, in October 1688, of the Magdeburg Concert of Saxony, Brandenburg, Hannover, Osnabrück, and Hessen-Kassel. This resolved to send one army to the Lower Rhine to help protect the Dutch Republic.

83 Peter H. Wilson, *German Armies. War and German Politics, 1648–1806* (London: UCL Press, 1998), p.160.

84 Heinrich Ludwig Gude, *Staat der Chur und Fürstlichen Hauser Braunschweig-Lüneburg* (Halle, 1701), p.64.

85 Peter H. Wilson, *German Armies. War and German Politics, 1648–1806* (London: UCL Press, 1998), p.184.

approximately 1,600 and 500 men respectively.[86] By 1642, the infantry formed field regiments, and after the reduction of the army in 1648, a regiment still existed for administrative purpose, despite the companies being assigned separately to the garrisons in the duchy. The cavalry, by contrast, formed independent companies. Although it was a modest force, its officers had served during the Thirty Years' War, when Wolfenbüttel had deployed four times that number during the 1640s.[87]

As with other medium-sized German principalities after 1648, Wolfenbüttel had to face the dual task of recovering from the war and securing its power within the Empire. In 1654, the Duke concluded a treaty of alliance with the Elector of Brandenburg, by which he pledged to keep 300 cavalry and 1,200 infantry on active service. In 1657, the Lower Saxon Circle requested troops to be sent to the borders of the Swedish territory of Verden-Bremen as an observation corps for Danish troops that had crossed the borders of the region.[88] The next year, Duke August joined the Rhenish League, and as head of the Guelph duchies, he also retained a prominent role in the Lower Saxon Circle. In the 1660s, he managed to lay the basis for raising a common army alongside the other Guelph princes. Collaboration among the members of the Brunswick House continued, and in 1662, Wolfenbüttel ceded three companies of infantry to the Bishopric of Osnabrück, ruled by his cousin Ernst August of Brunswick-Lüneburg.[89] In 1663, the Duke provided his quota of troops for Hungary together with Celle and Hannover for the *Deutsche Allianz*. This comprised 150 cavalry and 430 infantry, of which three infantry companies joined the regiments of the Lower Saxon Circle under *Obrist* Job Bernhard von Mücheln, for the campaign of 1664 under Hohenlohe and the Croatian Palatine Miklós Zrínyi.[90] The contingent from Wolfenbüttel included an artillery corps with 3 field guns, 8 *Constabler*, and a field train with 13 horses.[91] In the early phase of the campaign, the contingent suffered just 32 casualties, but by August, half of the contingent had been lost from both fighting and disease.[92]

In 1665, the Estates met the Duke's request to increase the Army's strength to 4,400 horse and foot.[93] One year later, Rudolph August succeeded his

86 Otto Elster, *Geschichte der stehenden Truppen im Herzogtum Braunschweig-Wolfenbüttel, 1600-1806*, band I (Leipzig: Heinsius, 1899), p.75.

87 Rainer Jakobs, 'Braunschweigisches Militärwesen 1641–1714. Heeresorganization in Spannungsfeld von landständischer Verfassung und Fürstlichem Absolutismus', in *Braunschweigisches Jahrbuch für Landesgechsichte*, 81 (Wolfenbüttel: Braunschweigischer Geschichtsverein, 2000), p.31.

88 Adolph Köcher, *Geschichte Von Hannover Und Braunschweig 1648 Bis 1714*, bande I-III (Leipzig: Hirzel, 1884–1895), band I, p.250.

89 Otto Elster, *Geschichte der stehenden Truppen im Herzogtum Braunschweig-Wolfenbüttel, 1600–1806* (Leipzig: Heinsius, 1899), band I, p.76.

90 See Bruno Mugnai, *Wars and Soldiers in the Early Reign of Louis XIV, volume 2, The Imperial Army 1657–1687*, (Warwick Helion & Co, 2019), p.113.

91 Otto Elster, *Geschichte der stehenden Truppen im Herzogtum Braunschweig-Wolfenbüttel, 1600–1806* (Leipzig: Heinsius, 1899), band I, p.81.

92 Otto Elster, *Geschichte der stehenden Truppen im Herzogtum Braunschweig-Wolfenbüttel, 1600–1806* (Leipzig: Heinsius, 1899), band I, pp.96 and 99.

93 Peter H. Wilson, *German Armies. War and German Politics, 1648–1806* (London: UCL Press, 1998), p.162.

Duke Anton Ulrich of Brunswick-Wolfenbüttel, portrait by Hyacinthe Rigaud (Herzog Anton Ulrich Museum, Brunswick). Although the history attributed to Anton Ulrich is a more warlike attitude compared to his brother Rudolph August, he was an erudite writer and poet, who protected arts and learning.

father as Duke, and found himself immediately involved in the geopolitical scenario of Northern Germany. In late spring 1666, the Duke sent three infantry companies in support of Bremen which was besieged by the Swedes. The new Duke was more interested in art than politics and only one year after his accession to the throne, he appointed his younger, power-conscious, brother, Anton Ulrich (1633–1714) as Governor.

In the following years, Rudolf August gradually withdrew from the affairs of government, which he left to his brother, and in 1685, he appointed Anton Ulrich as Duke and co-ruler, with equal rights. The two brothers jointly held the rule of Wolfenbüttel until the next century. Consequently, the military policy of the Duchy followed the progressive development of power management, with Rudolph August less interested in the military policy compared to his brother. However, in 1667–1668, talks were opened with Spain and later with the Dutch Republic for the hiring of auxiliary troops for the Triple Alliance against Louis XIV, but the Peace of Aix-La-Chapelle let the project fall. Nonetheless, by 1671 the strength of the army had climbed to 4,260 men.[94]

German musketeers depicted on the first page of the *Deutliche Beschreibung, Von dem Exerciren in der Mußquet* by Johann Georg Pascha (Halle: 1672). (Author's collection)
There is little information about dress and equipment of the Wolfenbüttel infantry, but the illustration for Pascha's treatise could be a reliable source for the Brunswick military types of late 1660s and early 1670s.

94 Otto Elster, *Geschichte der stehenden Truppen im Herzogtum Braunschweig-Wolfenbüttel, 1600–1806* (Leipzig: Heinsius, 1899), band I, p.103.

An accurate description of Wolfenbüttel's troops can be found in the *Reisen Diarium* (travel diary) of Duke Albrecht of Saxe-Coburg, who was a guest in Wolfenbüttel of Duke Rudolph August between 7 and 16 May 1670.

The city of Wolfenbüttel in an early seventeenth century print. (Author's collection)
In the Thirty Years' War, Wolfenbüttel was the strongest fortress in North Germany but survived the war heavily damaged. In 1635, Duke August the Younger took over power in the principality and founded the new line of Brunswick. Under his rule, Wolfenbüttel reached its cultural zenith. One of his greatest achievements was the building of the Wolfenbüttel Library, the largest in Germany in its day.

With the typical meticulous attitude of the seventeenth century traveller, Albrecht took note of the *Türkischbeute* (Turkish booty) captured in the campaign of 1664, and also described the artillery preserved in the arsenal. As for the troops, he wrote:

> The garrison (of Wolfenbüttel) consists of five companies, one mounted company commanded by *Kapitän* Kotwitz and four on foot, each consisting of 200–250 men. Of each company, 50 men serve as guard daily and are assigned in turn to honour duty. But only *Obrist* Schönberg's company is on guard duty inside the castle. They are mostly *unteroffiziere* and also act as *Trabants* when on duty in the duke's residence. Each of them receives 2½ thalers and 15 rations of bread monthly. The other soldiers receive 2 thalers and the same number of bread rations.[95]

95 Annette Faber, '… und besahe, was noch denckwürdiges darinne wahr. Zum Aufenthalt Prinz Albrecht von Sachsen-Gotha in Wolfenbüttel und Braunschweig in Mai 1670' in *Braunschweigisches Jahrbuch für Landesgeschichte* (Wolfenbüttel: Jahrbücher des Braunschweigischen Geschichtsvereins, 2004), band 85, p.84. Duke Albrecht also noted the

In 1671, the Dukes received the support of their cousin of Celle and Hannover when the city of Brunswick was besieged and forced to surrender. For the campaign against the rebel city, the professional army numbered 4,260 men.[96] In the same period, the dukes had three *ausschuss* (militia) companies.

The towns of Brunswick and Wolfenbüttel were the only two fortified places of the Duchy. After the siege of Brunswick, the town was manned by a permanent garrison, and also housed the army headquarters. In 1672, there was, in Brunswick, one company of mounted life guards, and one of foot guards, two companies of cavalry, three infantry regiments, and a company of artillery.[97] By the 1670s, Wolfenbüttel began providing auxiliaries for the Dutch Republic and, later, Spain and Austria once both became involved in 1673. Though in the Franco-Dutch War, the association of the Guelph duchies recorded the default of Hannover in June 1674, Wolfenbüttel and Celle met the request of Den Haag, Vienna, and Madrid-Brussels to provide auxiliary soldiers for the war against France in exchange for subsidy. On the basis of the treaty of 20 June 1674, the Ducal brothers agreed to provide 5,780 men, The Dukes had to assemble four regiments of cavalry, 2,480, three regiment of infantry, 3,000 men, and 300 artillerymen and drivers, who were entrusted to Rudolph August's brother-in-law – *Feldmarschall* Johann Adolph of Holstein-Ploen.[98] The contingent was badly affected by the events of the campaign in Alsace. At Entzheim, on 4 October 1674, the troops of Wolfenbüttel suffered losses of 396 dead, including 20 officers, and 696 wounded.[99]

By spring 1675, the strength of the contingent had fallen to about 3,000, but the war against Sweden opened the way to Wolfenbüttel for further trade in soldiers. In 1675, the professional troops comprised five companies of mounted life guards (*Rudolph August Garde zu Pferde* with 3 companies, which formed the *Leibregiment*, and *Anton Ulrich* with 2 companies); 30 cavalry companies divided into four regiments; 6 companies of dragoons; 84 infantry companies divided into infantry regiments each of 12 companies, and 12 free companies.[100] The total strength was 225 *Trabanten*, 2,530 cavalry and dragoons and 6,357 infantry.

---

uniforms. Schoenberg's company wore light grey coats with green cuffs, the 'major's company' dressed in the same coat, but with red facings, the *Stückhauptman*'s company (artillery captain) had blue facings and the fourth company had yellow facings.

96 Peter H. Wilson, *German Armies. War and German Politics, 1648–1806* (London: UCL Press, 1998), p.162.

97 Otto Elster, *Geschichte der stehenden Truppen im Herzogtum Braunschweig-Wolfenbüttel, 1600–1806*, band I (Leipzig: Heinsius, 1899), pp.105–111.

98 Robert Sichart, *Geschichte der Königlich-Hannoverschen Armee* (Hannover, Hahn'sche Hofbuchhandlung, 1866), band 1, p.369.

99 Otto Elster, *Geschichte der stehenden Truppen im Herzogtum Braunschweig-Wolfenbüttel, 1600–1806* (Leipzig: Heinsius, 1899), band I, p.141. According to Sichart, *Geschichte...*, pp.378–377, the casualties were lower, with197 dead and 309 wounded.

100 Carl Venturini, *Umriss einer pragmatischen Geschichte des Kriegswesens im Herzogtum Braunschweig* (Magdeburg, 1837), p.22. The author reports a probably inaccurate figure, as according to Elster and Sichart the number of regiments actually present was four in total, while Venturini increases the number to six. Possibly the further two regiments were field-battalions formed with the free companies.

'German cavalry' shown on a French playing card, after *Le Jeu des Treize Nations de l'Europe*, dating to the 1670s (Private collection). Brunswick cavalry followed the general trends introduced in Northern Germany in the matter of uniforms and equipment. Cloth coats had become common from the 1660s, and the only metal protection could be an iron secret under the headwear. The contract with the Dutch Republic in 1688 specified that the cavalrymen were to be armed with good carbines, pistols and swords. Dragoons were to have flintlocks, swords and bayonets.

The Swedish assault on Brandenburg opened the northern front and led to the recall of the Wolfenbüttel auxiliaries from the Rhine, and their concentration in the Westphalian and Lower Saxon Circles, where arrangements had to be made not to antagonise Hannover. The Dukes exploited the situation in the north, as Austria was unable to stem the influence of Celle, Münster, Brandenburg and Wolfenbüttel itself, all of which enjoyed diplomatic backing and subsidies, from Spain and the Dutch in return for their renewed contribution to the allied effort in the Spanish Low Countries.[101] With this subsidy, Wolfenbüttel's standing army increased to 7,749 horse and foot in 1677.[102] Troops were also sent against Sweden in Pomerania alongside those from Celle – these were the infantry regiments Wrede (BwI-3) and Schack (BwI-4), which participated in the siege of Stettin.[103] In the final years of the war, these troops were assigned to a secondary task of guarding the border with Verden-Bremen.

Further tensions in the region compelled the recall of Wolfenbüttel's troops in 1679 to counter the Danish attempt to take Hamburg. However, in 1680, the number of troops fell to just 1,972 men as the effect of the peace and post-war policy. Two infantry regiments were disbanded, while the other two were reorganised to 8 companies with 897 men. The cavalry retained a single regiment of 4 companies with 421 men, while the artillery numbered 1 officer and 40 *Büchsenmacher*, *Feuerwerker* and assistants.[104]

However, the army's strength increased again between 1683 and 1684 to 6,755 regular troops. In 1683, the artillery comprised 1 *Leutnant*, 2

101 Peter H. Wilson, *German Armies. War and German Politics, 1648–1806* (London: UCL Press, 1998), p.50.

102 Peter H. Wilson, *German Armies. War and German Politics, 1648–1806* (London: UCL Press, 1998), p.162.

103 Otto Elster, *Geschichte der stehenden Truppen im Herzogtum Braunschweig-Wolfenbüttel, 1600–1806* (Leipzig: Heinsius, 1899), band I, pp.168–171.

104 Otto Elster, *Geschichte der stehenden Truppen im Herzogtum Braunschweig-Wolfenbüttel, 1600–1806* (Leipzig: Heinsius, 1899), band I, pp.175–178.

Prince August Friedrich of Brunswick-Wolfenbüttel (1657–1676), in a print by Bartholomeus Kilian after the painting of Johann Burckhard. (Author's collection)
Eldest son of Duke Anton Ulrich, August Friedrich entered a military career in the Imperial Army aged 16, and one year later he became *Obrist* of the regiment *Sparr zu Fuss*. In March 1676, after a short stay in Wolfenbüttel, the prince joined his regiment for the siege of Philippsburg. On 9 August, he personally led the assault against the counterscarp but was seriously wounded in the head. He died in Speyer on 22 August, just two days before his nineteenth birthday.

Zeugwärter (supervisors), 1 *Zeugschreiber* (clerk), 1 *Feuerwerker*, 9 *Büchsenmeister* (constables), 13 *Schlangenschützen* (servants), 1 *Stückgiesser* (caster), 1 *Pulvermacher*, 1 *Zimmermann*, 4 *Rademacher* (wheelwrights), 1 *Zeugschmied* (blacksmith), 1 *Polierer* (polisher), and 5 workers.[105] In September 1684, alongside Celle and Hannover, Wolfenbüttel agreed to provide the auxiliary corps to the Emperor for the Hungarian campaign against the Ottomans. Rudolph August and Anton Ulrich agreed to raise 1,510 foot divided into two regiments each of 7 companies.[106]

As for the involvement on other fronts, by treaty of 18 August 1688, talks were opened with the Dutch Republic. William of Orange quickly secured the services of the north German armed princes by renewing the contracts made before his departure for England in 1688. After these subsidies the army numbered approximately 5,000 men in 1689. Along with Brandenburg, Celle, Hessen-Kassel and Saxe-Gotha, by 1690 Wolfenbüttel provided 1,400 soldiers – one regiment of horse and two of foot – as a part of the 15,000 strong corps for guarding west of the Meuse.[107] In the same year, Wolfenbüttel sent his quota of troops to the Rhine as his contingent of the Lower Saxony Circle.[108]

Now, at the forefront was Anton Ulrich, who, as a representative of the senior branch of the Guelphs, felt the title should have gone to him and was concerned that Hannoverian arrangements to inherit Celle would marginalise his own Duchy within the family's territories. Aided and abetted by Denmark, Anton Ulrich established the League of Corresponding Princes in May 1692, joined eventually by Münster, Saxe-Gotha, Ansbach, Würzburg, Hessen-Kassel and other middling territories. France encouraged these developments, hoping to bring these

105 Otto Elster, *Geschichte der stehenden Truppen im Herzogtum Braunschweig-Wolfenbüttel, 1600–1806* (Leipzig: Heinsius, 1899), band I, p.179.

106 Sich Robert Sichart, *Geschichte der Königlich-Hannoverschen Armee* (Hannover, Hahn'sche Hofbuchhandlung, 1866), band 1, p.451.

107 Peter H. Wilson, *German Armies. War and German Politics, 1648–1806* (London: UCL Press, 1998), p.90.

108 Georg Tessin, *Die Regimenter der Europäischen Staaten im Ancien Régime des XVI bis XVIII Jahrhunderts* (Osnabrück: Biblio Verlag, 1986), Teil 1, p.140.

principalities on board, but it proved impossible to find a basis for a stable 'Third Party'.[109] Nevertheless, resentment towards Vienna led Wolfenbüttel to side with France in the following years. The approach was sealed by the agreement made with Louis XIV in 1698 by Anton Ulrich, in order to increase the army and to use it against Hannover.[110]

109 Peter H. Wilson, *German Armies. War and German Politics, 1648–1806* (London: UCL Press, 1998), p.97.

110 *New Cambridge Modern History*, 'The Ascendancy of France, 1648–1688' (Cambridge: Cambridge University Press, 1968), vol. V, pp.445–446.

5

The Two Hessen

In 1567, the Landgraviate of Hessen was divided into four territories between the heirs of Philipp I 'The Magnanimous': the northern part, or Hessen-Kassel, the southern part or Hessen-Darmstadt, Hessen-Rheinfels, and Hessen-Marburg. The principality was further divided in order to also assign a fief to the sons of the second marriage, who received the County of Diez. After this branch died out in 1608, the four Landgraves von Hessen divided up the inheritance, but further changes occurred in the meantime. The rulers of Hessen-Rheinfels and Hessen-Marburg died childless in 1583 and 1604 respectively, and their territories passed to Hessen-Kassel and Hessen-Darmstadt. Another branch was established in 1622, when Ludwig V of Hessen-Darmstadt founded the Homburg line for his brother Friedrich, which survived as a parallel lineage until 1866. Meanwhile, while Hessen-Rheinfels was partitioned without conflict, the inheritance of Hessen-Marburg was the starting point of a dispute between the two Landgraves that lasted for decades. Although in the first partition of 1567, a pact binding on all had been suggested, no agreement was reached. In addition to the succession dispute, there was also the confessional conflict: while Hessen-Darmstadt remained Lutheran, Hessen-Kassel passed to the reformed branch of Protestantism – Calvinism.[1]

During the Thirty Years' War, the two landgraves fought on different sides, with Hessen-Darmstadt in the Catholic-Imperial coalition. This was the background to the unbalanced agreement of 24 September 1627, which awarded Darmstadt most of the former Landgraviate of Hessen-Marburg, with the territory in Upper Hessen, including the University of Marburg and its possessions, the County of Katzenelnbogen and the condominium of Umstadt in Hessen-Kassel. However, this was not to last, but rather led to further military conflicts between the two Hessian states – 'the Hessian War', a struggle within the Thirty Years' War. The conflict caused the loss of territories, since the Hessen-Homburg and Hessen-Rothenburg estates seceded from the opponents in 1622 and 1627. Though Hessen-Darmstadt

1 The dispute also affected the universities. In 1607, in response to the name change imposed by Moritz of Hessen-Kassel on the University of Marburg, Hessen-Darmstadt founded the Lutheran University of Giessen.

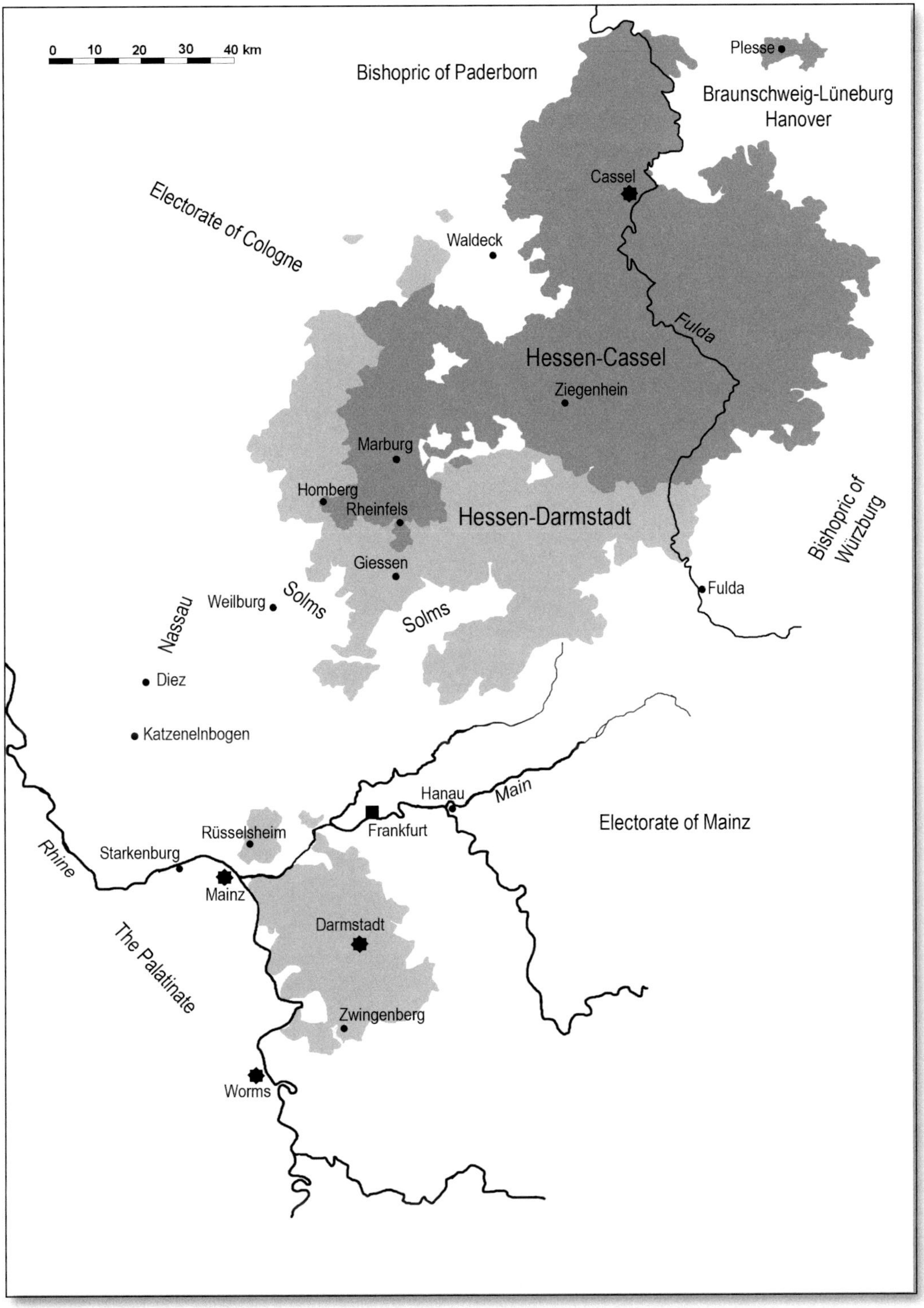

Together the two main Houses of Kassel and Darmstadt, in 1648 there were the collateral branches of Hessen-Rheinfels, Hessen-Homburg, and Hessen-Rotenburg, while others were created in the following decades, which, however, did not have the status of immediacy in the Empire.

and Hessen-Kassel reached an agreement, the quarrel rekindled, resulting in the siege of Dorsten and culminating in the campaign of 1645, when the Kassel Landgravine Amalie Elisabeth besieged Marburg. The conflict was finally settled on the eve of the Peace of Westphalia, more than 80 years after the division of the estates. Large parts of the disputed Upper Hessen territory, including Marburg, fell to the elder Kassel line, while Hessen-Darmstadt retained Giessen and Biedenkopf. The agreement was confirmed by the Peace of Westphalia concluded shortly afterwards. The conquests that Hessen-Darmstadt had obtained in 1627 were partially annulled.[2]

Scene of pillage during the Thirty Years' War in a contemporary German print (Author's collection). Like many of the Upper Rhenish states, both the Margraviates of Hessen had suffered the loss of more than half their population during the Thirty Years' War. The evacuation of Swedish, Spanish and French armies took time and it was not until 1653 that the foreign armies returned the cities and fortresses within the Circle they were occupying as pledges. The wars which followed, especially those of the 'Forty Years War' against Louis XIV intermittently from 1674 to 1714, prevented any reasonable chance of recovery and was one of the causes leading to the bankruptcy of several smaller states. On the other hand, the Circle association provided a basis for those small principalities to enter the ranks of the armed states and to gain some protection against the abuses practised by the larger states, who were in the habit of foisting their troops on the smaller states during marches and for winter quarters.

2 Jean Bérenger, 'Un texte inédit de Lisola concernent l'Affaire de Lorraine (1670)' in *Revue Ssemestrielle de Linguistique et Littératures Romanes*, vol. V, Nos 1–2 (2009, Institut d'études romanes de la Faculté des Lettres de l'Université de Bohême du Sud, České Budějovice), p.49.

Both states were among the major principalities in the *Oberreinischer Kreis* (Upper Rhine Circle), and in the next decades, their discontinuous relationship affected the Circle's affairs.[3] In 1658, Hessen-Kassel joined the *Rheinbund*, and in 1664, when the Diet called for the assembling of troops to face the Ottoman offensive in Hungary, only Hessen-Darmstadt honoured the request, since Hessen-Kassel sent its troop to the *Deutsche Allianz*.[4] In 1667, the War of Devolution alarmed the western states of the Upper Rhine Circle, but the pro-French members, including Hessen-Kassel, refused to call the Diet. In 1673–1674, the new emergency caused by the French invasion of the United Provinces of The Netherlands, favoured a re-approach of the Circle's member to a common military policy. This time, a General invitation was sent to all the Circle's states to participate in the assembly meeting in Friedberg in June 1674 to discuss the raising of the common contingent. The meeting was later solemnised as the *Partikularallianz*, but included only the northern part of the Upper Rhine Circle, namely the principalities of Hessen-Kassel, Hessen-Darmstadt, Nassau-Idstein, Nassu-Usingen and Nassau-Weilburg, the counties of Hanau-Münzenberg, Solms, Ysenburg, Leiningen-Westerburg, Wittgenstein, Waldeck, the Prince-Abbot of Fulda and the Imperial Cities of Frankfurt, Friedberg and Wetzlar.[5] The *matricel* (number of troops) amounted to 700 horse and 1,400 foot.[6] The talks were finalised at the meeting at Frankfurt, which agreed to the mustering of troops in September, but the final result was less than hoped, because the troops from Kassel and Darmstadt did not join the Circle's army.[7]

After the Peace of Nijmegen, on 19 September the states on the right bank of the Rhine signed the Frankfurt Union, comprising Hessen-Darmstadt, Fulda, Waldeck, and other small lordships; Hessen-Kassel entered the Union on 26 September. The treaty had a duration of six years, but it represented a decisive step to protecting the smaller members from the quartering of soldiers of the larger ones. It had been agreed that the members would be free from demands for quarters and other war related services of foreign states. However, in the next decades, Hessen-Kassel progressively separated from the Circle, becoming a supplier of mercenaries for the Dutch Republic, and only Hessen-Darmstadt continued to regularly join the Diet gathering troops for the *Reichsarmee*.

---

3 The Upper Rhine Circle mustered its contingent from 57 states including 6 secular and 4 ecclesiastical princes, 32 *Grafen* and Barons, 3 ecclesiastical lordships and 5 Imperial Free Cities.

4 For further information on the Upper Rhine contingent see Bruno Mugnai, *Wars and Soldiers in the Early Reign of Louis XIV, volume 2: The Imperial Army 1657–1687* (Warwick: Helion & Company, 2019), pp.112–113.

5 Bruno Mugnai, *Wars and Soldiers in the Early Reign of Louis XIV, volume 2: The Imperial Army 1657–1687* (Warwick: Helion & Company, 2019), p.116.

6 Winfried Dotzauer, *Die Deutschen Reichskreise 1383–1806* (Stuttgart: Franz Steiner, 1998), pp.232–233.

7 Bruno Mugnai, *W ars and Soldiers in the Early Reign of Louis XIV, volume 2: The Imperial Army 1657–1687* (Warwick: Helion & Company, 2019), p.116.

Hessen-Kassel

By the late sixteenth century, the Landgraviate of Hessen-Kassel could be rightly considered as one of the best administered states of Germany. As historians have noted, Landgrave Wilhelm IV appointed skilful officials and councillors who calculated the income and expenditure of the state through the first statistical recording of the towns and villages' economies.[8] The Landgrave created his own bodies for administrative and government purposes with a well-organised chancellery established between 1578 and 1580. Under Wilhelm IV's successor, the second Landgrave Moritz, Kassel's court became one of the most important in Germany when theatre, music and alchemy flourished. In terms of foreign policy, Moritz was long in search of an ally who could guarantee him independence from the Emperor and the German Catholic princes, but also from the other Lutheran princes. For this reason, he visited the French King Henri IV in Paris in 1602. The Landgrave maintained a close correspondence with the French monarch, but Henri IV's assassination in 1610 changed the balance of power in Europe and again weakened the position of the Landgrave. This scenario affected the military policy of Hessen-Kassel and consequently the formation of a permanent army began very early. Already by the early seventeenth century, in order to consolidate his position as an independent prince, Moritz began to establish a select militia consisting of four regiments of foot, probably totalling 4,000 to 5,000 men.[9] The Landgrave had exercised the right to organise the militia into an effective military force but it had the disadvantage of denying a significant portion of the workforce to the economy. For this reason, the Landgrave added an increasing number of regular soldiers, recruited from his own state and from other German principalities. These troops comprised the classic specialities of the time, *Arquebusier-Reiter*, *Cuirassier*, *Knechte*, *Landreiter*, and *Ausschuss Soldaten* (militiamen) organised in companies for administrative purposes, and which were assembled into regiments under professional officers in case of need. In 1619, the Landgrave Moritz had a force of 10,000 men, comprising a mounted *Leibguardia* company, six

Landgrave Wilhelm VI 'the Just' (1629–1663), portrait by an anonymous artist (Museumlandschaft Hessen-Kassel). Wilhelm became Landgrave after he came of age in 1637. Under his reign, Hessen-Kassel fought the short war against Darmstadt that established the border of the principality. In 1658, he joined the Rhenish League.

8 This statistic record took the name *Ökonomischen Staaten*, and it was celebrated in the *Renthof* of the town of Kassel, which became the centre of administration for the Landgraviate.

9 Gerhard Petri, *Das Militärwesen von Hessen-Kassel in der Zeit Landgraf Wilhelms V. und der Landgräfin Amalie Elisabeth 1627–1649* (Bonn: Rheinische Friedrich-Wilhelms-Universität, 1996), p.128.

cavalry companies and two infantry regiments of professional troops, to which were added five militia cavalry companies and five foot regiments of the *Landausschuss*.[10] The army also included a Swiss Guard of 20 foot.[11]

Despite the occupations by the Imperialists, Hessen-Kassel managed to maintain its own professional army thanks to the financial support of France, allowing the Landgraves to return to their state in 1640. However, after the Treaty of Westphalia, the army was drastically reduced to only 15 militia companies, four of which were cavalry, and a further three regular companies quartered in Kassel, Ziegenhain and Rheinfels. In 1650, under Landgrave William VI (r. 1637–1663), this force numbered about 1,500 men at all.[12]

The professional troops increased in 1655 after the raising of a further two companies of horse, and two companies of foot. Four years later the garrisons increased again to four with the establishment of one at Marburg, all manned by professional infantry.[13]

In 1664, Hessen-Kassel contributed 460 foot to the contingent raised by the *Deutsche Allianz* for the Hungarian campaign against the Ottomans, thus freeing itself from the obligation to provide troops for the Upper Rhine Circle. However, the troops arrived too late to join the army on the campaign and returned home in the winter, when the whole contingent was disbanded.[14] Soon afterwards, in 1666 another regiment of infantry was formed with the companies serving in the garrison when the Swedes besieged Bremen, but this was also disbanded on its return.

Landgrave Wilhelm VII (1651–1670) in a portrait by an anonymous artist (Museumlandschaft Hessen-Kassel). After the regency of Hedwig Sophie of Brandenburg, Wilhelm became Landgrave in 1668, but remained under the tutelage of his mother until 1670. In the same year, he embarked on a Grand Tour to the Dutch Republic, England and France. In Paris, he became very ill with a 'fever', the French physicians tried to cure the 19-year-old Landgrave with laxatives, emetics, enemas and bloodletting, but the treatment killed him. Hedwig Sophie again took over the government of Hessen-Kassel, until 1675, when her second son Carl succeeded his dead brother and reigned until 1730.

10 Various, *Stamm-und-Rang-Liste des kurfürstlich Hessischen Armee Corps von 16ten Jahrhundert bis 1866* (Kassel: Gg. Francke und Ponnaz. 1866), p.5.

11 Various, *Stamm-und-Rang-Liste des kurfürstlich Hessischen Armee Corps von 16ten Jahrhundert bis 1866* (Kassel: Gg. Francke und Ponnaz. 1866), p.111.

12 Petri, *Das Militärwesen von Hessen-Kassel*, p.129. The dismissed soldiers found new employment, mainly in agriculture, which had naturally suffered from the loss of population. Before 1648, the army comprised six cavalry regiments, 13 infantry regiments, 1 free-company of horse and 1 free-company of foot, equal to 3,000 horsemen and 13,000 infantrymen at all.

13 Friedrich Wilhelm Strieder, *Grundlage zur Militär-Geschichte des Landgräflich Hessischen Corps* (Berlin, Publisher not Specified, 1798), p.7.

14 On the participation of Hessen-Kassel troops in the 1664 campaign, sources are discordant. According to the *Stamm-und-Rang-Liste des kurfürstlich Hessischen Armee Corps von 16ten Jahrhundert bis 1866* (Kassel: Gg. Francke und Ponnaz. 1866), p.15, the Hessians fought at Szentgotthárd, 'contributing to the victory with their valour'.

In the 1670s, the Italian historian Galeazzo Gualdo Priorato published a description of the state including an accurate picture of its military. He emphasised the qualities of Kassel's arsenal, which was equipped with a large quantity of weapons and ammunition.[15] Gualdo Priorato mentions 31 localities with the status of towns, but only Kassel had a population of more than 10,000 and only the latter, Marburg and Spangenberg still housed a garrison worth mentioning. As far as fortifications were concerned, none of these could be considered modern, and apart from Kassel, which had a double curtain with modern bastions, and Marburg, Homberg and Zigenhein, which had recently built citadels, most of the towns had obsolete defences.

Kassel had the largest garrison with four infantry companies, as well as a 'permanent militia' of 800 bourgeois.[16] Gualdo Priorato states that in total, in 1668, the Landgrave had 2,000 'salaried infantrymen', but that in the event of war he could raise an army of 600 horse and 8,000 foot by recruiting them in his state.[17] With his knowledge as a military scholar, he examines the geostrategic scenario of Hessen-Kassel, noting that in the event of a conflict, the Landgrave could support his troops by levying contributions

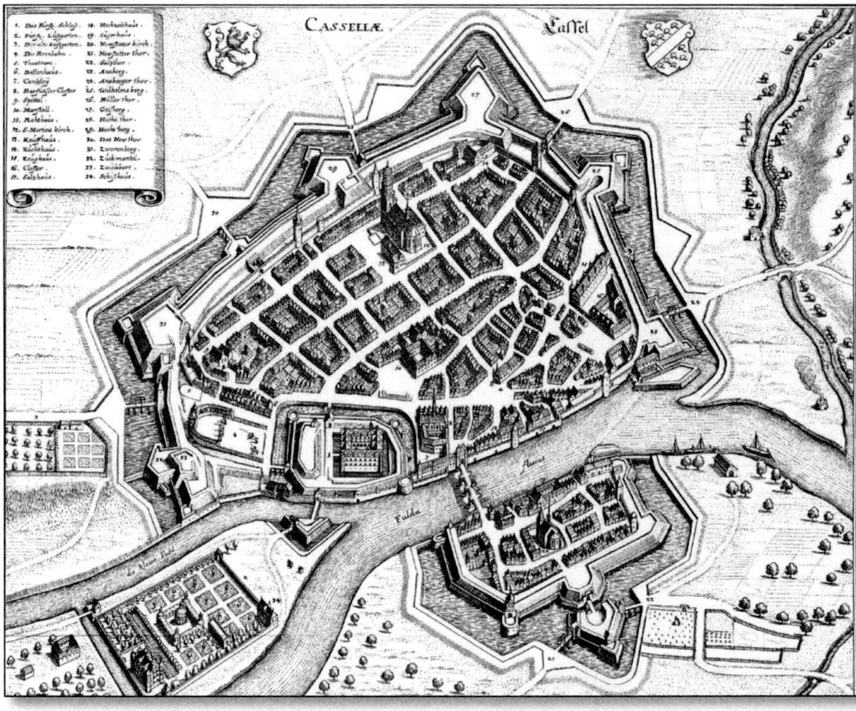

Kassel in 1648 in a print from the *Theatrum Europeum* by Matthäus Merian the Elder. (Public domain)

15 Galeazzo Gualdo Priorato, *Relationi delle Città Imperiali & Anseatiche di Colonia, Lubecca, Bremen, & Amburgo, ... delle Corti e Stati de' Serenissimi Elettor di Baviera, e de' Langravi d'Hassia in Kassel e Darmstadt* (Bologna, 1674), p.310.

16 Galeazzo Gualdo Priorato, *Relationi delle Città Imperiali & Anseatiche di Colonia, Lubecca, Bremen, & Amburgo, ... delle Corti e Stati de' Serenissimi Elettor di Baviera, e de' Langravi d'Hassia in Kassel e Darmstadt* (Bologna, 1674), p.314. The Landgrave also had 150 mounted Life Guards, and a palace corps of 24 *Trabanten*.

17 Gualdo Priorato, Galeazzo, *Relationi delle Città Imperiali & Anseatiche di Colonia, Lubecca, Bremen, & Amburgo, ... delle Corti e Stati de' Serenissimi Elettor di Baviera, e de' Langravi d'Hassia in Kassel e Darmstadt* (Bologna: 1674), p.314.

in the neighbouring territories of Mainz, Cologne, Paderborn and Fulda, which did not have strong garrisons, but the proximity to the territories under Brandenburg and Münster control severely limited his sphere of action.[18] Priorato also describes the structure of the state, governed by the Landgrave through six councils; the first of these, the *Geheimrat* (Secret Council), included the army commissioner.

Though the *Deutsche Allianz* guaranteed a relative security to its members, after the Peace of Aix-le-Chapelle in 1669 Louis XIV's foreign policy undermined its cohesion. This also had repercussions in Hessen-Kassel, where the Regent Hedwig Sophie of Brandenburg maintained a policy of neutrality that, however, hardly could be maintained. In 1672, the French invasion of The Netherlands forced Hedwig Sophie to modify her plans, but even more decisive for this change was the French plundering in the Palatinate in 1673, which caused great consternation. The nightmare generated by the presence of the belligerents' armies close to the borders persuaded the government to increase the size of the army. The prospect of having to house foreign troops on their own territory, and the resulting drain of money for billeting them, was enough on its own to force the estates to finance a new military policy. Decades of defending German Protestantism against the Counter-Reformation and then Germany itself against French aggression had cemented Hessen-Kassel's membership in a 'Protestant System' that embraced not only the northern German states but also England, the Dutch Republic, Sweden, and Denmark. Like most other small states Hessen-Kassel was very much subject to the limitations imposed by its size. Despite its standing army, it enjoyed little diplomatic advantage. Instead, it generally blended in with the bulk of smaller states that abided by the 'Imperial Peace', valued the stability afforded by the status quo, and helped make Imperial institutions work, especially at the regional, Circle, level. Therefore, like other small and medium states, Hessen-Kassel established relationships with states that largely predetermined its policies within the Empire.

By the late seventeenth century this was a relationship with which the dynasty, ministry, and

Musketeer of the *Leibgarde Compagnie* of Hessen-Kassel, 1664. (Author's reconstruction and artwork)
Martin Lezius and Richard Knötel, *Die Entwicklung des Deutschen Heeres von Seinen Frühesten Anfängen bis unsere Tage in Uniformtafeln* (Berlin: Verlag für Militärgeschichte und Deutsches Schrifttum,1936) give this unit a uniform of black hat, white cravat, dark blue coat with red 'Swedish' cuffs, tin buttons, dark blue breeches and red stockings. This uniform looks very similar to that of the Brandenburg *Markische Leibgarde* in the same years. It is possible that the Regent Hedwig Sophie – daughter of Friedrich Wilhelm of Brandenburg – took her father's unit as the model for her own company.

18 Gualdo Priorato, Galeazzo, *Relationi delle Città Imperiali & Anseatiche di Colonia, Lubecca, Bremen, & Amburgo, ... delle Corti e Stati de' Serenissimi Elettor di Baviera, e de' Langravi d'Hassia in Kassel e Darmstadt* (Bologna: 1674), p.315.

people felt comfortable. It had also given rise to a tradition of keeping a strong military in order to maintain the country's security against foreign threats. In 1672, three newly recruited companies of cavalrymen formed into a squadron, which took the name of *Carabinier* 'Cavalry Regiment' under *Major* Hörnumb, in order to have a mounted force to patrol the borders. When the Diet of the Upper Rhine Circle met in 1674, Hedwig Sophie sent her representatives, but she did not adhere to the raising of a *Kreiscontingent* for the Upper Rhine, and pursued a different goal. In the Landgravine's plans, the troops would have been a more valuable chip if they remained autonomous, avoiding the state being burdened by billeting costs as was happening in many of the Circle states.[19] During the Franco-Dutch War, Hessen-Kassel mobilised the militia to block Brandenburg's march to their winter quarters and opened talks with the Ernestine Saxon dukes for joint countermeasures to protect their zone of contribution.[20] The events of 1673–1674 led to the raising of a further 3 companies of cavalry and 11 companies of infantry. In July 1676, after the accession of Landgrave Carl an infantry regiment of 1,000 men was formed under *Obrist* Johann zur Brüggen, joining three of the existing companies with five new ones recruited in the spring.[21]

After further negotiations, in 1675 troops of Hessian-Kassel joined the allied army on the Rhine and the Saal Rivers against the French. These were the cavalry squadron *Hornumb* (hkc-ii) with three companies of 66 horsemen and the approximately 1,000 men of the infantry regiment *zur Brüggen* (HkI-3).[22] They fought at the siege of Philippsburg in 1676 and after this campaign, the cavalry had suffered the loss of 50 men and the infantry mustered just 304 privates.[23] In autumn 1676, Hedwig Sophie was unable to reach a new agreement with Emperor Leopold I and before the end of the year made a separate treaty with his son-in-law Christian V of Denmark to achieve armed status by fielding 2,000 auxiliaries against Sweden, a number later increased to 3,000. The infantry should have formed one regiment of 18 companies with a total of 2,776 men; the cavalry a regiment with 5 companies and 370 troopers, which with drivers, servants and other personnel exceeded the establishment figure.[24] The preparation of the contingent took a number of weeks.

19 The treaty was known as *Partikularallianz* (particular alliance). Georg Tessin 'Die Oberrheinische-Kreis und seine Kreistruppen' in *Zeitschrift für Heereskunde* I (1985). See also Bruno Mugnai, *Wars and Soldiers in the Early Reign of Louis XIV, volume 2: The Imperial Army 1657–1687* (Warwick: Helion & Company, 2019), pp.136–137.

20 Some regiments of Brandenburg troops were sent into Franconia to demand billets and contributions in October 1676, followed by another five regiments to Hessen-Kassel, Fulda, Anhalt and the Thuringian states the next month, while two more occupied Cologne's Westphalian territories.

21 Friedrich Wilhelm Strieder, *Grundlage zur Militär-Geschichte des Landgräflich Hessischen Corps* (Berlin, Publisher not Specified, 1798), p.8.

22 Various, *Stamm-und-Rang-Liste des kurfürstlich Hessischen Armee Corps von 16ten Jahrhundert bis 1866* (Kassel: Gg. Francke und Ponnaz. 1866), pp.16–17.

23 Carl von Stamford, *Die Feldzüge der Regimenter Ufm Keller und von Hornumb von Hessen-Kassel in dem Reichskriege Gegen Schweden, auf Schonen und auf Rügen; 1677 und 1678* (Kassel: Freyschmidt 1862), p.21.

24 Carl von Stamford, *Die Feldzüge der Regimenter Ufm Keller und von Hornumb von Hessen-Kassel in dem Reichskriege Gegen Schweden, auf Schonen und auf Rügen; 1677 und 1678* (Kassel:

Plate A. *Deutsche Allianz*, 1660–64

1 – Pfalz-Neuburg, Infantry Field Officer, early 1660s; 2 – Württemberg, Cuirassier Trooper, 1664; 3 – Electorate of Mainz, Pikeman, 1668

(Illustration by Bruno Mugnai © Helion & Company)

See Colour Plate Commentaries for further information.

Plate B – The Three Brunswick, 1660s–1670s

1 – Hanover, Öffener zu Pferd, Trooper, 1668–72; 2 – Celle, Leibregiment zu Fuss, Musketeer. 1668; 3 – Wolfenbüttel, Musketeer, 1675

(Illustration by Bruno Mugnai © Helion & Company)

See Colour Plate Commentaries for further information.

Plate C – The Three Brunswick, 1680s
1 – Hanover, Siegelberg zu Fuss, Musketeer, 1685; 2 – Celle, Bothmer Dragoner, Dragoon, 1688;
3 – Wolfenbüttel, Holle zu Fuss, Musketeer, 1689–90
(Illustration by Bruno Mugnai © Helion & Company)
See Colour Plate Commentaries for further information.

Plate D – Hessen-Kassel and Hessen-Darmstadt

1 – Hessen-Kassel, Ufm Keller zu Fuss, Pikeman with Kaputrock, 1677; 2 – Hessen-Kassel, Prinz Carl zu Fuss, Drummer, 1687; 3 – Hessen-Darmstadt, Leibgarde zu Fuss, Musketeer, 1678
(Illustration by Bruno Mugnai © Helion & Company)
See Colour Plate Commentaries for further information.

Plate E – Infantry, 1660s

1 – Frankfurt am Main, Militia's Officer, 1659–60; 2 – Lorraine, Infantry NCO, 1660–64; 3 – Palatinate, Musketeer, 1668–69

(Illustration by Bruno Mugnai © Helion & Company)

See Colour Plate Commentaries for further information.

Plate F – Infantry 1670–1680

1 – Baden (Swabian Circle), Montfort zu Fuss, Officer, 1672; 2 – Osnabrück, Leibregiment zu Fuss, Musketeer, 1676; 3 – Mecklenburg-Güstrow, Musketeer, 1672–75

(Illustration by Bruno Mugnai © Helion & Company)

See Colour Plate Commentaries for further information.

Plate G – Infantry Regiment Hohenlohe (Greece, 1691-94)

1-3) Hanover, 1660–80; 4) Celle, 1690s; 5) Wolfenbüttel, 1690s
(Illustration by Bruno Mugnai © Helion & Company)
See Colour Plate Commentaries for further information.

Plate H – Cavalry, 1660s–1670s

1 – Mecklenburg-Schwerin, Trooper, 1664–69; 2 – Lorraine, German Cavalry Regiment, Trooper, 1672–78; 3 – Osnabrück, Hitzfeld zu Pferd, Trooper, 1674–75; 4 – Hessen-Darmstadt, Riedesel zu Pferd, Trooper, 1677

(Illustration by Bruno Mugnai © Helion & Company)

See Colour Plate Commentaries for further information.

Plate I – Cavalry and Dragoons, 1680s–1690s

1 – Würzburg, Truchsess Cuirassieren regiment, Rittmeister, 1683–85; 2 – Hessen-Kassel, Prinz Philipp Dragoner, Corporal, 1684; 3 – Brunswick-Wolfenbüttel, Lippe Dragoner, Dragoon, 1688–89; 4 – Palatinate, Leibregiment zu Pferd, Trooper, 1685–90

(Illustration by Bruno Mugnai © Helion & Company)

See Colour Plate Commentaries for further information.

Plate J – Life Guards

1 – Lorraine, Mousquetaires de la Garde, 1664–69; 2 – Hessen-Darmstadt, Leibgarde zu Pferd, 1668; 3 – Celle, Garde zu Pferd, 1670–75; 4 – Württemberg, Leibgarde des Herzogs, 1673

(Illustration by Bruno Mugnai © Helion & Company)

See Colour Plate Commentaries for further information.

In June 1677, the Danish commissioners received the first 11 infantry companies. In total there were 33 officers, 240 NCOs and lance corporals, and 1,170 private soldiers; the companies numbered between 113 and 122 men of which one-third were pikemen. With them, there were also the *Stabpersonen* (staff) with *Regimentsquartiermeister*, *Adjutant*, *Regimentsschultheiss* (auditor), *Secretär*, *Feldgeistliche* (field chaplain), *Profoss* with his *Steckenknechten* (assistants), *Wagenmeister*, and the Landgrave's commissioner. Days later, the cavalry also arrived; they were of three companies, each with 1 *Rittmeister*, 1 *Lieutenant*, 1 *Cornet*, 1 *Wachtmeister*, 1 *Quartiermeister*, 1 *Trompete*, 3 *Corporalen*, and 55 *Einspännige* (troopers). The first company was under the command of the *Obristlieutenant* Wilhelm von Hörnumb, and included 1 *Adjutant*, 1 *Musterschreiber* (accountant) 1 *Reitschmiede* (smith) and 1 *Feldscherer* (surgeon). With the cavalry, there were also reformado officers and NCOs who served as volunteers increasing the companies to 80 or more men.[25]

In July, the infantry had increased to 1,500 men, and the cavalry numbered above 300, but in September the number had fallen to 1,525 in all.[26] Desertion and diseases further diminished the troops, which at the end of October numbered just 1,000 foot and half of the original cavalry strength.[27] The winter quarters established in the cold island of Rügen provoked many protests – not only from soldiers but also from officers. As this initial contingent was destroyed by Swedish action at Warksow on 7 January 1678, Denmark negotiated for a second force of 1,400 infantrymen in April, this time with Landgrave Carl I, with formal Imperial approval extending to the exemption of Hessen-Kassel from billeting.[28]

In June, this second contingent joined the Danish army in Scania. On 15 July, they numbered a total of 1,303 men, with an additional 70 to 80 not currently present.[29] In mid-September, the regiment had fallen to 1,261 men, of which 1,140 officers, NCOs and privates formed 8 companies, 41 grenadiers, 21 in the *Regimentstab*, and 119 sick in the hospitals.[30] This was a ratio of loss on campaign considered as acceptable, but three months later the situation appeared much worse – on 2 December, there were only 87

Freyschmidt 1862), p.27.

25 Carl von Stamford, *Die Feldzüge der Regimenter Ufm Keller und von Hornumb von Hessen-Kassel in dem Reichskriege Gegen Schweden, auf Schonen und auf Rügen; 1677 und 1678* (Kassel: Freyschmidt 1862), pp.39–40.

26 Carl von Stamford, *Die Feldzüge der Regimenter Ufm Keller und von Hornumb von Hessen-Kassel in dem Reichskriege Gegen Schweden, auf Schonen und auf Rügen; 1677 und 1678* (Kassel: Freyschmidt 1862), p.98.

27 Carl von Stamford, *Die Feldzüge der Regimenter Ufm Keller und von Hornumb von Hessen-Kassel in dem Reichskriege Gegen Schweden, auf Schonen und auf Rügen; 1677 und 1678* (Kassel: Freyschmidt 1862), p.102.

28 Peter H. Wilson, *German Armies. War and German Politics, 1648–1806* (London: UCL Press, 1998), p.53.

29 Carl von Stamford, *Die Feldzüge der Regimenter Ufm Keller und von Hornumb von Hessen-Kassel in dem Reichskriege Gegen Schweden, auf Schonen und auf Rügen; 1677 und 1678* (Kassel: Freyschmidt 1862), p.151.

30 Carl von Stamford, *Die Feldzüge der Regimenter Ufm Keller und von Hornumb von Hessen-Kassel in dem Reichskriege Gegen Schweden, auf Schonen und auf Rügen; 1677 und 1678* (Kassel: Freyschmidt 1862),.157.

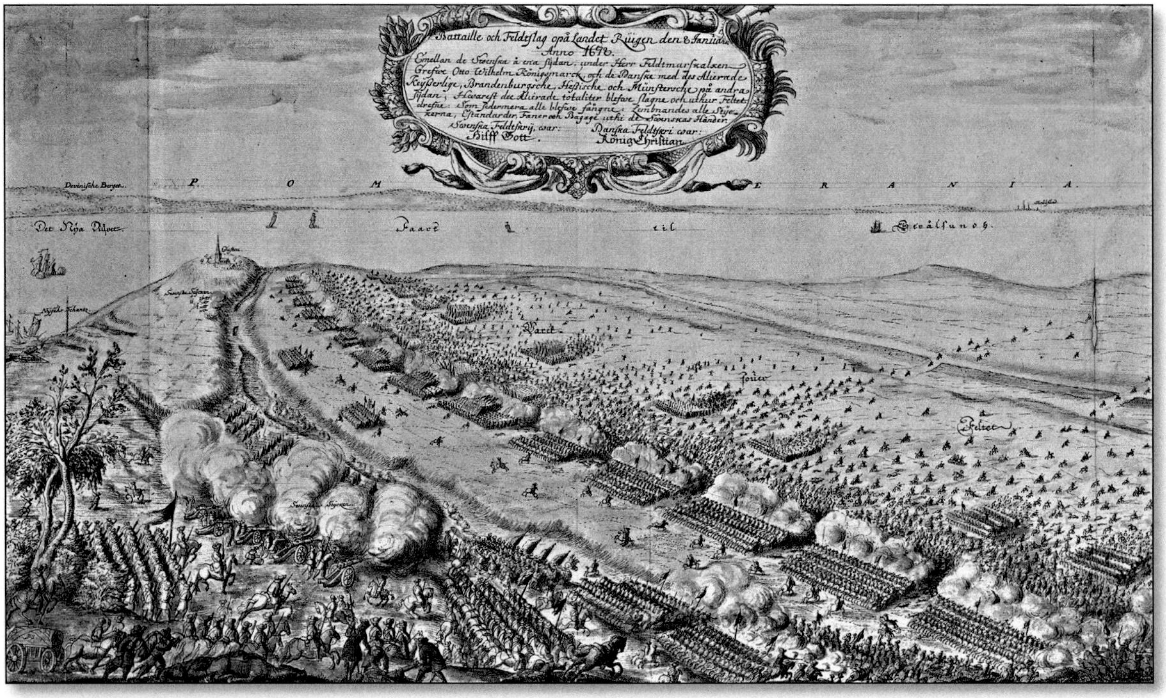

Print depicting the Battle of Warksow, fought on 7 January 1678 north-west of the village of Gustow, opposite Warksow Manor. (Author's collection)
In the battle, the Danish-German contingent was nearly destroyed by the Swedes under Otto Wilhelm von Königsmarck, who succeeded in retaking control of the Island of Rügen preventing the allied effort to isolate Stralsund. Only 245 foot and 149 horse of the original Hessen-Kassel contingent escaped death or capture.

officers and NCOs, and 458 privates, including 20 grenadiers and 42 assigned to other duties, still fit to serve, plus a further 246 were sick in the hospitals, where in the previous week 232 had died. At the end of the year, only 833 men returned to Hessen-Kassel.[31]

By 1679, the Landgrave reorganised and re-equipped his troops, putting in place the veteran August von der Lippe-Brake as Commander-in-Chief. The professional troops numbered 1,304 infantry, 150 cavalry and 115 dragoons; the household troops comprised 63 horse of the *Leibguardia*, and a further 98 soldiers served as artillerymen or permanent garrison troops.[32] In 1678, the artillery had already been formed into a company under *Hauptmann* Heppe.[33]

31 Carl von Stamford, *Die Feldzüge der Regimenter Ufm Keller und von Hornumb von Hessen-Kassel in dem Reichskriege Gegen Schweden, auf Schonen und auf Rügen; 1677 und 1678* (Kassel: Freyschmidt 1862), p.177.

32 Carl von Stamford, *Die Feldzüge der Regimenter Ufm Keller und von Hornumb von Hessen-Kassel in dem Reichskriege Gegen Schweden, auf Schonen und auf Rügen; 1677 und 1678* (Kassel: Freyschmidt 1862), p.185.

33 Various, *Stamm-und-Rang-Liste des kurfürstlich Hessischen Armee Corps*, p.187.

From this figure the professional army climbed to 4,000 men in a few years, underpinned by new funding agreements with the estates.[34] By 1680, a monthly contribution of 16,000 thalers was agreed as military tax, but like other German princes, Carl I managed to trade his troops. In March 1683, the professional army numbered 1,020 cavalry and 3,200 infantry, with 2 companies of horse and 22 of foot from the *ausschuss* (militia).[35] Each regiment fielded 8, 10 or 12 companies with 100 to 120 privates and NCOs and three officers as usual; by 1677 each company also had 6 or 7 grenadiers.[36] Cavalry regiments had 6 to 8 companies of 50 horsemen. The French threat forced the Landgrave to further increase the army by five infantry regiments between 1683 and 1684, and a further two cavalry regiments and one dragoon regiment in the same years. At the same time, the *Leibgarde* formed two companies with 167 men in all.

More or less in the same period, the diplomat Heinrich Ludwig Gude,[37] wrote a detailed report on Hessen-Kassel, updating Gualdo Priorato's information of the previous decades. He described the *Kriegsmacht* of the Landgrave Carl I, which he considered as 'remarkable'.[38] According to his knowledge, in the late 1680s Hessen-Kassel had 10 to 12 regiments of professional infantry and cavalry. As well as Kassel, Marburg and Spangenberg, permanent garrisons were also quartered in Rinteln, Rheinfels, and Rüsselsheim, supported by a regularly trained militia of horse and foot. Although approximate, these figures confirm that the army had strengthened considerably over the years, and that the troops represented the largest expenditure of the state. As occurred in other German principalities, it was a trend that indicated that Hessen-Kassel was also aiming to consolidate its role as an 'armed state'. In the early 1680s, renewed relations with the Upper Rhine Circle led to the appointment of the Landgrave as co-director, but Hessen-Kassel did not sent troops to join the relief army for Vienna in 1683, since negotiations with the Emperor had broken down.[39] Moreover, the states

34 Peter H. Wilson, *German Armies. War and German Politics, 1648–1806* (London: UCL Press, 1998), p.54.

35 Friedrich Wilhelm Strieder, *Grundlage zur Militär-Geschichte des Landgräflich Hessischen Corps* (Berlin, Publisher not Specified, 1798), pp.9–10. This number comprised 1,068 foot of the militia regiment raised in Kassel.

36 Various, *Stamm-und-Rang-Liste des kurfürstlich Hessischen Armee Corps von 16ten Jahrhundert bis 1866* (Kassel: Gg. Francke und Ponnaz. 1866), p.15.

37 Born at Rendsburg, in Schleswig-Holstein, Heinrich Ludwig Gude (1635?–1707) travelled through Europe and acquired considerable knowledge, especially in the languages and diplomacy; which gave him a position as Government Secretary in Copenhagen. He published a series of small volumes with descriptions of most European states, as well as some non-European ones, such as Algiers, together with an *Introduction to the European States and Their Decisions* (published after his death in 1708). These are genealogical and topographical treatises of remarkable precision and clarity, but without any higher historical or geographical interest. However, the works deal with the geopolitical scenario of the late seventeenth century and met the needs of the time primarily through their convenience and practical usefulness and they were continued after Gude's death by other unnamed authors.

38 Gude, Heinrich Ludwig, *Des Hochfürstl. Landgrafs. Hessischen Staats* (Halle, before 1708), p.106.

39 Leopold I asked Hessen-Kassel for 3 companies of cavalry and 1,800 infantry. Carl von Stamford, *Die Feldzüge der Regimenter Ufm Keller und von Hornumb von Hessen-Kassel in dem*

of the Upper Rhine were more concerned with a new French aggression than the Ottoman offensive, and they rejected the demand to send troops to the east. On the other hand, Landgrave Carl I opened talks with the Governor of the Spanish Low Countries, Ottone Enrico Del Grana, to supply 1,000 cavalry, 500 dragoons and 6,000 infantry for Flanders, but a shortage of resource forced the Governor to renounce the agreement.[40]

Despite divergences with Vienna and the other members of the Upper Rhine Circle, in the spring of 1685, the Landgrave sent troops to Hungary alongside the *Reichsarmee*, which served under Charles V of Lorraine until 1688. Hessen-Kassel contributed with infantry *Kreisregiment* of two battalions, and added three cavalry companies to form a regiment of horse with Hessen-Darmstadt and other Upper Rhine states.[41] The contingent also included artillery, consisting of constables and *knechte*, two 2lb guns with 50 round shot and 24 canisters of grape shot. With them, a further 1,500 infantry from three different regiments joined the Imperial Army in Hungary, where they also served until 1688. The troops of the Circle as well as those of Hessen-Kassel were sadly weakened during these campaigns, due more to neglect by the administrations at home and the disinterest of the Imperial command than to enemy action.

In 1685–86, through the mediation of Duke Ernst August of Hannover, the Republic of Venice turned to Hessen-Kassel for more infantry to be sent to Greece. Landgrave Carl I was initially less enthusiastic and rejected Venetian offers to hire four or five regiments, but eventually agreed to a single regiment in March 1687.[42] The regiment returned home in 1689 very chastened by the events of the campaigns.[43] From 1686 to 1689 the cavalry raised three new regiments, the dragoons two new regiments and the infantry four new regiments. Of the dragoons, that under Johann Ernst zu Nassau-Weilburg (HkD-2) entered the service of the Dutch Republic.[44] The infantry also comprised the battalions *Buttlarsch* and *Derenthalsch*, and a *Jäger* company from the militia.[45]

The War of The League of Augsburg marked a turning point for Hessen-Kassel. Already by 1688, Prince William III had secured the services of the north German armed princes by renewing the contracts made before his departure for England. About 2,000 troops from Hessen-Kassel were serving

Reichskriege Gegen Schweden, auf Schonen und auf Rügen; 1677 und 1678 (Kassel: Freyschmidt, 1862), p.31.

40 Friedrich Wilhelm Strieder, *Grundlage zur Militär-Geschichte des Landgräflich Hessischen Corps* (Berlin, Publisher not Specified, 1798), p.12.

41 The Hessian-Kassel contingent served in the *Regiment zu Fuss Nassau-Saarbrücken* and *Regiment zu Pferd Rau*. See Bruno Mugnai, *Wars and Soldiers in the Early Reign of Louis XIV, volume 2: The Imperial Army 1657–1687* (Warwick: Helion & Company, 2019), p.286.

42 Peter H. Wilson, *German Armies. War and German Politics, 1648–1806* (London: UCL Press, 1998), p.79.

43 Various, *Stamm-und-Rang-Liste des kurfürstlich Hessischen Armee Corps von 16ten Jahrhundert bis 1866* (Kassel: Gg. Francke und Ponnaz. 1866), p.17.

44 Various, *Stamm-und-Rang-Liste des kurfürstlich Hessischen Armee Corps von 16ten Jahrhundert bis 1866* (Kassel: Gg. Francke und Ponnaz. 1866), p.18.

45 Friedrich Wilhelm Strieder, *Grundlage zur Militär-Geschichte des Landgräflich Hessischen Corps* (Berlin, Publisher not Specified, 1798), p.12.

west of the Meuse by 1690.[46] Alongside commanders like Max Emanuel, Friedrich III of Brandenburg, Ernst August of Hannover and Johann Georg III of Saxony, Landgrave Carl I also wanted an independent command of his own, preferably incorporating as many other princely contingents as possible and deployed on the lower or middle Rhine sectors from where he could intervene either in Flanders or South Germany. This scheme became the core of the defence against France in the next years, and moved Hessen-Kassel into the Anglo-Dutch orbit. In the eighteenth century, the Landgraviate became one of the main suppliers of 'mercenaries' in Germany, a primacy which remained strong as when King George III of Great Britain turned to Hessen-Kassel for hiring most of the 'mercenaries' (actually auxiliaries) for the war against the American colonies.[47]

Hessen-Darmstadt

Reduced in terms of territory and population in favour of Kassel after the settlement of Westphalia, Hessen-Darmstadt managed with great difficulty to maintain a status capable of guaranteeing an autonomous policy. By 1648, the regular forces were reduced to a few companies of 80 to 90 men each, although increased to 150 in 1657, but reduced again to 99 the next year. Cavalry consisted only of the company of the *Leibgarde zu Pferd*, and the mounted militia, known as *Land-Ausschuß* or *Land-Reiter*.[48] In 1658, Hessen-Darmstadt also joined the Rhenish League and the *Deutsche Allianz* but in 1664 contributed to the formation of the Empire's contingent to Hungary with 150 foot, all musketeers.[49]

After Hessen-Kassel, Galeazzo Gualdo Priorato also provided a detailed report on Hessen-Darmstadt.[50] In 1668, during the reign of Landgrave Ludwig VI (r. 1661–1678), the army comprised one company of Foot Guards, which formed the stable garrison of Darmstadt and of the Landgrave's residence.

As for the cavalry, Darmstadt quartered the company of the *Leibcompagnie*, and a further 600 cavalry raised by the aristocracy served as a semi-permanent force.[51] The capital had no modern curtains, but could deploy a militia of 400 trained bourgeois. The only modern fortifications were those

46 Peter H. Wilson, *German Armies. War and German Politics, 1648–1806* (London: UCL Press, 1998), p.90.

47 For further reading on this topic, see Rodney Atwood, *The Hessians. Mercenaries from Hessen-Kassel in the American Revolution* (Cambridge, London, New York: Cambridge University Press, 1980), and Charles W. Ingrao, The *Hessian Mercenary State Ideas, institutions, and Reform under Frederick II, 1760—1785* (Cambridge, London, New York: Cambridge University Press, 1987).

48 Friedrich Hild, *Militärchronik des Großherzogthums Hessen von Anfang des Regierenden Hauses bis auf die neueste Zeit*, band I, 1567–1790 (Darmstadt: Friedrich Hild, 1828), p 277.

49 Friedrich Hild, *Militärchronik des Großherzogthums Hessen von Anfang des Regierenden Hauses bis auf die neueste Zeit*, band I, 1567–1790 (Darmstadt: Friedrich Hild, 1828), p 277.

50 Galeazzo Gualdo Priorato, *Relatione delle Corti e Stati delli Serenissimi Landgravii d'Hassia in Kassel e Darmstadt ....*, (Leyden, 1668), pp.6–42.

51 Galeazzo Gualdo Priorato, *Relatione delle Corti e Stati delli Serenissimi Landgravii d'Hassia in Kassel e Darmstadt ....*, (Leyden, 1668), p.16.

Landgrave Ludwig VI of Hessen-Darmstadt, in a portrait by Salomon Duarte dating to 1665 (Art Collection of the Gripsholm Castle in Mariefred, Sweden). Note the scarf in azure lined and fringed with white, which was presumably the older type of scarf also worn by the army's officers. To this, another of white silk with red and blue threads was introduced by the late 1680s.

of Giessen, and besides this latter, the Landgrave also had strategic strongholds at Zwingenberg, covering the Rhine crossing, Lichtenberg, Rüsselsheim near the River Main and the ones of Frankenstein and Starkenburg, overlooking the valley of the Rhine and surveying the important trading route along the right bank of the great river. Despite the modest size of the state, Gualdo Priorato describes the local aristocracy as more used to arms than to literature, and the Landgrave could raise a strong army and militia which would number12,000 men; then he closed his *Relatione* by stating that Hessen-Darmstadt could raise the best soldiers of Germany.[52] The Landgraviate was divided in two main parts: the *Oberfürstenthum*, comprising the territory around Giessen, and the *Obergrafschaft*, the area around Darmstadt.

When France invaded the Dutch Republic in 1672, the Landgrave increased his *Leib-Kompagnie* of foot to 198 men and renamed it *Leibgarde zu Fuss*. The cavalry included the *Leibgarde zu Pferd* and the *land-ausschuss* (state militia). The Landgraves devoted great care to the state militia, and this increased the military reputation of their principality. The foot militia, or *ausschuss*, consisted of all physically healthy adult male subjects and was divided into *junger ausschuss* consisting of people between 17 and 40 years of age and *alter ausschuss* comprising militiamen between 41 and 60 years of age. In order not to take too many people away from work, generally only the younger militiamen were subject to regular training. They were organised into companies which could be joined into a regiment like the regular troops, and met at intervals to practise with weapons, concluding each session by taking an oath to the Prince, and to perform their duty against internal and external enemies. At least in theory, militiamen could serve outside the territory.[53] Organisation and equipment of the *junger ausschuss* was as for the regular troops, since the militia were a pool for recruitment into the regular infantry.

In 1681, there were three companies in the *Oberfürstenthum* (Giessen), and two in the *Obergrafschaft* (Darmstadt). The duties of the captains were permanent and they were commissioned officers. In addition to his wages, the Commander-in-Chief of the militia had the right of free accommodation in Frankenstein. In 1687, the Regent Elisabeth Dorothea, ordered the foot

52 Galeazzo Gualdo Priorato, *Relatione delle Corti e Stati delli Serenissimi Landgravii d'Hassia in Kassel e Darmstadt ....*, (Leyden, 1668), pp.15–16.

53 August von Keim, *Geschichte des 4 Großherzoglich Hessischen Infanterie-Regiments Großherzogin (Prinz Carl) Nr. 118 und seiner Stämme* (Berlin: E.S. Mittler und Sohn 1879), p.2. In mid-1600, each company numbered 200 men and consisted of 1 *Hauptmann*, 1 *Leutnant*, 1 *Fâhnrich*, 1 *Führer*, 1 surgeon, 2 *Feldwebel*, 6 corporals, 12 *Gefreite* (lance corporals) 2 *Trommelschläger* (Drummers), 1 fifer, 62 pikemen and 110 musketeers.

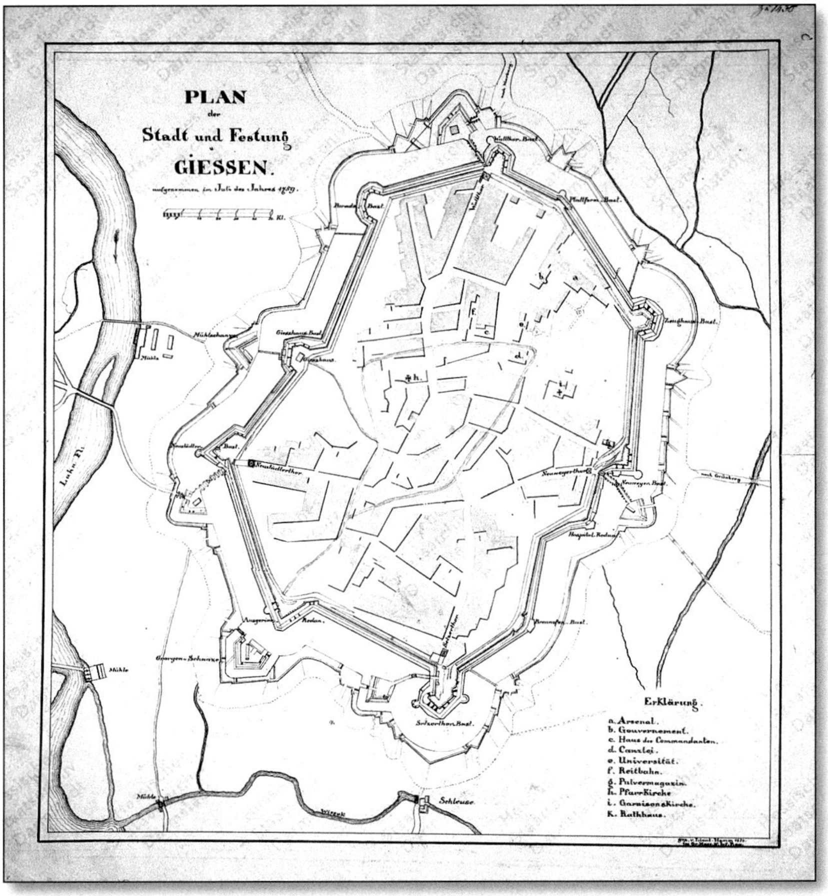

Plan of the city of Giessen, with the curtain dating to the late 1690s. (Author's collection) After 1648, the city became an important cultural centre and the seat of the University of Hessen-Darmstadt

companies to be uniformly dressed.[54] Even greater attention was paid to the mounted militia. In 1668, there is mention of a company of *Landreiter* in Giessen, and two years later, another company of 50 *einspânnige* under a *Rittmeister* entered service in the territory of Darmstadt. In 1671, both companies were mustered together with six others, to a total of: a staff with 1 *Obrist*, 1 *Obristlieutenant*, 2 *Obristwachtmeister*, 2 *Rittmeister*, 6 *Leutnants*, 6 *Quartiermeisters*, 18 corporals, 6 trumpeters, and 600 men.[55] In 1679, there were only five companies totalling 381 horsemen, and one year later the strength had fallen further to 278 rank and file. After decreasing to 145 horsemen in 1684, there are no further references to the presence of *Landreiter*, and thereafter this term designated only voluntary recruits for the regular cavalry.

Like other German states, by 1674 Hessen-Darmstadt had made bilateral arrangements with Vienna, supplying troops for the Imperial Army on the Rhine in return for limited cash assistance and exemption from billeting and

54 August von Keim, *Geschichte des 4 Großherzoglich Hessischen Infanterie-Regiments Großherzogin (Prinz Carl) Nr. 118 und seiner Stämme* (Berlin: E.S. Mittler und Sohn 1879), p.3.

55 Fritz Beck, *Die alten Hessen-Darmstädtischen Reiterregimenter bis zur Errichtung des 1. Großherzoglich Hessischen Dragoner-Regiments Garde-Dragoner-Regiment Nr. 23 1609–1790* (Darmstadt: Wittich, 1910), p.5.

provision of *Kreistruppen*.[56] In 1677, Landgrave Ludwig VI increased the professional force with two companies of Foot Guards, which assumed the title of *Leibgarde Bataillon*. In the same year, the Landgrave agreed to hire an auxiliary corps to the Emperor of 500 cavalry and 1,000 infantry to be sent to the army on the Rhine. The infantry included the three companies of the *Leibgarde*, the old company quartered in Giessen, and two other newly raised companies. The cavalrymen formed a regiment of 10 companies under colonel Riedesel.

Landgrave Ludwig VI died on 24 April 1678 and was succeeded by his son, Ludwig VII, who himself died on 31 August 1678 after a reign of only four months. Since his brother Ernst Ludwig was still a minor, their mother, Elisabeth Dorothea, governed as Regent for the next 10 years. During Ludwig VII's short reign the *Leibgarde zu Pferd* increased to two companies. In 1678, a new agreement with the Emperor established the auxiliary corps as 400 horse and 1,000 foot, who served under the Duke of Lorraine against France. The corps returned home at the end of that year although the Treaty of Nijmegen was only ratified by the Emperor in 1679. On their return the *Garde zu Fuß* was reduced by one company, the two others joined the existing garrisons. The cavalry regiment of 8 companies was also reduced. The edict for the reduction had already been signed by the Landgrave on 20 June 1678.[57]

Not having the resources of Kassel's cousins, the Regent of Hessen-Darmstadt did not pursue a rearmament policy, but nevertheless the overall professional strength increased, albeit slightly. In the early 1680s a new garrison was established in Giessen under *Oberstleutnant* Turkheim, while the younger son of the Regent Landgravine, Prince Georg, took the command of the *Garde zu Fuß*, which was the largest unit with 216–300 men between 1680 and 1682.[58] In 1684, a company was added to the *Garde zu Fuß*, now under *Oberstleutnant* Ludwig Balthasar von Weitolhausen-Schrattenbach, and a fourth company was added in 1687. Meanwhile, Prince Georg took command of an infantry regiment of 1,000 men as a part of the contingent provided by Regent Prince Carl Friedrich of Württemberg for service with the Republic of Venice. Prince Georg held the office until 1690 and served with his regiment in Greece, where he participated to the siege of Athens, Negroponte (Chalkis) and the blockade of Malvasia (Monemvasia).[59]

56 Peter H. Wilson, *German Armies. War and German Politics, 1648–1806* (London: UCL Press, 1998), p.53.

57 Carl Christian Röder von Diersburg, *Geschichte des 1. Großherzoglich Hessischen Infanterie (Leibgarde) Regiments Nr. 115*, 1621–1899, (Berlin: Ernst Siegfried Mittler & Sohn, 1899), p.67.

58 Carl Christian Röder von Diersburg, *Geschichte des 1. Großherzoglich Hessischen Infanterie (Leibgarde) Regiments Nr. 115*, 1621–1899, (Berlin: Ernst Siegfried Mittler & Sohn, 1899), p.69.

59 See Bruno Mugnai, Wars *and Soldiers in the Early Reign of Louis XIV, volume 6, Armies of the Italian States 1660–1690, part 2* (Warwick: Helion & Company, 2023), p.301.

In 1689, Hessen-Darmstadt maintained a regular force of 1,600 soldiers.[60] Artillery was also strengthened. Field cannon, mortars and siege pieces were collected in Rüsselsheim. However, at the end of October 1688, all the artillery was lost, when a strong French corps under General Louis François de Boufflers appeared before the fortress. After receiving a refusal to surrender from the Hessian commander, the French opened a fierce artillery fire against the fortress. A prolonged defence was out of the question, and therefore Captain-Lieutenant Blegt surrendered in accordance with the instructions received from Darmstadt, on the condition that the garrison would be freely evacuated.[61]

In 1683 and again in 1685–1688, Hessen-Darmstadt also supplied troops for the Upper Rhine Circle with two companies of cavalry and two of infantry.[62] Despite the relatively small number, provision of the *Kreistruppen* represented a considerable burden, particularly for the smaller principalities like Hessen-Darmstadt, which paid 103,710 thalers by 1685, equivalent to nearly half its annual revenue.[63]

Landgrave Ernst Ludwig came into his majority on 15 February 1688 and was soon involved in the Nine Years' War. His domains were threatened by the French and escaped the fate suffered by the Palatinate thanks to the providential arrive of the Allied contingents on the Rhine.

Prince Georg of Hessen-Darmstadt (1669–1705), in a portrait by Thomas Murray (Public Domain via Wikipedia Commons). As brother of the reigning Landgrave, he had no immediate prospect of political power, and like many junior princes had served as a volunteer in Hungary in 1687. After obtaining command of a regiment, the logical next step was to advance his military career as an entrepreneur. Similar motives prompted other small German Houses to enter the business of mercenaries.

60 Peter H. Wilson, *German Armies. War and German Politics, 1648–1806* (London: UCL Press, 1998), p.91.

61 Fritz Beck, *Geschichte des Großherzoglich Hessischen Feldartillerie-Regiments Nr. 25 und seiner Stämme, 1460–1883* (Berlin: Siegfried Mittler und Sohn, 1884), p.36.

62 Georg Tessin *Die Regimenter der Europäischen Staaten im Ancien Régime des XVI bis XVIII Jahrhunderts* (Osnabrück: Biblio Verlag, 1986), Teil 1, p- 165: The companies joined the infantry regiment Nassau- Saarbücken and cavalry regiment Spiegel.

63 Peter H. Wilson, *German Armies. War and German Politics, 1648–1806* (London: UCL Press, 1998), p.77.

6

The Palatinate

In October 1649, Prince Carl Ludwig of Wittelsbach-Simmern (1617–1680), the eldest son of the erstwhile King of Bohemia, Friedrich V, left his exile in London and regained possession of his states. The Peace of Westphalia confirmed the agreement with the Emperor signed in May 1635 with the Peace of Prague, and reinstated Carl Ludwig as the legitimate Prince-Elector. Thus ended one of the most dramatic chapters in the history of the Palatinate, marked by foreign occupations and devastations. The economic condition of the state was so bad that the Imperial Diet freed the Palatinate from supplying its quota of soldiers or money for the *Reichsarmee*: a condition that lasted until 1663.[1]

Carl Ludwig, Elector of the Palatinate (r.1649–1680), in a print from Anselmus van Hulle, *Les Hommes Illustres* (Amsterdam, 1717). (Author's collection)

The Palatinate was the smallest and least populous of the secular Electorates, and during the Thirty Years' War suffered some territorial amputations with the loss of the Upper Palatinate to Bavaria. Except for the principalities of Simmern and Lauter, the other domains were fragmented into a number of enclaves located on both banks of the Rhine, some of which bordered on more than one state, while the counties of Sponnheim and Veldenz were shared *in condominium* with other Wittelsbach princes.[2] This made the Electorate another geographic nightmare in the Empire: an actual buffer state constantly exposed

1 The case of the Palatinate, whose debts were catastrophic, was referred to the *Reichshofrat* (the council of finance for the Empire) and thus to the Emperor, who granted a moratorium of 10 years followed by a 50 percent reduction of interest payments for a further 10 years. See Joachim Whaley, *Germany and the Holy Roman Empire. From the Peace of Westphalia to the Dissolution of the Reich, 1648–1806* (Oxford: Oxford University Press, 2012), p.18.

2 Bruno Mugnai, *Wars and Soldiers in the Early Reign of Louis XIV, The Imperial Army 1657–1687* (Warwick: Helion & Company, 2019), p.243. Electoral Palatinate was entirely in the Upper Rhine Circle.

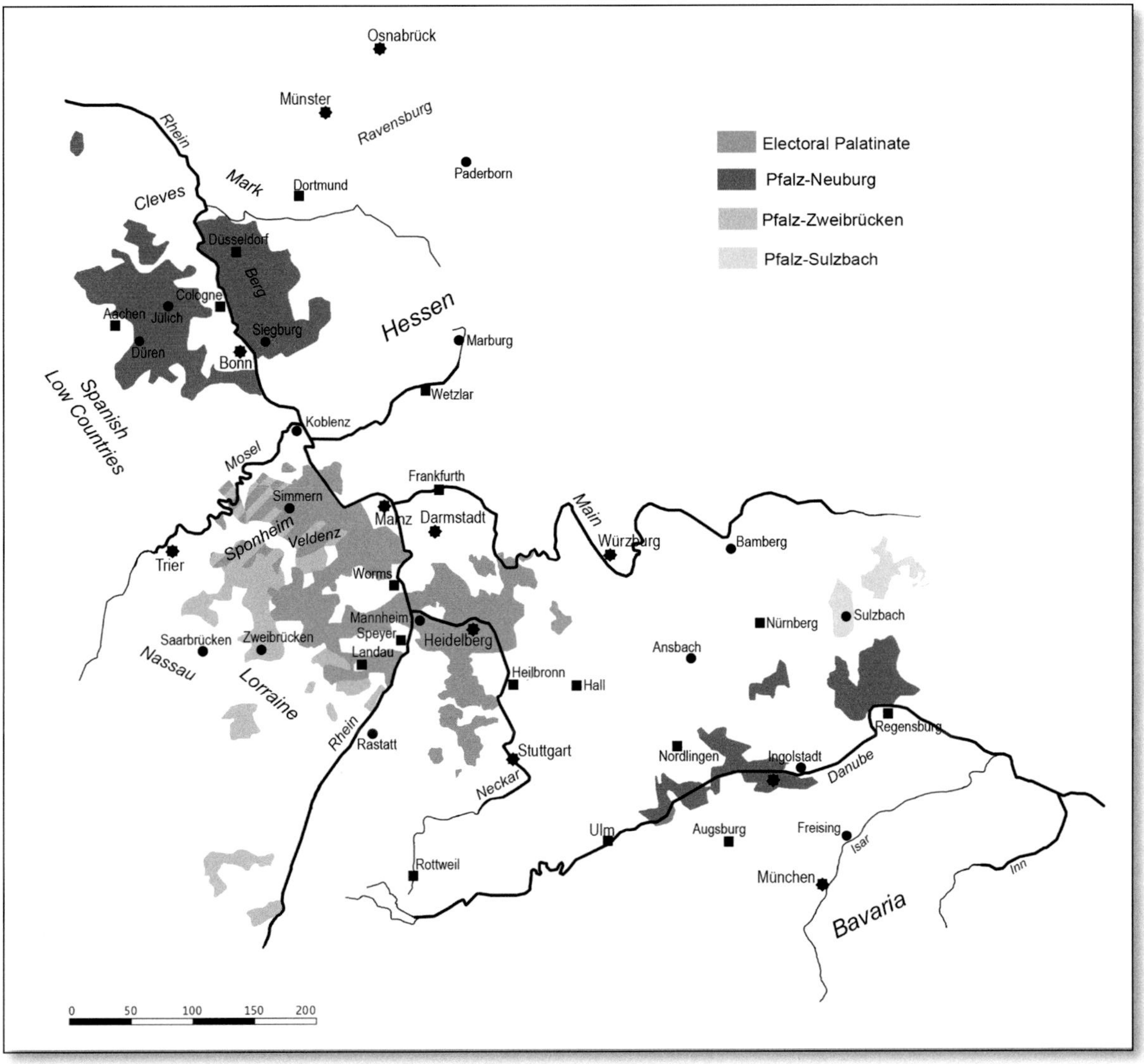

Map of the Palatinate

The territories belonging to the four Houses of the Palatine-Wittelsbach after the Peace of Westphalia. By 1676, the Allies occupied the Swedish territories of Zweibrücken. During the negotiations at Ratisbon in 1684, Sweden failed to gain support for her claim that the restitution of Palatinate-Zweibrücken and Holstein-Gottorf should be included in the settlement, and Swedish diplomacy was equally unsuccessful in demanding that a specific guarantee of her possessions should be included in the armistice. Hence Sweden continued negotiations with other powers trying to find support for its demands; then in 1686, talks with the Emperor led to Sweden's accession to the League of Augsburg.

to foreign invasions and virtually indefensible. This weakness was partially counterbalanced by the paternal links with the Dukes of Pfalz-Neuburg, while the relations with those of Sulzbach were less strong, or even openly hostile as with the Bavarian Wittelsbachs. As for the Protestant House of Pfalz-Zweibrücken, the abdication of Christina Wasa gave the Swedish throne to the line of Kleeburg in 1654, an event that considerably affected the geopolitical scenario of the Palatine territories, bringing a significant support to the Elector in the European arena.

How the security of the state was based on an unstable balance can be deduced from the alternating residences of the princes, who were forced to move their residence on several occasions. Heidelberg was the major fortress of the Electorate, but its fortifications could be considered as just relatively modern. Further, small, fortified places, notably Oppenheim, Friedrichsburg, Kaiserslautern, and Frankenthal, guarded the Rhine and the western border, while Mosbach controlled the routes east of the River Neckar.

The Army Under Prince-Elector Carl Ludwig.

On his arrival in Heidelberg in early 1650, Carl Ludwig showed uncommon energy in restoring prosperity in his domains. Marked by the setbacks he had experienced during his youth in exile, the Elector's first aim was to ensure the security of his country, and support for the recognition of his rights. From the outset, financial policy was closely linked to geostrategic objectives, as the Palatinate required high levels of investment, such as the maintenance and construction of strongholds. The more prosperous the country became, the greater the revenue would be to achieve his plans. It was therefore necessary to wait for better times and focus on one project at a time, since, as yet, the Electorate did not have the means to pursue an ambitious foreign policy. The Elector thus had the choice between taking a powerful ally and giving weight to his alliance through a policy of armament, or sticking to armed neutrality, a solution that suited his tastes better but required more effort. Therefore, among the matters he had to deal with, one of the first was the army, since the general weakness of the Empire required a military force strong enough to achieve his goals. In March 1650, the Elector raised his mounted *Kurfürstliche Leibcompagnie* in order to have a core of trustworthy young nobles to be initiated into a military career as army officers. The *Leibcompagnie* was 50 to 60 horsemen armed with sword and carbine, along with the customary pair of saddle pistols.[3] It is from that date that the actual history of the Palatine Army begins. The Bavarian Wittelsbachs' annexation of the Upper Palatinate was the first topic that he tried to resolve *manu military*. Professional soldiers were recruited, but the shortage of resources did not allow for the recruiting of a large army, leaving Carl Ludwig without the necessary means to win.[4] In

3 Oskar Bezzel, *Geschichte des Kurpfälzischen Heeres von Seinen Anfängen bis zur Vereinigung von Kurpfalz und Kurbayern* (Munich: Lindauer LTR-Verl, 1925), Band I, p.90.

4 Oskar Bezzel, *Geschichte des Kurpfälzischen Heeres von Seinen Anfängen bis zur Vereinigung von Kurpfalz und Kurbayern* (Munich: Lindauer LTR-Verl, 1925), Band I, p.91. In September 1650,

1652, the regular troops did not exceed 1,000 men under the command of the Friulian Giulio Antonio Frangipane.[5] Other forces were gathered using the *Freiwillige Landreiter* (militia horsemen), but their contribution was not enough to expel the Bavarian cousins from the Upper Palatinate. The dispute continued intermittently until 1662, when a truce was signed thanks to the mediation of Duke Philipp Wilhelm of Pfalz-Neuburg.

After 1648, any diplomatic manoeuvre could not be separated from the relationship with France: the main guarantor of the Peace of Westphalia. In 1658, Carl Ludwig discussed a treaty with Mazarin to protect the interests of his House, particularly against Bavaria. The treaty was to remain separate from the Rhenish League, and this aroused the suspicion of the Elector of Mainz, Johann Philipp von Schönborn, who wanted to extend and expand the alliance as widely as possible. Carl Ludwig's policy displeased von Schönborn even more when he rejected all proposals to join the Rhenish League and even afterwards, he remained insensitive to all suggestions of joining the alliance, and after the expiry of the French treaty in 1661, he turned to Brandenburg.[6]

However, unlike the Grand Elector, Carl Ludwig did not have the primary instrument of politics – a large standing army. In the early 1660s, single companies of regular troops garrisoned Heidelberg, Frankenthal, Ladenburg, Oppenheim, and other minor places on the borders.[7] In September 1663, Carl Ludwig answered the call of Emperor Leopold I for the war against the Porte. Before the end of the year, the Elector agreed to provide one cavalry company and one infantry company, 100 horse and 300 foot, as auxiliary corps for the *Reichsarmee*. In April 1664, they were ready to head for Hungary, some accompanied by wives and children. Difficulties in allocating quarters and other problems caused delays and therefore it was only in June that the column marched from Heidelberg. They were destined for Komárom, in Hungary, to join the Allied corps under Souches. From Neuburg, the troops sailed to Vienna via the Danube, and on 27 July, not far from the Austrian capital, a boat with about 100 people overturned and 64 passengers, including three women and one child, drowned.[8] The Palatine troops remained in Upper Hungary until September, without having taken part in any of the encounters of the fateful campaign, but still suffered some losses. In early September, three infantrymen died of natural causes and another 21 were sick. On 19 September, the 200 survivors were re-embarked by river and remained on Schutt Island for a week, until Carl Ludwig agreed

a corps of Palatine troops marched via Heilbronn and Schwabach to the Upper Palatinate, but it was ambushed near Auerbach by the Bavarians. Further small clashes occurred in the following years.

5 Oskar Bezzel, *Geschichte des Kurpfälzischen Heeres von Seinen Anfängen bis zur Vereinigung von Kurpfalz und Kurbayern* (Munich: Lindauer LTR-Verl, 1925), Band I, p.93.

6 Karl Brunner, *Der Pfälzische Wildfangstreit unter Kurfürft Karl Ludwig (1664–1667)* (Innsbruck: Wagner´schen Universität-Buchhandlung, 1896), p.22.

7 Georg Tessin, *Die Regimenter der Europäischen Staaten im Ancien Régime des XVI bis XVIII Jahrhunderts* (Osnabrück: Biblio Verlag, 1986), Teil 1, p.260.

8 Oskar Bezzel, *Geschichte des Kurpfälzischen Heeres von Seinen Anfängen bis zur Vereinigung von Kurpfalz und Kurbayern* (Munich: Lindauer LTR-Verl, 1925), Band I, p.94.

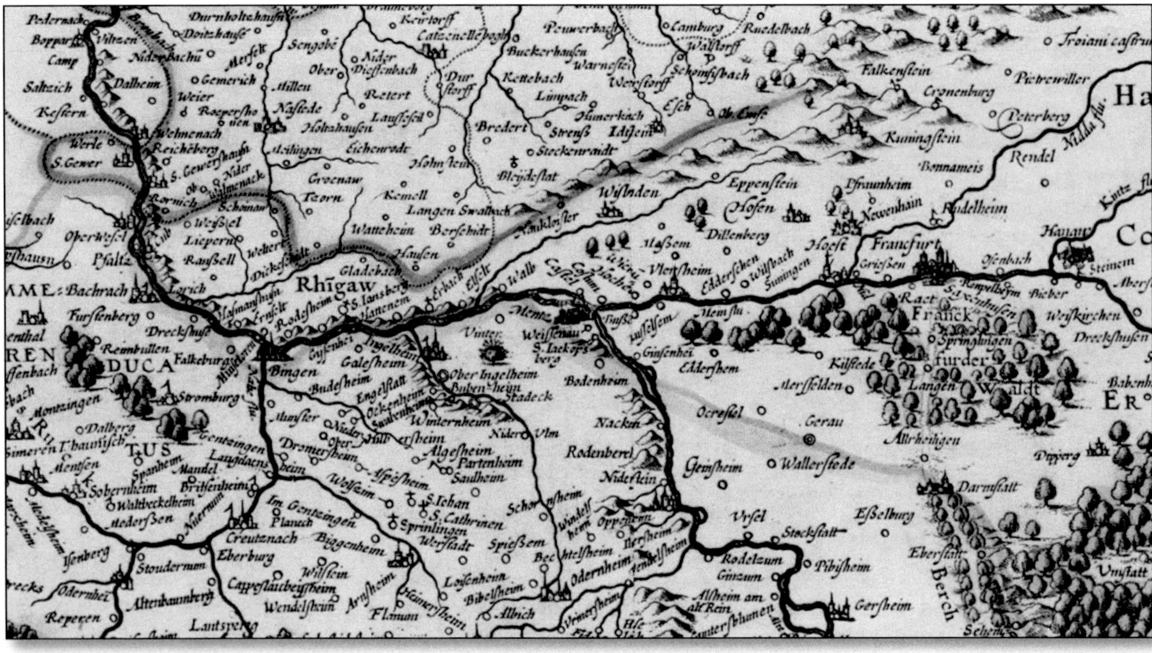

Detail from a map showing the border between the Palatinate and the Electorate of Mainz. The *Wildfangrecht* worked in this area; this was a medieval right that allowed the ruling prince to grant people who were homeless or engaged in seasonal activities the status of subjects. However, the conflict evolved into a dispute between the Electoral Palatinate and Lorraine over the County of Falkenstein on the Donnersberg. This lay in the territory of the Electoral Palatinate, but was a fief of Lorraine.

with the Emperor to let them enter Austrian service.[9] The cavalry company remained in Hungary until February 1665.

After a decade of negotiations, in late 1663, the dispute with Mainz concerning the *Wildfang*'s rights came to an increasingly serious outcome.[10]

Carl Ludwig had no other armed forces except the *Kurfürstliche Leibcompagnie*, the small infantry garrisons, the *ausschuss* (infantry militia) and the *landreiterei* (cavalry militia). The growing tension convinced him to increase the regular troops. The muster of 21 April 1664 registered 1,544 infantry in six large companies, and 75 cavalry excluding the troopers already marching to Hungary.[11] The Elector also enlisted a senior commander, *Generalmajor* Johann Gories Gorgas,[12] with a staff comprising 4 *obristleutnante*, 1 *major*, 3 *kapitäne*, 10 *leutnante*, 6 *fähnriche* and 1 technician

9 Oskar Bezzel, *Geschichte des Kurpfälzischen Heeres von Seinen Anfängen bis zur Vereinigung von Kurpfalz und Kurbayern* (Munich: Lindauer LTR-Verl, 1925), Band I, p.95; the Palatine infantrymen were amalgamated in the Imperial regiment *Kayserstein*.

10 See Chapter 3: The Electoral Prince-Archbishopric: Mainz, and Chapter 10: Wars and Factions in Germany, The *Wildfang* War, 1665–68.

11 Oskar Bezzel, *Geschichte des Kurpfälzischen Heeres von Seinen Anfängen bis zur Vereinigung von Kurpfalz und Kurbayern* (Munich: Lindauer LTR-Verl, 1925), Band I, pp.95–96. In detail they were 24 *Sergenten*, 15 *Unteroffiziere*, 30 *Corporale*, 8 surgeons, 23 drummers and fifers, 129 *Gefreite*, 2 officers' servants and 1,313 private infantrymen. The cavalry comprised 3 corporals, 1 blacksmith, 4 officers' servants and 67 troopers.

12 This is the same officer who entered the service of Münster in 1665.

with the rank of *ingenieur-kapitän* as senior officer, alongside with other 2 *ingenieuren*. The professional army included the artillery, with 1 *stückkapitän*, 2 *stückleutnante*, 1 *stückfähnrich*, 3 constables and 1 *minierer*.[13]

Although a homogeneous body of troops was available, the army still lacked a fixed organisation. Initially, the regular troops were organised as independent companies, just as officers were temporarily assigned to command a garrison. Naturally, the distribution of soldiers followed the importance attributed to the major places, 17 garrisons in all. Only the cavalry received a regular organisation. In 1664, all new recruits were incorporated into the *Leibgarde*, but they did not have a *kapitäne*, a rank held by the Elector in person, being replaced by two *leutnantes* who alternated in command. The army remained in a provisional organisation for a long time, to the point that the council of war of 1 June 1665, was forced to limit the total number to six infantry companies because of the lack of captains, although it established the same number of men for all companies, a strength of 30 horse or 180 foot. However, before the end of the year, the number of infantry companies increased to 12, including the *Leibcompagnie zu Fuss*. In the cavalry, two companies of 60 men were formed, one of horse and one of dragoons.[14] In late 1665, the regular army numbered about 2,000 men, comprising 75 mounted *Leibgarde*, two cavalry companies, one dragoon company, one *Leibcompagnie* of infantry and a further 12 companies of foot.[15] In early 1666, Elector Carl Ludwig hired mercenaries from Osnabrück, Hannover and from Bremen, and added them to his own troops to expel the enemies from his territories.[16] The growing military involvements in the *Wildfang* Dispute forced the Elector to further strengthen his army, and for the first time the infantry was organised into a field regiment. In September 1666 there were 24 cavalry companies with 1,056 men, two companies of dragoons totalling 380 men, and three battalions of foot, 1,980 men.[17] The *Leibcompagnie* of foot also included a small squad of Swiss guards who served in Heidelberg as a palace guard.

Despite many difficulties, the regular force did not stop growing. In September 1667, 17 cavalry companies numbered 3,000 horsemen including the hired contingents, along with 600 dragoons, and 3,000 infantrymen.[18]

13 Oskar Bezzel, *Geschichte des Kurpfälzischen Heeres von Seinen Anfängen bis zur Vereinigung von Kurpfalz und Kurbayern* (Munich: Lindauer LTR-Verl, 1925), Band I, p.96.

14 Oskar Bezzel, *Geschichte des Kurpfälzischen Heeres von Seinen Anfängen bis zur Vereinigung von Kurpfalz und Kurbayern* (Munich: Lindauer LTR-Verl, 1925), Band I, p.97.

15 Oskar Bezzel, *Geschichte des Kurpfälzischen Heeres von Seinen Anfängen bis zur Vereinigung von Kurpfalz und Kurbayern* (Munich: Lindauer LTR-Verl, 1925), Band I, p.97; three companies were still under formation without weapons and clothing.

16 'Carl Ludwig expected Sweden to send a large number of troops. He also asked Württemberg for military assistance. In the same period, the Elector initiated consultations with the Rhenish principalities gathered in Baden through the Heidelberg's best jurist, Johann Friedrich Böckelmann, with the aim to obtain a financial support.' Karl Brunner, *Der Pfälzische Wildfangstreit unter Kurfürft Karl Ludwig (1664–1667)* (Innsbruck: Wagner´schen Universität-Buchhandlung, 1896), pp.28–29.

17 Georg Tessin, *Die Regimenter der Europäischen Staaten im Ancien Régime des XVI bis XVIII Jahrhunderts* (Osnabrück: Biblio Verlag, 1986), Teil 1, p.260.

18 Oskar Bezzel, *Geschichte des Kurpfälzischen Heeres von Seinen Anfängen bis zur Vereinigung von Kurpfalz und Kurbayern* (Munich: Lindauer LTR-Verl, 1925), Band I, p.99. Possibly this figure

In late summer 1668, the army still numbered 6,500 men, and this force fought at Bingen on 25 September 1668.[19] After the Peace of Heilbronn, signed in December, the army's strength fell to 153 horse, 2,820 foot and 70 artillerymen, miners and engineers; seven reformado officers were also included.[20] These troops performed garrison duties in strategic places, with Heidelberg and Kaiserslautern quartering the largest corps. To these regular troops, the Elector could add 400 horsemen of the *Landreiterei* (militia) for the patrolling of the borders.[21]

Musketeers and Pikemen after Johann Andreas Böckler, *Schola Militaris Moderna* (Frankfurt am Main, 1668). These figures provide a good idea of the military clothing from Central and Northern Germany in the 1660s. The musketeers wear coats of different length, which could be classified as an early *Rock* or *Pyerock* – as it was commonly called at the time – and consisting of a single breasted coat with small turned up cuffs, and occasionally with pockets. The German term *Pierock* also indicates that it could be of two or even three different colours. Note the unusual headgear of the third figure in the first print. The pikemen are wearing breastplates and helmets, which were becoming rare in several German states by the 1660s. Wide breeches and stockings, often worn with overstockings, continue to be the universal clothing for the legs.

The lesson learned in the *Wildfang* War persuaded Carl Ludwig to develop his military policy in order to achieve the status of regional power for his principality: a very difficult mission with the limited budget of his state, and the only solution was to gain the support of a powerful ally.[22] In September

---

did not include the hired troops.

19 Oskar Bezzel, *Geschichte des Kurpfälzischen Heeres von Seinen Anfängen bis zur Vereinigung von Kurpfalz und Kurbayern* (Munich: Lindauer LTR-Verl, 1925), Band I, p.100.

20 Oskar Bezzel, *Geschichte des Kurpfälzischen Heeres von Seinen Anfängen bis zur Vereinigung von Kurpfalz und Kurbayern* (Munich: Lindauer LTR-Verl, 1925), Band I, pp.101–103.

21 Oskar Bezzel, *Geschichte des Kurpfälzischen Heeres von Seinen Anfängen bis zur Vereinigung von Kurpfalz und Kurbayern* (Munich: Lindauer LTR-Verl, 1925), Band I, p.97.

22 An analysis of the financial capacity of the Palatinate cannot disregard the distinction between ordinary and extraordinary revenues that was common to all western European states in the

1671, the marriage of the Electorate's heir Prince Carl to the Prinsesse Wilhelmine Ernestine of Denmark was a first step. As a sign of welcome for the bride, and to show his military might, Elector Carl Ludwig gathered the regular troops and militia at Ladenburg, and they carried out a great parade of 9,000 horse and foot under the *Obermarschall* Count Sayn-Wittgenstein, the newly appointed Commander-in-Chief.[23] The units of the horse and foot are mentioned in the chronicle of the event. The cavalry comprised the company of the *Hoffstaats*, formed by the teachers and students of Heidelberg, two companies recruited by the nobility, and the *Landcompagnien* of Heidelberg, Bretten, Alzey, Mosbach and Germersheim. The infantry was represented by the three battalions of the Heidelberg's *ausschuss*, along with those of Mosbach, Alzey, Bretten, Oppenheim and other territories.[24]

The other royal marriage between the Elector's daughter Elisabeth Charlotte, and Philippe d'Orleans, brother of Louis XIV, was supposed to seal the rise of the line, but was ultimately a choice that backfired on the Palatinate in the following years.[25] Unlike his relatives of Pfalz-Neuburg and Bavaria, Carl Ludwig tried, as far as possible, to maintain a policy of neutrality without joining Germany's pro-French princes. However, the Electorate remained unable to effectively protect its territories, and Carl Ludwig did nothing that might help a collaboration with other principalities of the Upper Rhine and Rhenish Electoral Circles, notably Mainz, Trier and Cologne.[26]

In the opening phase of the Franco-Dutch War, Carl Ludwig avoided any involvement and pursued his neutral policy, but this proved to be an illusory choice. In June 1672, the arrival of the Bavarian contingent hired by Cologne meant standing-to of both regular troops and militiamen.[27] The foreign soldiers crossed the Electorate sailing on the Rhine: in July the emergency

---

seventeenth century. Ordinary revenues were collected through taxation and were normally related to military expenditure. Another part of the revenue was collected in kind, mainly wine and grain, and could amount to up to 20 percent of the value of other revenues. One of the few surviving accounts from 1671 shows that the total income of the Palatinate was about 500,000 florins, and 200,000 florins were earmarked for military expenses, which corresponded to half of the cash resources. The army therefore weighed heavily on the budget, and it should be noted that 1671 was a year of peace. This was the price of the military policy developed by the Elector, which show that the military expenditure of the Palatinate was proportionally comparable to that of Brandenburg. On this see also Volker Sellin, *Die Finanzpolitik Karl Ludwigs von der Pfalz: Staatswirtschaft im Wiederaufbau nach dem Dreissigjährigen Krieg* (Stuttgart: Klett-Cotta,1978), pp.97–115.

23 Oskar Bezzel, *Geschichte des Kurpfälzischen Heeres von Seinen Anfängen bis zur Vereinigung von Kurpfalz und Kurbayern* (Munich: Lindauer LTR-Verl, 1925), Band I, p.102.

24 Oskar Bezzel, *Geschichte des Kurpfälzischen Heeres von Seinen Anfängen bis zur Vereinigung von Kurpfalz und Kurbayern* (Munich: Lindauer LTR-Verl, 1925), Band I, p.103.

25 Hostility was heightened by French interference in the Neuburg inheritance of the Palatinate in 1685, when Louis XIV advanced claims to the Electorate on behalf of his brother's wife in an effort to force recognition of the 1680s' *Réunions* as permanent.

26 Peter H. Wilson, *German Armies. War and German Politics, 1648–1806* (London: UCL Press, 1998), p.46.

27 Karl Staudinger, *Geschichte des Kurbayerischen Heeres Insbesondere unter Kurfürst Ferdinand Maria, 1651–1679* (Munich: J. Lindauer, 1901), band I, p.613. The Bavarian troops crossed the border of the Electorate of the Palatinate between Lorch and Bacharach. The local authorities refused the passage, even though two captains offered to stay as hostages for the time necessary

Palatine *Leibgarde*, *c.* 1672–78. (Author's reconstruction and artwork)
According to Oskar Bezzel, in March 1650, 50–60 horsemen, all dressed in blue with wide silver lace, black hats and blue plumes, were raised by Elector Carl Ludwig from men belonging to the Palatinate's aristocracy. The *Leibgarde* maintained these colours in the following years, although obviously updating the style of the clothing. The company assumed the name of *Leibgarde zu Pferd* becoming the premier cavalry unit of the army. In 1680, the *Leibgarde* comprised 1 *Kapitänleutnant*, 1 *Kornett*, 1 *Quartiermeister*, 1 *Musterschreiber*, 2 *Trompeter*, 57 *Einspännige* and 4 *Diener* (servants) – 69 men at all.

ceased, but the Elector increased the infantry with 687 new recruits. By the end of summer, the regular army numbered 153 horse and 2,593 foot.[28]

The First Devastation (1672–1678).

Though the regular army was gradually increasing in strength, it could do little against a major power. In autumn 1672, about 3,000 French troops coming from Lorraine, entered the territory of Oppenheim to take up winter quarters. Carl Ludwig had no choice but to accept the French demands, and the Palatine garrisons were ordered not to react. After the invasion of Trier in the summer of 1673, the French crossed the border again, and this time demanded forced labour for the army.[29] The situation became even worse in the autumn during Turenne's retreat from the Main to the Neckar, as the *Lieutenant Général* Vaubrun approached with 4,000 men from Alsace to join the main army.[30] The Elector continued to submit to the French dictats, in the vain hope of sparing his

---

to cross the territory of the state. The troops had to abandon the ships and continue on land to circumvent the borders with the Palatinate, which were heavily guarded by soldiers and militia.

28 Oskar Bezzel, *Geschichte des Kurpfälzischen Heeres von Seinen Anfängen bis zur Vereinigung von Kurpfalz und Kurbayern* (Munich: Lindauer LTR-Verl, 1925), Band I, pp.103–104.

29 'The transit of troops and their violence constantly harassed the population, and when Turenne turned from Westerwald to the River Main, the Palatine peasants were forced to build entrenchments and, if they refused, were plundered in the most shameless manner.' Oskar Bezzel, *Geschichte des Kurpfälzischen Heeres von Seinen Anfängen bis zur Vereinigung von Kurpfalz und Kurbayern* (Munich: Lindauer LTR-Verl, 1925), Band I, p.107.

30 'Although Carl Ludwig welcomed the French so much that he helped to build a bridge in Ladenburg, they remained in the area between the Neckar and the Bergstrasse for a few days, and when they finally retreated, continued their acts of violence across the Rhine in an even more ruthless manner. For weeks the enemy hordes, carrying plunder and destruction far and wide, headed for Kreuznach on the Rahe and devastated one of the most beautiful areas of the Electorate with theft, fires and atrocities of all kinds.' Oskar Bezzel, *Geschichte des Kurpfälzischen Heeres von Seinen Anfängen bis zur Vereinigung von Kurpfalz und Kurbayern* (Munich: Lindauer LTR-Verl, 1925), Band I, pp.107–108.

subjects from the reprisals threatened by the Louis XIV's generals. In early 1674, Louis XIV turned his attention to the German principalities and ordered his army to invade the Palatinate, which remained virtually undefended. In February, French troops under Vaubrun and Rochefort occupied the territories of Germersheim and Kaiserslautern imposing contributions, and soon these turned to depredations by out of control French troops that devastated villages and countryside in the most appalling manner.[31]

Illustration by Maurice Leloir depicting the French invasion of the Palatinate in 1688. (Author's collection)
When the French army invaded the Electorate for the first time in February 1674, it was impossible to ignore the obligation to assist Elector Carl Ludwig. In March, the Diet neatly sidestepped the issue by expelling the French Ambassador from Regensburg and informing all the states that, by their actions, the French had made themselves an enemy of the Empire. Emperor Leopold I allowed the general mood of anti-French opinion to push the assembled delegates into sanctioning aid to the Palatinate and other threatened areas on 31 March 1674.

This time it was impossible to ignore the provocation. Before the end of the month, Carl Ludwig called on the Triple Alliance for support, and in March, an Imperial corps under General Caprara quartered in Oppenheim, while further troops from the Swabian and Franconian Circles marched to join them. Carl Ludwig mustered the cavalry, which numbered approximately 350 horsemen. The Imperialists and their allies moved to engage the enemy, and on 24 March faced them in a skirmish near Mannheim. On 31 March, the Diet of Regensburg proclaimed the *Reichskrieg* against Louis XIV. On 13 May, the Elector reviewed his cavalry in Frankenthal and four days later, at Friedrichsburg, he solemnly signed a treaty of alliance with the Emperor. On 18 May, the Palatine cavalry was assigned to guard the pontoon bridges at Speyer, while the Imperialists with the Circles' troops marched to join the allies at Rastatt. The Elector gathered his cavalry the next day in front of Mannheim, where the infantry, numbering 1,000 men

31 'The Elector sent some of his officers to Germersheim to negotiate with the French, but the latter imprisoned them and, after stripping them naked, released the officers days later.' *Relation des Violences Exercées au Palatinat, à la fin de l'Année 1673 & au Commencement de 1674* (Cologne, 1675), p.44.

Contemporary Austrian playing card depicting Elector Carl Ludwig as a field commander. (Author's collection)
The Elector himself led the response of the Electoral troops to the French invasion of 1674. However, according to Bezzel, 'Carl Ludwig, in impotent rage, watched his life's work, the reconstruction of the country, crumble into rubble. In July, in order to avenge the invasion, the Elector meditated to personally challenge Turenne to a duel, since, as he himself wrote, he could not raise an army equal to that of his enemies and could therefore only receive satisfaction that way.'

with some field guns, had also arrived.[32] This force faced the French parties which were looting the countryside, and in late May they defeated a corps of enemy cavalry near Weissenburg capturing six standards, a pair of kettledrums, 50 horses and 2 troopers, and forcing the remnants to withdraw to Kaiserslautern.[33] Further engagements occurred in June, even in French territory. The Palatine cavalry again joined the Imperialists under Caprara and on 16 June fought at the unsuccessful Battle of Sinsheim. The Palatine casualties are unknown, but the news of the defeat reverberated through the Electorate causing great concern. The Palatinate had to bear the costs of the Imperial Army, and furthermore found itself once again at the mercy of Turenne's army, which was advancing from Philippsburg. The French general diligently carried out Louis XIV's order to devastate the Electorate.[34]

With the allied troops, Carl Ludwig could defend Heidelberg and other locations, but this did not prevent the devastation of the countryside. Unfortunately, only the allied cavalry was of good quality, while the infantry, especially the ones from the Franconian Circle, had poor discipline and performed their duties badly, since they had not been paid for a some time, and they soon they turned on the inhabitants with terrible consequences.[35]

In August 1674, Carl Ludwig signed a new agreement with the allies, committing to provide 2,000 men for the field army that was being gathered in Alsace under *Feldmarschall* Bournoville. This was already a considerable effort for the Palatinate, but the number was increased to 2,500. The infantry would be formed as two battalions, while the cavalry, 500 men, would have been united in one regiment. In the meantime, differences emerged between the Elector and the allied commanders. Disappointed, Carl Ludwig returned to Heidelberg with his son and heir Prince Carl, while the Electoral contingent was quartered in Swabia before

32 Oskar Bezzel, *Geschichte des Kurpfälzischen Heeres von Seinen Anfängen bis zur Vereinigung von Kurpfalz und Kurbayern* (Munich: Lindauer LTR-Verl, 1925), Band I, p.108.

33 Oskar Bezzel, *Geschichte des Kurpfälzischen Heeres von Seinen Anfängen bis zur Vereinigung von Kurpfalz und Kurbayern* (Munich: Lindauer LTR-Verl, 1925), Band I, p.108.

34 Oskar Bezzel, *Geschichte des Kurpfälzischen Heeres von Seinen Anfängen bis zur Vereinigung von Kurpfalz und Kurbayern* (Munich: Lindauer LTR-Verl, 1925), Band I, p.109: 'From Weinheim, which had just gained protection from plundering and nevertheless fell victim to the crudest destructive fury of the enemy, with the most vain pretence of disarming the citizens, the incursions poured in like molten lava flows from the Bergstrasse to the Neckar region. In a single day, seven towns in the Palatinate and 19 villages were set ablaze.' Oskar Bezzel, *Geschichte des Kurpfälzischen Heeres von Seinen Anfängen bis zur Vereinigung von Kurpfalz und Kurbayern* (Munich: Lindauer LTR-Verl, 1925), Band I, p.109.

35 Oskar Bezzel, *Geschichte des Kurpfälzischen Heeres von Seinen Anfängen bis zur Vereinigung von Kurpfalz und Kurbayern* (Munich: Lindauer LTR-Verl, 1925), Band I, p.110.

returning home at the turn of the year. Furthermore, fearing the arrival of the Brandenburg corps heading to Alsace, Carl Ludwig called back his troops from across the Rhine to save the Electorate from contributions and billets.[36]

Consequently, except for a cavalry squadron assigned to the army under Bournonville for the campaign in Alsace, the Palatines were unaffected by the events that led to the unfortunate winter campaign of 1674–1675, and the retreat of the Allies from the left bank of the Rhine. In May 1675, Carl Ludwig agreed to send 600 infantry to the Upper Rhine Circle's contingent, while the rest of his force guarded the Rhine outposts between Mannheim and Speyer. This assignment exempted the Palatine troops from any involvement in the campaign of 1675, but they were involved in minor engagements anyway.

On 17 February, a party of 150 infantry surprised the French cavalry encamped at Saint-Abold, in Lorraine, and captured 112 officers and men. At the end of the month, on the orders of the Elector, who feared new French incursions along the Rhine, the *Obristwachtmeister* Hennoy with 500 infantry seized the small town of Gernsheim in the Electorate of Mainz, and destroyed the walls.[37] The town and castle of Kirchhorn were occupied on 7 March by a storming party sent from Heidelberg. Soon afterwards, the Palatine troops entered the enemy territory and took a transport column which was escorted by 80 French dragoons and as many infantrymen, but on 23 April the Electoral soldiers were ambushed by an enemy party that pursued them to Alzey, on the western bank of the Rhine, where the Palatine soldiers surrendered. On 12 June, a corps of 300 Palatine horse, as a vanguard of a stronger infantry column that was escorting wagons from Frankenthal to Mannheim, faced the assault of a French mixed-arms party. The fighting involved other allied troops, and they succeeded in repulsing the enemy assault but suffered high casualties. In April 1676, Elector Carl Ludwig agreed with the Allies to provide one chief-engineer, artillerymen and heavy guns for the siege of Philippsburg.[38] This was the Elector's second and last attempt to provide troops in exchange for subsidies, as many German principalities did, and to raise the Electorate from the status of minor power.

In October 1676, the strength of the cavalry had fallen to 240 horsemen (3 companies) but there were now 345 dragoons in 5 companies, which had been raised in the spring. The infantry numbered 3,308 men in two field regiments, distributed between Friedrichsburg (13 companies), Frankenthal (4 companies), Bacharach (2 companies), Neustadt (2 companies), Kaiserslautern (1 company), and further minor detachments. The artillery deployed 66 *Constabler*, 23 *Artillerie und Zeugbediensteten*, and 31 drivers,

36 Peter H. Wilson, *German Armies. War and German Politics, 1648–1806* (London: UCL Press, 1998), p.47.

37 Oskar Bezzel, *Geschichte des Kurpfälzischen Heeres von Seinen Anfängen bis zur Vereinigung von Kurpfalz und Kurbayern* (Munich: Lindauer LTR-Verl, 1925), Band I, p.110; the commander was mortally wounded in the head.

38 Oskar Bezzel, *Geschichte des Kurpfälzischen Heeres von Seinen Anfängen bis zur Vereinigung von Kurpfalz und Kurbayern* (Munich: Lindauer LTR-Verl, 1925), Band I, p.112. The Palatine artillery comprised 2 *Halbkartaune* and two heavy mortars.

Prince-Elector Carl II (1657–1685), in a portrait by an unknown artist (Collection of the Middachten Castle, Rheden, The Netherlands). His parents separated after an unhappy marriage, and the mother retreated to Kassel after his birth; as a result, Carl grew up under his authoritarian father. However, the talented scholar Samul Pufendorf led the prince's education. In 1670, during his European tour, Carl fell ill with smallpox, which permanently disfigured his face. According to contemporaries, the prince was of weak and timid nature, but with a brilliant mind. Like his father he also had a problematic marriage, that remained childless. Increasing financial difficulties caused by oversized households, a passion for theatre and music, as well as military spending, could no longer be regulated by tax increases. To face the state's debts, he pledged the town of Germersheim to France for 20 years. He was the last Protestant Elector of the Palatinate.

with 7 officers under 1 *Stückmajor*; 8 *Mineuren* with 1 *Korporal*, and also included 1 *Ingenieur* as the senior officer.[39]

By February 1677, the Palatine troops guarded the fords on the Lauter River between Kusel and Zweybrücken under *Generalmajor* Count of Leiningen. Their concerns, however, came not only from the French, but also from the allied troops who demanded provisions for winter quarters. The war was having disastrous side effects in the Empire. Most of the smaller states quickly experienced serious difficulties, especially as their foreign partners sought to reserve the best billets for their own men. Soon, the cost sustained for quartering the troops fuelled a political crisis and this accelerated the collapse of the alliance between the German states.

Louis XIV did not, however, take advantage of this crisis. The only significant engagement occurred on 27 February, when a French cavalry party advancing to Kaiserslautern was sighted. About 200 Palatine cavalrymen moved to intercept the enemy, but the French avoided a fight and withdrew behind their lines. In the following winter, the Palatine cavalry and infantry held the positions between Kaiserslautern and Kreuznach together with Celle's troops, which received in exchange provisions from the Electorate. There were no major military actions involving the Palatine troops in 1678. Meanwhile, the Palatinate's debts accumulated to become dramatic and this did not allow the pursuit of a consistent military policy, nor to try any significant trade of soldiers with the major powers in exchange for subsidies. In 1679, after the Peace of Nijmegen, Carl Ludwig disbanded the cavalry, except for the 69 horsemen of the *Kurfürstliche Leibgarde*, and retained 353 dragoons and 3,365 infantry.[40] The infantry companies were organised as two regiments, while the Foot Guards still formed two companies; the one of the Elector, numbering 224 men, also comprised 28 Swiss Guards, the one of the Prince,

39 Oskar Bezzel, *Geschichte des Kurpfälzischen Heeres von Seinen Anfängen bis zur Vereinigung von Kurpfalz und Kurbayern* (Munich: Lindauer LTR-Verl, 1925), Band I, p.104.

40 Oskar Bezzel, *Geschichte des Kurpfälzischen Heeres von Seinen Anfängen bis zur Vereinigung von Kurpfalz und Kurbayern* (Munich: Lindauer LTR-Verl, 1925), Band I, p.104.

the Elector's heir, had 170 German and 16 Swiss soldiers.[41] In 1680, the *Leibgarde zu Pferd* formed a detachment of 25 horsemen for the service of the Elector's widow.

This was one of the last acts of government by Elector Carl I, who died on 28 August 1680, and was succeeded by his son, who assumed the title of Carl II.

The new Elector had to face a critical scenario since the French troops were still quartered just across the frontiers, and, like the other Rhenish principalities, he wished to do nothing that might antagonise Louis and thus rejected the Austrian offers of a new alliance.[42] The army's strength was further reduced due to the shortage of funds, but the Elector introduced some reforms to update the structure of the army. The two *Leibgarde* companies were joined in a grenadier corps, while by 1683 the 28 infantry companies still in service formed four permanent regiments. The first regiment, the *Kurpfalz-Leibregiment*, comprised the two grenadier companies and a further 10 companies to a strength of 1,063 men in all; the other regiments had a different number of companies and consequently their strength varied from 740 to 500 men. In 1684, a similar reform was introduced for the dragoons, which formed the *Leibregiment*. With regards to the technical corps, Carl II raised one *Pionierbataillon*, of 104 men in 1685, while the artillery received a new organisation which comprised a new officer staff, 56 *Constabler* and 30 *Handlanger*. All this brought the regular army's strength to 4,720 men.[43] The militia included 400

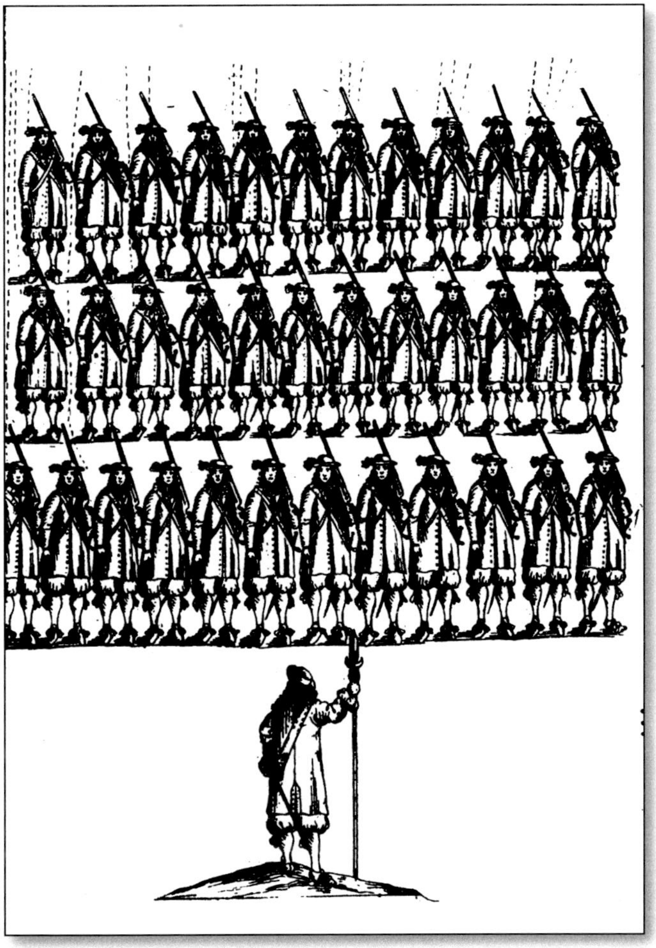

Infantry attending training, after the manual of military exercises by Johann Georg Pascha (1668). In 1681, Elector Carl II ordered the training of his soldiers yearly in a military camp of manoeuvre. In 1684, the soldiers received training in trench and siege warfare, and the event involved the inhabitants of Heidelberg as 'the sparring partner'. In relation to this Bezzel wrote: 'The fact that the enemy garrison, made up of students from the university, was disguised as Ottomans was part of the taste of the time, but the besieged city was called Negroponte, and this name blatantly recalled the military exploits of the Degenfeld family, formerly in the service of Venice. All this suggests that the training session was fully carried out.'[44]

41 Oskar Bezzel, *Geschichte des Kurpfälzischen Heeres von Seinen Anfängen bis zur Vereinigung von Kurpfalz und Kurbayern* (Munich: Lindauer LTR-Verl, 1925), Band I, p.106.

42 Peter H. Wilson, *German Armies. War and German Politics, 1648–1806* (London: UCL Press, 1998), p.62.

43 Oskar Bezzel, *Geschichte des Kurpfälzischen Heeres von Seinen Anfängen bis zur Vereinigung von Kurpfalz und Kurbayern* (Munich: Lindauer LTR-Verl, 1925), Band I, pp.115–117.

44 Oskar Bezzel, *Geschichte des Kurpfälzischen Heeres von Seinen Anfängen bis zur Vereinigung von Kurpfalz und Kurbayern* (Munich: Lindauer LTR-Verl, 1925), Band I, p.119.

horse of the *Landreiterei*.[45] The Elector also recruited officers with up-to-date knowledge from the 'German market'. Among these, were the brothers Ferdinand Christoph and Maximilian Degenfeld, sons of Ferdinand, who had served in the Palatine Army under Carl Ludwig, and were members of the renowned military family with relations all over Germany. In the plans of the Elector, the army was to receive regular training and each year to be trained in the most modern field tactics in a 'camp of manoeuvre'.[46]

The promising prince died unexpectedly on 16 May 1685 at the age of 34, leaving the House of Wittelsbach-Simmern without direct descendants.

The Palatine Army after 1685

The arrival of the new Elector, Philipp Wilhelm of Pfalz-Neuburg, marked a period of contrasts inside the Palatinate, since he was a Roman-Catholic, and despite the agreement in matters of religion, the Electoral estates refused to collaborate with him.

Prince-Elector Philipp Wilhelm, of the House of Wittelsbach-Neuburg (1615–1690), in a portrait by an unknown artist. (Collection of the Stadtmuseum Düsseldorf) The dynastic agreements of the family, discussed when Carl II was still alive, stipulated that upon extinction, the electoral branch would hand over the title to the dukes of Pfalz-Neuburg. Carl II managed to reach a compromise with the Estates on the question of religion, and received the agreement of his cousin Philipp Wilhelm of Pfalz-Neuburg. However, the Calvinists' distrust for the new government nevertheless grew. The Elector strove for legal equality of all confessions in the Palatinate, but this was not well received by the Protestants. Just after becoming Elector in 1685, Philipp Wilhelm tried to stop the ecclesiastical dispute, but tensions remained strong. Furthermore, unresolved questions concerning the inheritance of the late Elector Carl II quickly led to tensions with France. Louis XIV claimed parts of the Palatinate inheritance on behalf of his sister-in-law, the Duchesse d'Orléans. The negotiations were unsuccessful and the dispute escalated when Philipp Wilhelm in bitterness retired to Neuburg. Then, in the autumn of 1688, the French invaded the Palatinate and occupied the major towns included Heidelberg. The following year they repeated their systematic destruction of the country.

45 Oskar Bezzel, *Geschichte des Kurpfälzischen Heeres von Seinen Anfängen bis zur Vereinigung von Kurpfalz und Kurbayern* (Munich: Lindauer LTR-Verl, 1925), Band I, p.97.

46 Oskar Bezzel, *Geschichte des Kurpfälzischen Heeres von Seinen Anfängen bis zur Vereinigung von Kurpfalz und Kurbayern* (Munich: Lindauer LTR-Verl, 1925), Band I, p.119. In the summers of 1682 and 1683, the infantry performed exercises and manoeuvers at Friedelsheim and Ilvesheim; then in 1684 the regiments moved to Mannheim, and this time the training also included the construction of trenches and sessions of siege warfare.

However, from a political point of view, the union of the two principalities would have resulted in a substantial improvement, especially with regards to territorial extension and resources, but unfortunately it opened dangerous turmoil, because Louis XIV intervened to support his sister-in-law, Elisabeth Charlotte, Duchesse d'Orléans, for the inheritance of the late Elector Carl II.[47] All these matters remained unresolved and persuaded Philipp Wilhelm to keep the government of the principalities separate. For the time being, he allowed his third son, Ludwig Anton, to take possession of the principality as Governor in his place. In August 1685, the prince took up residence in Heidelberg and met the Palatine Estates for an agreement.

However, the Elector reserved the right to decide on all matters concerning the army and militia of both states. The matter was not easy due to the separation of the Electoral and the Ducal administration, and then the organisation of the military was rather complicated. In summer 1685, the Elector joined the troops with the ones that the Regent of Jülich and Berg, the heir prince Johann Wilhelm, had gathered. In his hope, this force could keep the principality from foreign interference. Before the end of 1685, the cavalry regiment *Erbprinz* (PnI-4) was transferred from Düsseldorf to Heidelberg, becoming the *Leibregiment zu Pferd* (KpC-2). After this, the dragoons formed one regiment of 410 men under *Obrist* Jungheim, which assumed the title *Leibdragoner* (KpD-1). Moreover, realising that the horizon was becoming darker, the Elector met the Estates of the principalities to discuss the raising of further troops. Relations with the Upper Rhine Circle were strengthened by agreeing on a quota of troops for the *Reichsarmee*.[48] At the organisational level, the Elector established a chain of command without, however, setting up new offices. All matters concerning the army were submitted to the Elector in the Court War Council, also known as the Private Cabinet or Private Conference, while ordinary affairs were managed by the governors or commanders.

Count Ernst Philipp of Nassau-Weilburg (1664–1719), in a portrait by an unidentified artist (Collection of the Weilburg Castle, Germany).
Count Ernst Philipp entered service in the Palatine Army in 1680, and in 1685 became *General Wachtmeister* and commander of the Upper Rhenish Circle's contingent in Hungary. In the *Reichsarmee* serving as a volunteer was Prince Carl Philipp of Pfalz-Neuburg (1661–1742), the younger brother of Elector Johann Wilhelm, and who distinguished himself at the siege of Buda in 1686.

47 Other claims to the inheritance came from the *Pfalgraf* Leopold Ludwig of Veldenz, but the Emperor confirmed the House of Neuburg as the legitimate successors (Author's note).

48 In 1686, about 800 infantrymen and 200 cavalry from the Palatinate joined the Imperial Army at the siege of Buda. These troops served in Hungary until 1688 as a part of the *Nassau-Saarbrücken zu Fuss* and *Nassau-Weiburg zu Pferd* regiments. See Bruno Mugnai, *Wars and Soldiers in the Early Reign of Louis XIV, volume 2: The Imperial Army 1657–1687* (Warwick: Helion & Company, 2019), p.286.

In November 1685, the Elector appointed Graf Maximilian Lorenz von Starhemberg, the Austrian Governor of Philippsburg, as his private adviser and at the same time entrusted him with the supreme command of the Palatinate Army and Militia, as well as the supervision of all the Palatinate fortresses. However, Starhemberg never achieved an important role in the Electorate, due to the immediate French blockade of Philippsburg at the outbreak of the War of The League of Augsburg. In 1687 a regular *Commissariat* was established under the direction of 1 *Oberkriegskommissär* who ranked as *Obrist*. He had a staff comprising two *Kriegskommissäriatsräten*, one chancellor and some office personnel.

On the eve of the French invasion of 1688, the regular army could deploy approximately 10,000 men in 2 cavalry regiments, 2 dragoon regiments, 8 infantry regiments and the artillery corps.

Detail from the medal commemorating the second French invasion of the Palatinate in 1688 (Author's collection). In September 1688, the French Army marched into the Palatinate without declaring war. With quick military forays, Louis XIV attempted to take the region by storm. By this method, the French generals could avoid large, open and costly battles and could operate with a relatively small army of 40,000 men. Once the Allies were able to push the French out of the Neckar valley, Louis XIV decided to render the deployment zone unusable for the advancing enemy army. With the cry: *Brûlez le Patinat!* (Burn the Palatinate!), Louis XIV's soldiers razed towns, castles and houses and countryside.

7

The Armed States

> Even the youngest scion of a princely line, imagines himself to be a little Louis XIV: he builds his Versailles, kisses his Maintenon and maintains his army.
>
> (Friedrich the Great)

This judgement, from a man who was to proclaim himself as the archetype of a new kind of reforming ruler, seems to justify the assessment of German princes of the last quarter of the seventeenth century that is often found in the traditional narrative of German history. This was allegedly an age in which German princes achieved a new degree of control and power through their own military.[1] They rode roughshod over the rights of their subjects, extracted as much money from them as they could and spent large sums on armies that were often hired out to foreign powers.[2] This negative sentence came from historians at the end of the next century, who blamed Germany's situation on the absolutism of these princes. However, at the heart of this policy was the aim to escape from the 'unarmed state' rank, as bitterly experienced by most of the German principalities in the 1670s, during the war against France. Relieved of their obligation to gather troops, the unarmed territories had made large cash payments to support the troops of their armed neighbours.[3] Thus, if a prince wanted to get out of this condition and achieve his dynastic and political aims, he required an army – and a full treasury.

---

1 *Deutsche Militär-Geschichte. 1648–1939* (Munich: Bernhard & Graefe, 1983), vol. I, pp.14–15.

2 Joachim Whaley, *Germany and the Holy Roman Empire. Vol. 2: from the Peace of Westphalia to the Dissolution of the Reich. 1648–1806* (Oxford-New York, NY: Oxford University Press, 2012), p.186.

3 See also *Wars and Soldiers in the Early reign of Louis XIV, volume 7: German Armies 1655–1690, part 1* (Warwick: Helion & Company, 2024), pp.21–27, 'Armed and Unarmed States'.

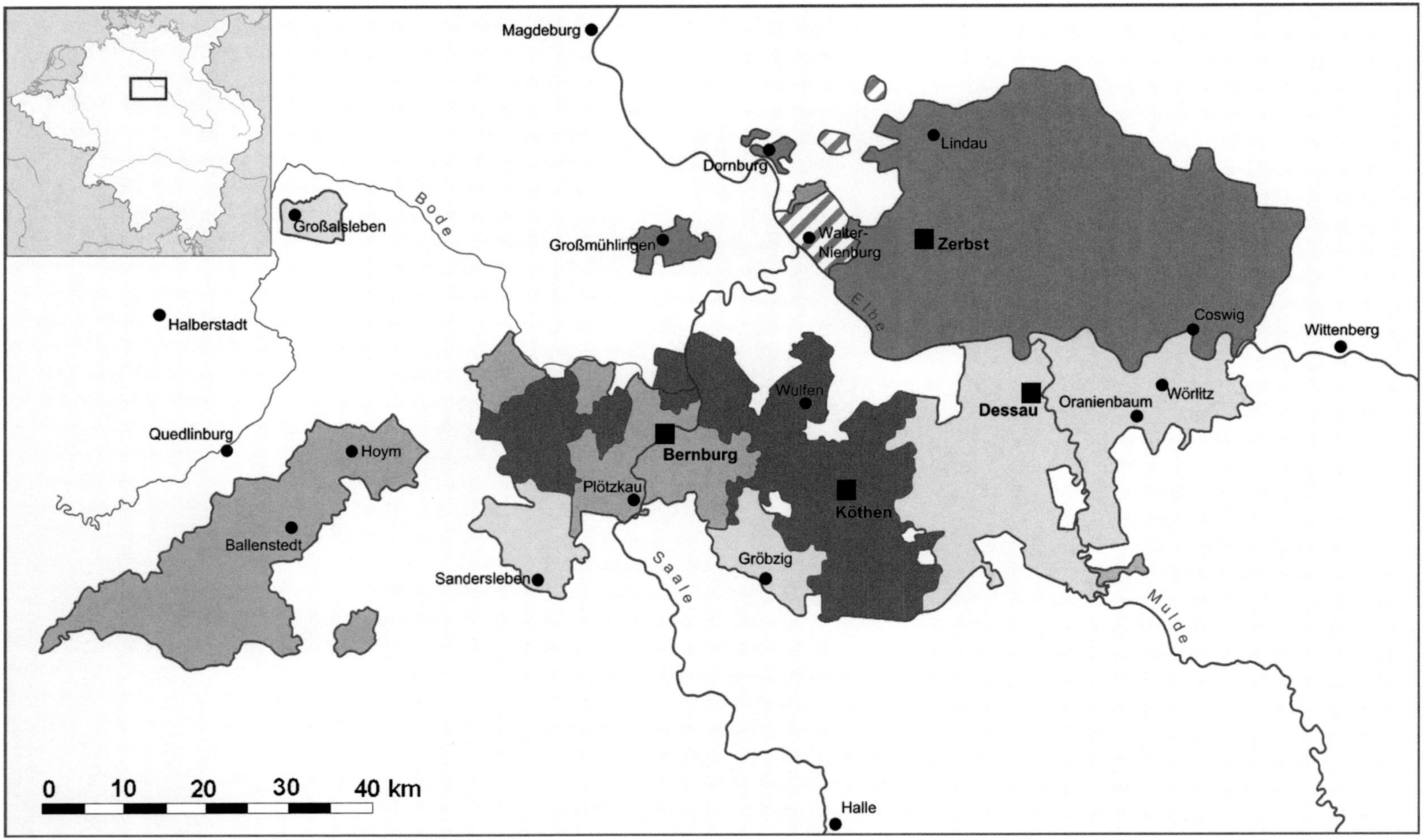

In 1648, the Duchy of Anhalt was divided into four: Dessau, Zerbst, Bernburg and Köthen. During the wars between 1664 and 1679, Anhalt provided its *Reichskontingent* of 27 cavalry and 48 infantry to the regiments of the Upper Saxon Circle. Most of the states of the Empire contributed even smaller quotas, and this is why they were called *Nicht-Armierten* (unarmed). The distinction between armed and unarmed territories emerged as many of the weaker princes paid stronger neighbours to take over their obligations. This occurred in Swabia, for example, where Württemberg, Baden, Fürstenberg, Ulm, Augsburg and Esslingen all fielded troops on behalf of other *Kreis* members, many of whom had been reluctant to contribute at all.

This title becomes clearer when examining the position of the small to middling territories that had been arming themselves in the 1670s such as Hessen-Kassel, Württemberg, Holstein-Gottorf, Mecklenburg, Osnabrück, Paderborn, and Pfalz-Neuburg. All these had raised permanent units to escape the exploitation of powerful neighbours, thus embarking on the same course as the larger territories, which had begun arming 10 or 20 years earlier. Some principalities already maintained small life guard and garrison companies that could be expanded by inducting militiamen or recruiting additional mercenaries, to serve in offensive operations as field regiments. A minimum level of permanent defence was provided in both large and small territories by the trained militias, which could be mobilised by the of ringing church bells to repel attacks or the transit of foreign troops. The Estates generally contributed to the upkeep of the militia, though the local communities were often expected to bear part of the cost directly, while most princes maintained their professional forces through heavy taxation. Old feudal obligations often still existed formally, including that of mass mobilisation (*landsturm*) as a last resort along with personal service by the nobility as cavalrymen (*lehns* or *ritterpferde*).

However, with the partial exception of Württemberg, Mecklenburg and Pfalz-Neuburg, states found it increasingly difficult to compete with Brandenburg, Bavaria, Saxony, the Guelph Duchies et cetera, which had economic resources, larger forces, and better international connections. Some principalities, like Holstein-Gottorp, Mecklenburg, Württemberg, Ansbach and Bayreuth, Paderborn and Reuss managed to place one or two units each in foreign service, but were unable to match the brigades provided by the large territories and so had proportionately less influence. Others were forced to subcontract to other German rulers: Hessen-Darmstadt provided the Guelph's contingent to the *Reichsarmee,* while Schwarzburg and Reuss collaborated in hiring a regiment to Franconia to meet its Association quota.

Such transfers became the Austrian Habsburgs' preferred way of obtaining military assistance and it often spun out negotiations for auxiliaries in the hope that financial exhaustion would force princes to sell them soldiers at less than it would cost their own officers to recruit them. The Emperor also offered to reduce the obligations for the *Reichsarmee* in return for drafting soldiers directly into his own army.[4] This would have gone a long way towards achieving the monarchical solution, converting the *Kreise* into recruiting districts for the Austrian army. Not surprisingly, when this was put to the Upper Rhine principalities in 1687, some rulers, notably Georg Friedrich of Waldeck, objected vehemently, claiming it would ruin their military structure and 'be a gross ingratitude to the honest soldiers' to turn them over to the Austrians, whose pay and conditions were far worse than at home. Some principalities, especially in Franconia, were less particular, already transferring part of their forces at the end of 1685 by which time Würzburg was in such dire straits, no longer able to pay its own contingent. As a result, the mobilisation of the *Reichsarmee* already displayed many of

4 Peter H. Wilson, *German Armies. War and German Politics, 1648–1806* (London: UCL Press, 1998), p.41.

Count Johann Friedrich I of Hohenlohe-Öhringen (1617–1702), a print by Johann Wolfgang Stichling after an engraving by Andreas Matthäus Wolfgang. (Landesarchiv Baden-Württemberg)
By 1635, the County of Hohenlohe was ruled in condominium between six branches, who also shared their seat in the Diet as immediate Princes of the Empire. Though Hohenlohe did not belong to the actual German armed states, in 1691 Count Johann Friedrich I entered the trade in soldiers, raising one infantry regiment of 1,000 men for Venice. The House of Hohenlohe also provided several officers to German and foreign armies: Georg Adolf (1623–1656), field officer in the Bavarian army, Wilhelm Heinrich (1624–1656), *Obristlieutenant* in the Swedish army, Christian zu Hohenlohe-Waldenburg-Bartenstein (1627–1675) and Joachim Albert (1628–1656) respectively a field officer and an ensign in the Swedish Army, Ernst Otto (1631–1664) *Obristlieutenant* of the Franconian cavalry, and the aforementioned Feldmarschall Wolfgang Julius von Hohenlohe-Neuenstein (1641-1698).

the features that were to characterise collective security after the great reform of 1681–1682.

However, the gathering of the *Reichsarmee* had remained subject to changes and adjustments since the 1660s. The official strength of 30,000 men decreed by the Diet of Regensburg on 4 February 1664 was cut by the decision to deduct the contingents already serving in the *Deutsche Allianz* corps. The remaining 20,993 men were apportioned to the individual Circles anticipating later mobilisation arrangements, with the Austrian *Kreis* omitted because the Emperor already had soldiers in the field. The distinction between armed and unarmed territories was clearly emerging, as many of the weaker princes paid stronger neighbours to take over their obligations. This occurred in Swabia, for example, where Württemberg and Baden, as well as the Free Imperial Cities, all fielded troops on behalf of other Circle members, many of whom had been reluctant to contribute at all. Nonetheless, this participation was fairly impressive. Even the Swabian Imperial Knights consented to the inclusion of their 220 infantry in the Empire's contingent, although they were under no obligation to cooperate.[5]

5 Peter H. Wilson, *German Armies. War and German Politics, 1648–1806* (London: UCL Press, 1998), p.77.

Ansbach-Bayreuth and Brandenburg-Bayreuth Kulmbach

Ruled by the Franconian branches of the Hohenzollern House, the two Margraviates were repeatedly in personal union until 1603, but the territories continued to remain independent up to the dissolution of the Empire in 1804. Although fragmented and divided into several enclaves lacking in territorial continuity, the Margraves benefited from their family ties with Brandenburg to consolidate their political status in the Empire. They shared the Protestant executive post in the Franconian Circle and as for foreign policy, and similarly to other small principalities, they saw opportunities to find security and act as spokesmen for regional interests.

From the beginning of the seventeenth century, Ansbach and Bayreuth both regularly contributed troops to the Circle contingent.[6] Initially, quotas were calculated according to the terms established in 1663 by the Diet of Worms, but from 1681 the new *Reichsmatricel* replaced this and both principalities agreed to retain in arms the *simplum* strength, namely a third of the required military force in peacetime.[7] This made the principalities two minor armed states that earned them a considerable authority in the next decades. The Margraves not only succeeded in securing their lands, but also managed to establish members of their Houses as reputed military leaders. Between 1664 and 1714, six princes served as senior officers in the *Reichsarmee* or in the Imperial Army,[8] while a further two entered the Brandenburg service as cavalry colonels.[9] The Margraves also acted as military entrepreneurs hiring troops to both German and foreign princes. In 1661, Albrecht II of Ansbach, agreed with the Republic of Venice to raise an infantry regiment of 800 men. The

Margrave Albrecht II of Ansbach-Bayreuth (1620–1667), shown on the obverse of a coin. (Digital Collection of the Baden-Württemberg Museum)

6 In 1610, Ansbach sent a cavalry regiment and two infantry regiments as part of the Franconian contingent. In 1620, the Franconian Circle raised two cavalry regiments and one infantry regiment composed of troops from the two Margraviates. In 1631, Kulmbach also supplied one infantry regiment for Sweden, which was disbanded after the Battle of Nördlingen in 1634.

7 Georg Tessin *Die Regimenter der Europäischen Staaten im Ancien Régime des XVI bis XVIII Jahrhunderts – Teil 1* (Osnabrück: Biblio Verlag, 1986), pp.67–68. (Author's note) According to the division established by the Franconian Diet, the contingents were distributed equally among all five *Kreis* regiments (1 cuirassier, 1 dragoons, and 3 infantry regiments). In 1691 Ansbach provided 114 horsemen (57 cuirassiers and 57 dragoons) in two companies and 384 footmen, Bayreuth the same number of horsemen and 468 footmen in 3 companies.

8 Antonio Schmidt-Brentano, *Kaiserliche und k.k. Generale (1618–1815)* (Vienna-Munich: Österreich Staatsarchiv, 2006), pp.13–14.

9 Bruno Mugnai, *Wars and Soldiers in the Early Reign of Louis XIV. volume 7: German Armies, 1655–1690, part 1* (Warwick: Helion & Company, 2024), pp.310 and 312.

regiment served in Crete until 1667–1668, and fought in the early phase of the dramatic siege, after which records of it are lost.[10]

In 1672, a single company of 150 cavalry from Bayreuth-Kulmbach joined the Brandenburg troops on the Rhine, and the next year it was sold to the Great Elector. In January 1687, Margrave Christian Ernst of Bayreuth raised two regiments, each of 10 companies of musketeers – 2,000 men in all – for the Republic of Venice, which served in Greece between 1687 and 1688.[11]

Equestrian portrait of Margrave Christian Ernst of Brandenburg-Bayreuth Kulmbach (1644–1712). Like many members of his House, the Margrave took up a military career, and by 1668 held the rank of *general* in the Franconian Circle and later in the Imperial Army. To face the financial crisis of 1672, Christian Ernst entered the trade of soldiers with Electoral Brandenburg.

10 Bruno Mugnai, *The Cretan War, The Venetian-Ottoman Struggle in the Mediterranean. 1645–71* (Solihull: Helion & Company, 2018), p.111.

11 Jochen Koch, *Johann Philipp Winheim, Kriegskommissair der Bayreuther Regimenter im'Großen Türkenkrieg' (1687–1695) und Späterer Reichspostmeister in Coburg (1698–1717)* (Regensburg: Roderer Verlag, 1998). Among the accounts dealing with the Venetian service, the relation of Johann Philipp Winheim is particularly accurate and includes much information about equipment and uniforms. He accompanied the troops as *Kriegskommissar* and his main task was to settle with Venice the soldiers' wages, rations and, obviously, their transfer to Greece, as well as the accounting of the money for the Margrave. The contingent sailed to Dalmatia and after stops at Dulcigno, Korcula, and Split, it then moved on to Morea, taking quarters in Nauplia. In 1688, both regiments fought at the siege of Negroponte, where they lost two-thirds of their strength. My thanks to Aris Kosionidis for this information.

Due to the high number of soldiers required, the contingent was also recruited in the Spanish Low Countries with special permission from the Spanish Governor to allow the recruiting of volunteers in Brussels and Brabant. One of the regiments was under the command of the Crown Prince Georg Wilhelm, and took the name *Venediger* (the Venetian). However, according to the Venetian sources, the quality of these troops left much to be desired, as they had never been in combat before.[12]

In August 1687, another contract was signed with the Emperor, who hired 950 dragoons from Bayreuth-Kulmbach. They entered the Imperial Army one year later as regiment *Brandenburg-Bayreuth Dragoner*.[13] Apart from the troops hired for foreign powers, and those for the *Reich* contingent, the only permanent forces of the Margraves were two companies of mounted life guards, which served as a military school for the local nobility.

Musketeer, infantry regiment *Prinz Georg Wilhelm*, 1687 (author's reconstruction).
The contract concluded by the Republic of Venice and the Margrave of Brandenburg-Bayreuth contains a detailed description of equipment and dress of the regiments raised for the Greek campaigns against the Ottomans. Count Carl von Sparre was commissioned by the Margrave to negotiate the terms, and he added on the contract some notes on the composition of the regiments in his own hand. The uniform consisted of grey *Rock* with cuffs and lining of red for regiment *Sparre* and blue for regiment *Prinz Georg Wilhlem*; natural leather breeches, grey stockings, black hat with red or blue ribbon, white-red or white-blue lanyard on the right shoulder, brass buttons, ammunition pouch, bayonet and waist belt with sword. Both regiments were only of musketeers, and in each company, 24 privates and lance corporals carried flintlocks (With thanks to Aris Kosionidis for this information).

12 Archive of State of Venice (ASVe) *Senato da mar*, reg. n. 154 (1688). After campaigning for a year in Greece, the *Venediger* regiment had just 13 officers and 663 NCOs and private soldiers. ASVe, *Senato da mar*, reg. n. 154 (1688).

13 Alphons von Wrede, *Geschichte der K.u.K. Wehrmacht von 1618 bis zum Ende des XIX Jahrhunderts* (Vienna, 1898–1905), band III, p.657.

Ansbach and Bayreuth avoided the direct involvement in the wars against France, but as generally occurred in the weaker territories, the actual situation was precarious. During the Franco-Dutch War, the billeting of troops in the winter 1674/1675 represented a considerable burden, with the cost of accommodating 12 Brandenburg regiments in Franconia for four months amounting to no less than 400,000 thalers, or nearly three times the annual tax revenues of Ansbach and Bayreuth combined.[14]

Baden-Baden and Baden-Durlach

The Margraviate of Baden-Baden was ruled by the Catholic branch of the Zähringen House (*Bernhardinische Linie*), which shared the territories with the Protestant cousins of Durlach. Both Margraviates belonged to the Swabian Circle, which comprised a total of 96 secular, ecclesiastical and free cities' territories. As with the majority of the dwarf states involved in the Thirty Years' War, after 1648 the Margraviates wished to avoid anything that involved an additional drain on their meagre resources, or might lead to conflict with more powerful neighbours. Baden-Baden and Baden-Durlach appreciated that they could only overcome their individual weakness through collective action and so remained receptive to schemes emphasising security, peace and maintenance of their territorial integrity. In 1658, both Margraviates negotiated for their membership in the Rhenish League but they were refused because of their exorbitant demands.[15] Baden-Baden, the larger of the Margraviates, regularly contributed its own quota of soldiers to the Circle contingent. In 1664, Margrave Wilhelm (r. 1622–1677) contributed with 50 horse and 50 foot for the Circle contingent which marched to Hungary, while 100 foot were provided from his cousin Friedrich VI of Baden-Durlach (r. 1659–1677), but the respective forces served in separate regiments according to their differing religion.

Margrave Friedrich VI of Baden-Durlach in a print from the *Theatrum Europeum*, by Matthäus Merian the Younger. (Author's collection)
In 1664, the Margrave actively contributed to raise the Swabian contingent for Hungary. In 1674, after an attempt to remain neutral, as did his relative of Baden-Baden, he joined the Dutch-Spaniards-Imperialists in the war against France.

Both Margraviates actively supported the formation of the Circle contingent in 1674 for the *Reichskrieg* against France. Baden-Baden contributed with 82 horse for the *Kreis-Regiment*

14 Peter H. Wilson, *German Armies. War and German Politics, 1648–1806* (London: UCL Press, 1998), p.51.

15 Peter H. Wilson, *German Armies. War and German Politics, 1648–1806* (London: UCL Press, 1998), p.171.

Württemberg, and on this occasion another 146 men from Baden-Durlach served in the same regiment, although this was exceptional since Baden-Baden put its foot into the Catholic regiment *Montfort*, which served separately from the Circle contingent. This was essentially recruited in Baden-Baden in exchange for subsidy from the other lesser Swabian Catholic territories, which agreed to pay for the 1,100 foot who joined the 100 directly recruited by the Margrave.[16] The confessional separation continued in the next decades, and in 1683 the cavalry also formed one Catholic and one Lutheran regiment.

The Swabian contingent joined the Allied army on the Upper Rhine, but soon conflict emerged over the assignment of the winter quarters. Matters reached a crisis by October 1676, as the shortage of assigned quarters and contributions began to undermine the decisive war effort of the Allies. Believing that they were being sacrificed to preserve the Emperor's relations with Brandenburg, Swabia and Franconia decided to pull out of the war altogether. By April 1677, the respective contingents were withdrawn in protest at the quartering of Imperial troops in their territories, and unilaterally both Circles declared their neutrality.[17] Baden and Durlach suffered again in the war, especially when the campaigns moved to their borders in 1677–1678. After seizing Freiburg in November 1677, French parties criss-crossed the countryside looting and extorting contributions.

Portrait of Georg Merius, *Hauptmann* in the infantry regiment Montfort, 1674. (Author's collection) The regiment had been recruited by Baden-Baden for the *Reichsarmee* jointly with the Catholic states of the Swabian Circle.

In 1680, as the Swabian Circle held to the Laxenburg Alliance, the Margraves Ludwig Wilhelm (Baden), and Friedrich VII Magnus (Durlach), agreed to maintain a third of the troops in active service as *Haustruppen*.[18] In the same years, the two Badens were also capable of mobilising approximately 3,000 militia.[19] The decision not to demobilise regular troops was a consequence of the damages suffered during the Franco-Dutch War, when both territories had become a battlefield in 1677. As for the strategic places, Baden-Baden updated the fortifications guarding the Rhine. In the 1680s the most important, and garrisoned, locations were Eberstein, Pforzheim and Stollhofen.[20] This latter was a small fort, but due to its location halfway between Strasbourg and Rastatt, increased in importance in the following years, becoming one of the mainstays of the defence on the Upper Rhine. Unfortunately, all these measures proved insufficient to save the territories from a new invasion and a further bitter destruction in 1688,

16 Georg Tessin *Die Regimenter der Europäischen Staaten im Ancien Régime des XVI bis XVIII Jahrhunderts* (Osnabrück: Biblio Verlag, 1986), Teil I, p.73.

17 See Bruno Mugnai, *W ars and Soldiers in the Early Reign of Louis XIV, volume 2: The Imperial Army 1657–1687* (Warwick: Helion & Company, 2019), p.120.

18 Bruno Mugnai, *Wars and Soldiers in the Early Reign of Louis XIV, volume 2: The Imperial Army 1657–1687* (Warwick: Helion & Company, 2019), p.122.

19 Peter H. Wilson, *German Armies. War and German Politics, 1648–1806* (London: UCL Press, 1998), p.56.

20 Heinrich Ludwig Gude, *Staat der Marck-Graffen von Baden-Baden und Baden-Durlach* (Halle, before 1708), p.58.

when the French army crossed the Rhine for the first campaign of the War of The League of Augsburg. The Margraviate of Baden-Durlach suffered the most damage compared to the territories of Baden-Baden.

As with many other German princely families who could not provide large auxiliary contingents, the Margraves managed to place one or more members as military officers in the foreign armies. The two Badens always provided skilled captains, who generally served in the armies of the Spanish and Austrian Habsburgs, Durlach and even in Sweden. Members of both families held commanders' posts in the Swabian Circle's military *Direktorium*. Prince Leopold Wilhelm of Baden-Baden and Margrave Friedrich IV of Baden-Durlach held the rank of *general* in the Imperial Army between 1651 and 1677, while Prince Hermann of Baden became president of the Austrian Aulic War Council in 1681, after a career spent in the Spanish and in the Empire's armies. After them, Margrave Ludwig Wilhelm of Baden-Baden became the most famous soldier of the dynasty in the 1690s.

Margrave Ludwig Wilhelm of Baden-Baden (1655–1707), also known as *Türkenlouis* after his victory over the Ottomans at Szlankamen in 1691, print after an engraving by Elias Heiss. (Author's collection) As ruler of his state, by the 1680s, Ludwig Wilhelm pursued an active military policy aimed at defending his lands against France.

Baden-Baden also managed a small but significant trade in soldiers with Spain, In 1663 Prince Leopold Wilhelm raised 600 horse and 900 foot as a contingent for the Circle of Burgundy.[21] This force should have participated in the campaign against the Ottomans in Hungary, but delays and other mishaps postponed the departure until late summer 1664, by which time the Truce of Vasvár had been signed. Instead of disbanding it, in September 1664 Prince Hermann moved this contingent to the Low Countries and then entered the Spanish service as colonel proprietor of a German cavalry regiment.[22] Since the 1650s, Baden-Baden had granted permission to the Emperor to recruit soldiers in its territory.

21 Georg Tessin, 'Reicharmee und Allianzkorps in Türkenfeldzug 1663–64', in *Zeitschrift für Heereskunder* 308/309, 1983; pp.133–137.

22 Bruno Mugnai, Wars *and Soldiers in the Early Reign of Louis XIV, volume 4: The Armies of Spain, 1659–1688* (Warwick: Helion & Company, 2021), p.328. In 1672, Prince Hermann also became colonel proprietor of an infantry regiment in the Imperial Army and in 1673 of another in the Spanish Army of Flanders.

Holstein-Gottorf

The law of 1544, which had established the principality as 'eternally indivisible', but ruled by two lines of the same dynasty, regulated the Duchy of Holstein, belonging to the German Empire, and the Duchy of Schleswig, a vassal of the Kingdom of Denmark: the Oldenburg-Gottorf (Oldenburg-Gottorp in Danish). The agreement, however, produced many complications, because the Ducal territories were mixed with the Danish ones, and the estates of the aristocracy of Schleswig and Holstein contributed to complicate the sovereignty over certain territories. As time went on, Denmark disputed sovereignty with the Dukes, and this moved Holstein-Gottorf to side with Sweden. This alliance constituted a great strategic opportunity for Sweden, because Gottorf was an ideal base to access the territories between the Rivers Weser and Elbe, and also offered an excellent location to assemble forces for an attack on the southern flank of Denmark. This position had been further strengthened by Carl X Gustav of Sweden's marriage to Hedvig Eleonora of Holstein-Gottorf, which became the foundation of an alliance destined to last into the eighteenth century, and the cornerstone of Swedish policy towards Denmark. The duchy therefore became an important pawn in the hegemony of the region.

After the Westphalian Settlement, economic contingencies forced Duke Friedrich III to reduce his expenses, including that for the military. Until 1657, the only regular troops were the garrison companies of Tönning and of Friedrichsburg. These were the main strategic locations of the duchy, which respectively guarded the access to the harbour of Eiderstedt – the duchy's principal trade's terminal – and the town of Schleswig with the manor of Gottorf, where the Princes had their residence. Increasing Danish pressure and the Second Northern War of 1655–1660 caused a drastic change in the military situation. An alliance was signed with the King of Sweden, Carl X Gustav, who promised full independence from Danish control in return for military assistance.[23] Meeting the Swedish request, Friedrich III demanded that the Estates provide the resources to increase the professional army. In December 1657, the Estates agreed to provide funds to raise an army of 5,500 horse and foot before March 1658.[24] From these troops, Sweden had to take 1,500 men, but the total figure was never fulfilled, forcing the Duke to mobilise the peasant militia. The regular troops, in autumn 1658, numbered only 2,450 men.[25] One infantry regiment entered the Swedish army, while another regiment manned the fortress of Tönning along with the cavalry regiment Osten, both transferred into Swedish service by October 1658. The Duke retained one infantry company for his own *Leibgarde zu Fuss*.

23 Peter H. Wilson, *German Armies. War and German Politics, 1648–1806* (London: UCL Press, 1998), p.36.

24 Friedrich Carl Rode, *Kriegsgeschichte Schleswig-Holsteins* (Neumünster: K. Wachholz 1935), p.27.

25 Günter Knüppel, *Das Heerwesen der Fürstentums Schleswig-Holstein-Gottorf, 1600–1715* (Neumünster, Karl Wachholtz, 1972), p.89.

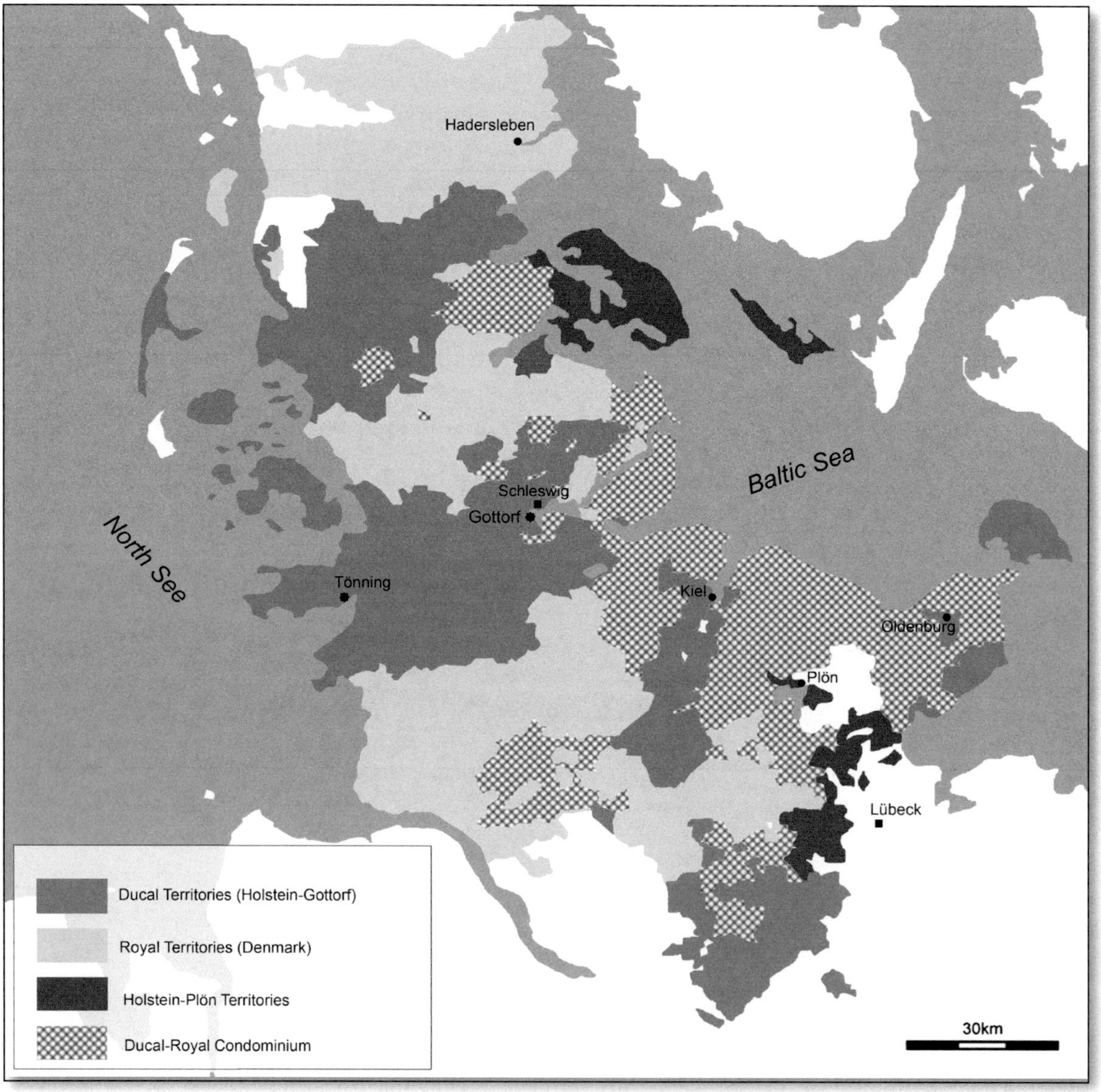

Map of Schleswig-Holstein (1657-60)

The Swedes struck at the Danes in February 1658, crossing the frozen Baltic to besiege Copenhagen and forcing the Danes to grant full sovereignty to the Gottorf parts of Schleswig as well as to abandon the war. By the Treaty of Roskilde, signed 26 February 1658, and again two years later with the Treaty of Copenhagen, Denmark renounced its feudal rights to, and recognised the full independence of, Holstein-Gottorf, retaining only the territory of Schleswig. However, sovereignty remained fragmented, with the Danish King ruling 5,800 square kilometres of Holstein, including 3,850 within the Empire, while the Duke of Holstein-Gottorf held the rest, which formed the narrow peninsula between Scandinavia and the European mainland. Schleswig, which lay outside the Empire immediately to the north, was also split, with the King owning one-third directly and exercising overlordship over the remainder. The agreement put an end to the Danish-Swedish struggle, but Holstein-Gottorf had suffered serious damage. In 1658, the Duchy was crossed by the Imperial and Brandenburg army which caused the inhabitants to flee in terror as conditions returned to those experienced during the Thirty Years' War. Duke Friedrich III was killed during the defence of Tönning Castle against the Danes in 1659.

Duke Christian Albrecht of Holstein-Gottorf (1641–1695), a print from Matthäus Merian's *Theatrum Europeum*. (Author's collection) Christian Albrecht became Duke after the dramatic death of his father in 1659, just as he came of age. In the following decades, he tried to strengthen his position against the Danish aims on the duchy. In foreign policy, he sought to balance his actions between Sweden and Austria.

Christian Albrecht, already Lutheran bishop of Lübeck, succeeded to the Duchy and he ruled until 1695.[26] The reign of the new Duke, however, was anything but easy. Though thwarted by Sweden during the Second Northern War, Denmark retained ambitions to impose its rule over the entire region. However, the internationalisation of German politics brought the Anglo-Swedish guarantee for Holstein-Gottorf's territorial integrity in 1665 to counter potential Danish claims. Despite such tensions with Denmark, the first 10 years of Christian Albrecht's reign remained peaceful, and enabled him to realise cultural projects and undertake a number of diplomatic trips. In 1661, the post-war reduction of the Army by Christian Albrecht fixed the regular force to the infantry garrisons and the life guard, about 1,000 foot in all, while the militia strength fell to 1,057 men in

26 It was not until 1666 that the Duke handed over the Bishopric to his 20-year-old brother August Friedrich, but had himself elected coadjutor, a position he held until the end of his life.

five companies of foot.[27] Under the new Duke, the military of Holstein-Gottorf received a new organisation with the appointment of a permanent *Kriegcommissariat*, which also managed the funds for the troops. Duke Christian Albrecht retained the rank of Commander-in-Chief for himself, but managed military matters with the assistance of a *General der Miliz*, with the *Festkommando* of the fortress of Tönning, and the *Oberkriegsgericht* (high court-martial).[28]

In 1664, Denmark and Holstein-Gottorf acceded to the Imperial request to provide troops for the Lower Saxony Circle for the upcoming campaign against the Ottomans in Hungary. They jointly sent a company of 101 horse and two 150-strong foot companies to the *Kreisregiment* Ende.[29] The Holstein-Gottorf troops were assigned to the *Obristlieutenant* Görtz and fought at Szentgotthárd on 1 August 1664. They formed the centre of the Imperial-German-French army, which in the early morning was overwhelmed by the Ottoman assault. The cavalry suffered 72 casualties, while the infantry was almost destroyed. In early 1665, the survivors returned home at half of their original strength.[30]

The scenario changed again in 1667, when the King of Denmark inherited the Duchy of Oldenburg, increasing the geostrategic weight in favour of Copenhagen. When Christian V of Denmark came to power in 1670, hostilities soon broke out. Christian V attempted to regain feudal sovereignty and control over Schleswig-Holstein-Gottorf supporting the claims of Joachim Ernst of the Holstein-Plön (Sodenburg) line, who considered himself the rightful inheritor. Christian V concluded a settlement with Joachim Ernst, in which the latter ceded his claimed shares in Oldenburg's inheritance to Christian V, and in return was granted territories in the Duchy of Holstein. After Joachim Ernst's death in 1671, his son Johann Adolf continued to contest the legitimacy of Christian Albrecht as Duke of Holstein-Gottorf, and turned his complaints to Vienna. In 1673, the Emperor decided in his favour, whereupon Johann Adolf ceded his claims to the Danish King, who from then on administered Oldenburg and Delmenhorst in personal union, leaving Christian Albrecht empty-handed.

This approach prompted Christian Albrecht to renew the alliance with Sweden, and in 1674, he travelled to Stockholm to negotiate personally with his nephew and King, Carl XI. Already by 1672, an agreement with Sweden established the mustering of 3,200 standing troops as 'practised militia'. A senior officer from Sweden was appointed as military adviser, in order to organise the Ducal troops according to the Swedish pattern. He, *Generalmajor* von der Wieck, supervised the improvement of the defences of Eiderstedt and the construction of an extensive net of earthworks. However,

27 Georg Tessin *Die Regimenter der Europäischen Staaten im Ancien Régime des XVI bis XVIII Jahrhunderts* (Osnabrück: Biblio Verlag, 1986), Teil I, p.185.

28 Günter Knüppel, *Das Heerwesen der Fürstentums Schleswig-Holstein-Gottorf, 1600–1715* (Neumünster, Karl Wachholtz, 1972), pp.64–65.

29 Bruno Mugnai, *Wars and Soldiers in the Early Reign of Louis XIV, volume 2: The Imperial Army 1657–1687* (Warwick: Helion & Company, 2019), p.288.

30 '1663–1664, Für das Reich gegen die Türken', in *Neu und Alte Zinnfiguren*, VI, June 1975, pp.26–27.

The life guard company of Holstein-Gottorf in 1665, from Günter Knüppel, *Das Heerwesen der Fürstentums Schleswig-Holstein-Gottorf, 1600–1715* (Neumünster: Karl Wachholtz, 1972). (Author's collection)
Contemporary accounts state that the Duke issued to his life guards a red 'livery'. As usual, officers dressed according their personal taste, but among the rank and file the clothing also seems to be far from an actual uniform. Some soldiers are wearing *Pyerock* with plain sleeves or with a variety of turned up cuffs, while others seem to wear doublets and short jackets. As for the neckwear, cravats are the most common item, but some NCOs and the drummer prefer to wear the *rabat* collar. Note in the first picture, two *enfants de trupe* armed, equipped and dressed as the privates.

the plan to raise regular field regiments failed, and only one was actually formed. Again, the established strength was not reached, therefore, in 1674 a new treaty was signed, by which the Duke pledged to maintain a regular force of 1,834 infantry divided in 11 companies of 100 musketeers and 50 pikemen, plus officers.[31] The militia was also reorganised and established in companies under experienced officers. In the original plan, the militia was to form a reserve corps, whose strength should be determined simply by the number of the conscripts aged between 18 and 60, net of exemptions granted to certain categories. The Duke hoped that this kind of compulsory recruitment would have allowed him to gather 30,000 men,[32] which could

31 Günter Knüppel, *Das Heerwesen der Fürstentums Schleswig-Holstein-Gottorf, 1600–1715* (Neumünster, Karl Wachholtz, 1972), p.89.

32 'From a military point of view, the militia performed their assigned defence tasks at all points of the territory until 1675. They were ready wherever no recruited soldiers were available, but

face any enemy assault taking advantage of well-designed earthworks and trenches. In 1674, the practical result resulted in the company of the Life Guards of horse, 1 regiment of foot of six companies, 7 companies of the *ausschuss* (militia), 2 companies of *Landwolk* and 36 artillerymen.[33]

In 1675, the Scanian War brought Holstein-Gottorf back into opposition to Denmark. The final break came when the King of Denmark demanded funds from the Schleswig-Holstein Estates in Kiel to finance the war, whereupon the Duke dismissed the assembly. Under the pretext of wanting to negotiate the replacement for Oldenburg-Delmenhorst, Christian V lured the Duke to the fortress of Rendsburg, where he forced him to sign the *Rezess* on 10 July 1675, in which Christian Albrecht gave up sovereignty and all foreign alliances. The *Rezess* also obliged the Duke to pass his soldiers over to Denmark.

Gottorf's share of the Duchy of Schleswig was occupied from 1675 to 1679 and the fortress of Tönning was razed. After this act, Christian Albrecht fled to Hamburg, where he lived in exile. Due to the occupation of his domains, Christian Albrecht lost all the revenues, so that he even had to pawn his personal jewellery in Hamburg.[34] The Danish occupation strongly affected the Duchy and the economy ran into major problems. In 1679, after the Peace of Fontainebleau, with the help of the Emperor, the Guelphs and their allies, Christian Albrecht forced Denmark to sign the agreement which restored him to the throne. A mounted life guard and two infantry companies were re-established in 1679, while Sweden added an infantry regiment of about 600 men assigned to garrison duty.[35]

The peace, however, was of short duration. Having failed to seize Hamburg in 1679, Denmark turned its attention to Holstein-Gottorf again. In 1682, Christian V changed sides and allied himself with France. Now, he tried to force Christian Albrecht to accept a compromise that would have prohibited him from pursuing any independent policy. When the Duke refused, Danish troops overran Holstein-Gottorf in May 1684, forcing Christian Albert to return into exile in Hamburg. Before the Danish invasion, the Duke handed over his troops to Hannover as a contingent for the Lower Saxony Circle. The Duke no longer felt safe in Hamburg either, as Christian V was also re-laying claims to the Free Imperial City. It was only after the second Danish siege of Hamburg in 1686 that Emperor Leopold I intervened and forced the two parties to negotiate a truce. As Christian Albrecht refused financial compensation for Oldenburg-Delmenhorst on Swedish advice and Christian

later the right to bear arms, so coveted as proof of service to the state's sovereignty, required the employment of permanent regular troops.'Günter Knüppel, *Das Heerwesen der Fürstentums Schleswig-Holstein-Gottorf, 1600–1715* (Neumünster, Karl Wachholtz, 1972), pp.91 and 99.

33 Günter Knüppel, *Das Heerwesen der Fürstentums Schleswig-Holstein-Gottorf, 1600–1715* (Neumünster, Karl Wachholtz, 1972), p.141.

34 Friedrich Carl Rode, *Kriegsgeschichte Schleswig-Holsteins* (Neumünster: K. Wachholz 1935), p.55. Even his sons and chancellor-minister Johann Adolf Kielmannsegg were deported to Copenhagen, where the latter died. Friedrich Carl Rode, *Kriegsgeschichte Schleswig-Holsteins* (Neumünster: K. Wachholz 1935), p.55.

35 Georg Tessin, *Die Deutschen Regimenter der Krone Schwedens*, Veröffentlichungen der Historischen Kommission für Pommern, Reihe V, Heft 13 (Cologne-Graz, 1965), pp.161–162.

V refused to hand over the Holstein-Gottorf territories, the negotiations dragged on for two years. Only the involvement of France in the War of The League of Augsburg, forced the King of Denmark to sign the Treaty of Altona on 20 June 1689 in order to avoid being completely isolated.[36] At the end of the year, Christian Albrecht returned to Gottorf, where he was to deal with the state's debt, which had increased considerably.[37] This scenario was little different to the one experienced 40 years ago, when the Duchy emerged from another foreign occupation. To reconstitute the army, Hannover and Sweden each ceded 8 and 18 infantry companies respectively to Holstein-Gottorf.[38] From this core of troops, two infantry regiments were raised between 1689 and 1690, which along with 509 cavalry brought the total of the professional troops to 3,372 men.[39]

Mecklenburg-Schwerin and Mecklenburg-Güstrow

In 1650, after 22 years of exile, Adolf Friedrich I of Mecklenburg-Schwerin (r. 1628–1658), and Gustav Adolf, of Mecklenburg-Güstrow (r. 1636–1695), regained their territories.[40] Both lineages had been deposed by Emperor in 1626 for having sided with Denmark, and then with Sweden, against Emperor during the Thirty Years' War.[41] However, the success did not resolve the poor economic situation of their domains, and among the first measures taken, the Dukes ceded all their troops to Sweden.[42] This was not the only loss, because Sweden annexed Wismar, the island of Poel and Neukloster. With Wismar, Mecklenburg lost its main sea port, which became the 'door to Germany' for Sweden, and in exchange received the territories belonging to the Bishoprics of Schwerin and Ratzeburg. These new lands were not an actual gain, since

36 'Brokered by the maritime powers, who also wished to be rid of the crisis, the treaty limited Gottorf and Danish military presence in their respective territories and established a demilitarised zone along the strategic Flensburg-Rendsburg-Hamburg highway. International assistance helped preserve the Gottorf plug in the Danish bottle, preventing further spillage of Copenhagen's ambitions into Northern Germany. To ensure adherence, Danish and Gottorf troops should be hired by the maritime powers in the event of a new war in the west.' Peter H. Wilson, *German Armies. War and German Politics, 1648–1806* (London: UCL Press, 1998), p.133.

37 Jens Martin Neumann: 'Das Schloss aus Ruinen wieder zu erwecken. Friederike Amalie von Gottorf und ihr Witwensitz zu Kiel', in *Mitteilungen der Gesellschaft für Kieler Stadtgeschichte* 87 (2013), pp.1–30.

38 Georg Tessin *Die Regimenter der Europäischen Staaten im Ancien Régime des XVI bis XVIII Jahrhunderts* (Osnabrück: Biblio Verlag, 1986), Teil I, p.187.

39 Günter Knüppel, *Das Heerwesen der Fürstentums Schleswig-Holstein-Gottorf, 1600–1715* (Neumünster, Karl Wachholtz, 1972), p.137.

40 When Gustav Adolf died without male heirs in 1695, Mecklenburg was reunited under Friedrich Wilhelm of Mecklenburg-Schwerin. In 1701, the Duchy was divided again between Mecklenburg-Schwerin and Mecklenburg-Strelitz. The principle of primogeniture was reasserted, and the right was reserved to the ruler of Mecklenburg-Schwerin.

41 Mecklenburg was granted by the Emperor to Albrecht Wenzel Eusebius von Wallenstein as a personal fief.

42 Georg Tessin, *Die Regimenter der Europäischen Staaten im Ancien Régime des XVI bis XVIII Jahrhunderts* (Osnabrück: Biblio Verlag, 1986), Teil 1, p.221. The Mecklenburg contingent comprised two cavalry and four infantry regiments recruited between 1631 and 1634.

they increased the territorial fragmentation making Mecklenburg another buffer territory.

As with other German principalities, the Duchy of Mecklenburg was a dual state with several domains shared in condominium. Among these, the town of Rostock belonged to both Duchies.

According to a contemporary account, Rostock had a medieval curtain but some modern improvements like ravelin and bastions made the city strong.[43] A second major fortress, Warnemünde (today part of the modern Rostock), guarded the shores of the Baltic Sea, and in 1669 still had a Swedish garrison.[44] The same account celebrated the city as prosperous, however, the state's economy was still recovering from the damage caused by the Second Northern War, which in 1658 had disastrously involved Mecklenburg, notwithstanding the Duchies had proclaimed their neutrality.

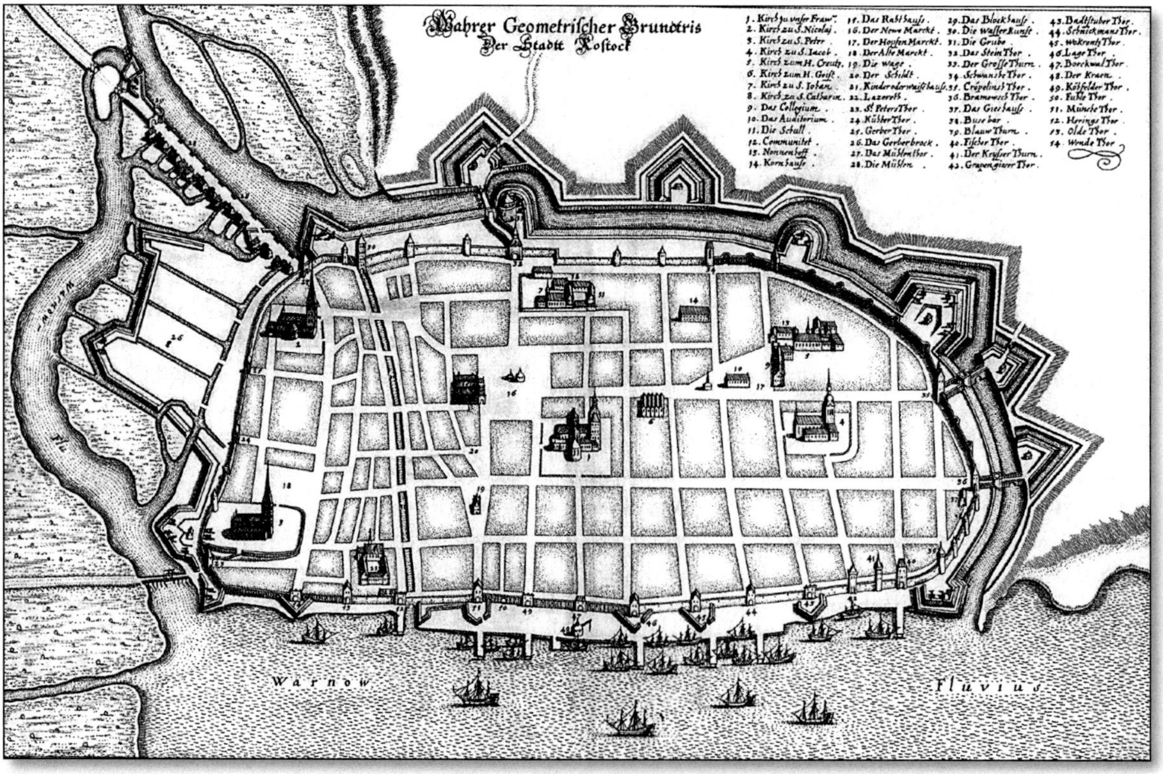

Plan of Rostock in 1653, shown with north at the bottom. (Author's collection)

In the 1650s, both Duchies maintained a very modest military strength. In 1652, Mecklenburg-Schwerin had three garrisons quartered in Schwerin, Dömitz and Bützow with 14 horse and 95 foot in all. In comparison, Mecklenburg-Güstrow had only 31 horse and 57 footmen of the *Leibgarde*

43 Galeazzo Gualdo Priorato, *Relatione della Corte e Stati del Serenissimo Gustavo Adolfo Duca di Meckelemburg* (Cologne, 1669), p.10.

44 Gualdo Priorato, *Relatione degli Stati del Serenissimo Filippo Guglielmo Duca di Juliers, Neuburg* (Cologne: 1668), p.10.

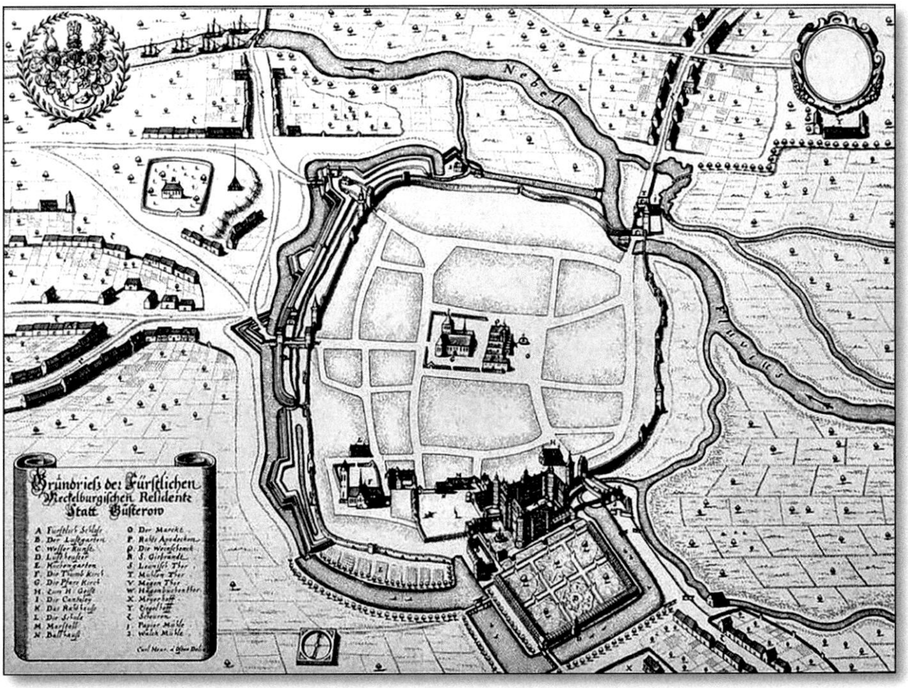

The little town of Güstrow with, below, the residence of the local House of Mecklenburg, print by Matthäus Merian the Younger. (Author's collection)
Güstrow gave its name to the ruling House, otherwise it was an insignificant settlement.

zu Fuss.[45] Both Dukes also contributed to the *Reichskontingent* as members of the Lower Saxony Circle. Until 1663, their contribution was minimal, due to the poor economic conditions of their lands. However, participation in the common defence was not without its problems, since the Circle was dominated by the Brunswick's princes and Mecklenburg. In 1657, during the Danish invasion of Bremen-Verden, Schwerin and Güstrow did not join the request to gather troops to support the Swedes.

In 1664, the Lower Saxony Circle's Diet discussed the formation of the contingent to support Emperor against the Ottomans. The Diet assigned to the Mecklenburg Duchies 60 cavalry and 100 infantry each. The final result saw the Duchies gathering only 109 horse but 227 foot in total.[46] The infantry formed a company in the *Kreisregiment zu Fuss* Ende, while the cavalry joined the regiment Schack.[47] After marching through Thüringen, Bohemia and Lower Austria, Mecklenburg's soldiers arrived at Vienna on 16 June along with the Lower Saxony contingent and joined the corps under Hermann von Baden. At Szentgotthárd, the Mecklenburg contingent suffered heavy casualties fighting alongside the Lower Saxony Circle's troops.[48] By the end of September the cavalry had only 25 officers and NCOs,

45 Klaus-Ulrich Keubke, *Kleine Militärgeschichte Mecklenburgs* (Schwerin: Stock & Stein, 1995), p.7.

46 Klaus-Ulrich Keubke, *Kleine Militärgeschichte Mecklenburgs* (Schwerin: Stock & Stein, 1995), p.7.

47 *War and Soldiers in the Early Reign of Louis XIV, Volume 2: The Imperial Army*, pp.287–288. On leaving for Hungary, the cavalry numbered 924 trooper and NCOs, while the infantry formed two regiments with 3,160 men in all.

48 Georg Tessin, 'Reicharmee und Allianzkorps in Türkenfeldzug 1663–64', in *Zeitschrift für Heereskunder* 308/309, 1983; pp.133–137. Only two officers were still able to serve, including

Duke Gustav Adolf of Mecklenburg-Güstrow (1633–1695), in a portrait by David von Krafft. (*Statens Porträttsamling*, Mariefred, Sweden) An enlightened prince and forerunner of social reforms ahead of his time, in 1661 Gustav Adolf ordered a population census, one of the first to be carried out in Germany. In 1671, he introduced new regulation for school education and in 1684, he was among the first to provide compulsory education for all children of all social classes, at least up to primary school level. In 1682, in order to combat superstition and witchcraft, he had a huge bonfire built in the main square of Güstrow where all confiscated books on magic were burnt, and he took care to hinder witchcraft by distributing free medicines to the population and to farmers for their livestock. Gustav Adolf died in 1695 without a direct heir and with his death, the line of Güstrow became extinct and the Duchy was reunited with Mecklenburg-Schwerin.

and 66 troopers, while the infantry numbered only 2 officers and 74 NCOs and privates. In mid-October, they marched back to Mecklenburg, where the infantry arrived on 12, and the cavalry on 15 December.[49] In the late 1660s, the regular force increased with the formation of the *Leibgarde zu Ross* of Mecklenburg-Güstrow numbering 100 horse.[50] The military weakness of the Duchies was, however, no impediment to the appointment of Duke Gustav Adolf of Mecklenburg-Güstrow as *Generallöjtnant* of the Lower Saxony's *Kreis-Directorium*.

Contemporary accounts emphasised that the Mecklenburg Duchies were almost without troops, but also remarked that 'the people here are strong and they are generally good soldiers' adding that they lived in harmony and loved their sovereigns. According to the same account:

> the nobility was the most illustrious of Germany and is particularly dedicated to the sciences, although recent wars have favoured the profession of arms. If necessary, the duke (of Mecklenburg-Güstrow) may call to arms 500 mounted gentlemen, all veterans, not counting the large number of subjects who could serve as officers, as many have served in Sweden and learned that military school.[51]

The author closed stating, with questionable truthfulness, that the Duke retained his veteran soldiers in their homes at the expense of the state, 'with the obligation to take up arms when ordered to do so by the prince'. This was an easy

the Mecklenburger *Hauptmann* Siegfried von Bibow who took over command of the survivors; his company claimed the loss of 2 officers, 3 NCOs and 68 men dead, wounded or missing.

49 '1663–1664, Für das Reich gegen die Türken', in *Neu und Alte Zinnfiguren*, VI, June 1975, pp.26–27.

50 Gualdo Priorato, Galeazzo, *Relatione della Corte e Stati del Serenissimo Gustavo Adolfo Duca di Meckelemburg* (Cologne: 1669), pp.22–23. The Duke also had 12 *Trabanten* as palace guards.

51 Gualdo Priorato, Galeazzo, *Relatione della Corte e Stati del Serenissimo Gustavo Adolfo Duca di Meckelemburg* (Cologne: 1669), p.13.

matter, because 'even the villagers are more accustomed to the musket and the sword than to the plough and the spade.'[52]

The military-political ambitions of the Dukes were not such as to provoke opposition from the estates, and no significant conflicts occurred about the economic management of the respective states. In the 1660s, the Duchies pursued a low profile policy, and it was not until 1670 that Mecklenburg-Schwerin took a clear position by joining the *Extendisten* group together with Bavaria, Cologne, Brandenburg, and Pfalz-Neuberg.[53] However, the military policy of Mecklenburg changed considerably under Duke Christian Ludwig of Schwerin.

Ten years previously, he travelled to Paris and was welcomed at the court of Louis XIV becoming a loyal supporter of France. Although neither of the Mecklenburg Duchies joined the Rhenish League, the Duke pursued a personal pro-French policy, and in February 1672 he signed an agreement with Louis XIV for the supplying of a cavalry contingent in exchange for subsidies. Christian Ludwig pledged to gather 600 horsemen and 150 dragoons and send them to join the French army for the upcoming war against the United Provinces of The Netherlands. This force was under the command of the *Obrist* Balthasar Gebhard von Halberstadt, colonel of the cavalry regiment and already Governor of the fortresses in Mecklenburg-Schwerin.[54] On 21 February, the Duke issued the order to raise 12 companies of horse in addition to his life guard, which was also doubled in strength. The colonel had under him the customary two field officers and staff, while each company included 1 *Rittmeister*, 1 *Lieutenant*, 1 *Kornett*, 1 *Quartiermeister*, 3 corporals, 1 surgeon, 1 clerk, 1 saddler, 1 smith, 1 trumpeter and 70 troopers – 82 horsemen in all. Eight companies of horse and the dragoons headed to The Netherlands sailing on the Elbe River and accompanied by the Duke, and in July the force joined the French army under Turenne. Meanwhile, Christian Ludwig expanded his trade to Münster, where the

Duke Christian Ludwig I of Mecklenburg-Schwerin (1623–1692), in a print after Claude Perrin (Österreichische Nationalbibliothek, Vienna). An admirer and supporter of France, in 1662, he travelled to Paris, to the court of Louis XIV. On 29 September 1663, he converted to the Catholic faith and his godfather, Louis XIV, gave him the second name Louis-Ludwig. Later, however, he often signed simply with 'Christian'. In 1672, his attempt to ingratiate himself as an ally of Louis XIV in the war against the Dutch Republic came to nothing.

52 Gualdo Priorato, Galeazzo, *Relatione della Corte e Stati del Serenissimo Gustavo Adolfo Duca di Meckelemburg* (Cologne: 1669), pp.25–26.

53 See Chapter 2: 'The German Chessboard'.

54 Klaus-Ulrich Keubke, *Kleine Militärgeschichte Mecklenburgs* (Schwerin: Stock & Stein, 1995), p.8.

martial Prince-Bishop Bernhard von Galen was recruiting the army for the upcoming war against the United Provinces. In April, the Duke signed a contract with the Prince-Bishop to supply 300 cavalry in four companies, but the agreement was not ratified because the men could not be raised in time for the start of the campaign.[55]

By the late summer of 1672, the French had achieved such a success that the presence of the Mecklenburg contingent faded into the background. The solution proposed by the French was probably not the one desired by the Duke, who agreed to reduce his auxiliary corps to just three companies of horse and the *Leibgarde zu Pferd*; the rest of the cavalry and the dragoons would join with the Cologne and Münster Army in the province of Groningen. In July, under *Obrist* Halberstadt, the Mecklenburg horse marched into Bentheim and then arrived before Groningen in early August.[56] Here, the treatment received by the allies was not the best. The horses were requisitioned and the troopers were assigned to the trenches along with the infantry. On 27 August, the Cologne and Münster Army abandoned the siege and followed a bitter retreat from Groningen. It was a poor consolation that during the siege the Ducal troops had lost only one man.[57] In September, desertion and disease considerably reduced the strength and in October, the horse, still without actual horses, were transferred to Lippstadt in Westphalia. In December, the regiment entered the Cologne Army together with its commander and *Obrist Inhaber* Halberstadt.[58]

The change of programme occurred in July favoured another agreement, this time directly with the Elector of Cologne, for the hiring of an infantry regiment. In a short time 800 men in six companies (one-third of pikemen and two-thirds of musketeers) was mustered and entrusted to the newly appointed *Obrist* Sigfried von Bibow, a veteran of the Hungarian campaign of 1664.[59] In late September, the regiment marched to join the Cologne troops but the negative outcome of the siege of Groningen changed its destination to Menschede, where it formed the garrison. The Mecklenburg infantry, like all the Electoral troops, suffered much from the poor treatment received during their winter quarters. By early 1673, the regiment had lost two-thirds of its strength through desertion and disease, and consequently, in April, it joined the cavalry under Obrist Halberstadt, and was transferred to Hildesheim, entering the Army of Cologne for a few months before being disbanded.[60]

As for the cavalry serving with the French army, its destiny was no better. In July, angered at seeing his troops poorly-used, the Duke, escorted by his

55 Tessin, 'Mecklenburgisches Militär in Türken und Franzosenkriegen', p.34.

56 Georges Bernard Depping, *Geschichte des Krieges der Münsterer und Cölner im Bundnisse mit Frankreich gegen Holland in den Jahren 1672, 1673 und 1674* (Münster: Theissing, 1840), pp.79–80.

57 Georg Tessin, 'Mecklenburgisches Militär in Türken und Franzosenkriegen 1648–1718' in *Mitteldeutsche Forschungen*, vol. 42 (Cologne: Böhlau, 1966), p.76.

58 Georg Tessin, 'Mecklenburgisches Militär in Türken und Franzosenkriegen 1648–1718' in *Mitteldeutsche Forschungen*, band 42 (Cologne: Böhlau, 1966), p.77.

59 Tessin, *Die Regimenter der europäischen Staaten im Ancien Régime*, p.222.

60 Georg Tessin, 'Mecklenburgisches Militär in Türken und Franzosenkriegen 1648–1718' in *Mitteldeutsche Forschungen*, band 42 (Cologne: Böhlau, 1966), p.79.

life guards, headed to Paris to meet personally with Louis XIV. The move was not the best, since among officers and troopers rumours began to circulate that they would be amalgamated in some French regiment.[61] The situation degenerated to the point that, on 11 August 1672, a quarrel broke out with some French cavalry involving a Mecklenburg trooper; Turenne personally intervened with his officers to restore order but the German soldier pointed a pistol at the French *Maréchal*. The reaction of Turenne's escort was immediate and the trooper disarmed – he was hanged the next day.[62] When Turenne crossed the Rhine at Wesel to enter Germany on 10 September, desertion among the Mecklenburg troops increased dramatically. In 19 days, 3 corporals and 66 troopers had deserted, the remainder were barely enough to form 3 companies. The little force followed the French in their march into the Electorate of Trier where Turenne entered winter quarters. In early January, upon news of the Prince of Orange advancing to join the allies on the Rhine. the French descended along the Rhine again and reached Bonn on 5 January, then moved on to Neuss. Here, on 23 January, Turenne ordered the transfer of what remained of the Mecklenburg cavalry under the newly appointed *Obrist* Antoine de Pas de Feuquières.[63] The protests of the Ducal officers induced Turenne to stop, but in return he asked the captains to personally contribute for recompleting and rearming the regiment. After they refused, Turenne ordered that the Mecklenburg troopers be amalgamated into the regiment *Schomberg Allemand*. Two months later, Duke Christian Ludwig managed get them released from French service.[64]

Finally, the dragoons faced less dramatic events. In July, they were transferred to Westphalia and assigned to the garrison of Werl, which in January 1673 was besieged by the Brandenburg Army. They succeeded in repulsing the enemy, and in the last phase of the siege received 30 deserters from the Brandenburg cavalry regiment *Mecklenburg*, whose colonel was Duke Christian Ludwig's brother Friedrich.[65] In spring 1673, the dragoons entered the army of Electoral Cologne. Used to negotiating on several tables and keeping relations open with other European courts, on 21 October 1672, Christian Ludwig hired four cavalry companies, 253 horsemen, to Denmark. As occurred for the auxiliary troops provided to Cologne, they also entered foreign service in 1673, and later formed the core of the Danish Life-Regiment

61 Georg Tessin, 'Mecklenburgisches Militär in Türken und Franzosenkriegen 1648–1718' in *Mitteldeutsche Forschungen*, band 42 (Cologne: Böhlau, 1966), p.80: 'They were even reluctant to accept pay from the French for fear that it would be seen as conscription.'

62 Georg Tessin, 'Mecklenburgisches Militär in Türken und Franzosenkriegen 1648–1718' in *Mitteldeutsche Forschungen*, band 42 (Cologne: Böhlau, 1966), p.80.

63 The episode is confirmed by the French *colonel* in Jules de Pas, Compte de Feuquières, *Mémoires de Monsieur le Marquis de Feuquières, Lieutenant Général des Armées du Roi: Contenans ses Maximes sur la Guerre, & l'Application des Eexemples aux Maximes* (London: 1736), p.47.

64 Tessin, 'Mecklenburgisches Militär in Türken und Franzosenkriegen', p.84. On 25 March 1673, 8 NCOs, 2 trumpeters and 44 troopers remaining joined the regiment Halberstadt in Meschede, who numbered 401 men in all.

65 Georg Tessin, 'Mecklenburgisches Militär in Türken und Franzosenkriegen 1648–1718' in *Mitteldeutsche Forschungen*, band 42 (Cologne: Böhlau, 1966), p.76.

of horse.[66] The departure of troops had left only two weak cavalry companies in Schwerin, known as *Reichcompagnie* and *Kreiscompagnie*, respectively with 56 and 58 horsemen in late 1672, and the infantry numbered 199 men divided into two companies.[67]

By contrast, Gustav Adolf of Mecklenburg-Güstrow did not join the French side, and nor did he take part in the trade in soldiers. The events of the war persuaded the pro-French Christian Ludwig of Schwerin to join the common cause, and in the spring of 1674 he contributed his troops to the Lower Saxony Circle. In May 1674, 100 cavalry and 1,000 infantry were was sent to Hildesheim to replace the occupying Brandenburg and Imperial troops, or at least to limit their claims for contributions. Both Mecklenburg Duchies sent one company of infantry under *Obristlieutenant* Joachim Friedrich von Barner, which comprised 8 officers and NCOs and 61 privates, who joined the Lower Saxony contingent marching to the Bishopric, 1 corporal of horse and 12 troopers were also added to the force. In early 1675, a further 25 officers and NCOs with 97 troopers, and a company of infantry with 124 rank and file marched along with the Lower Saxony contingent to the River Neckar, but they were not involved in the engagements of the campaign. The Mecklenburg troops performed limited actions escorting prisoners and facing some skirmishes with French parties on the Upper Rhine. As occurred in other contingents, late payment of wages and poor logistics negatively affected the troops, causing the mutiny of the Mecklenburg cavalry. Every attempt to restore order failed and soon the mutiny involved soldiers of the Saxe-Lauenburg contingents as well, who joined the mutineers and refusing to return into the ranks.[68] The small but resolute group of mutineers took the standards and marched back home by way of Heilbronn, Ochsenfurt and Magdeburg demanding free quarter in the villages they passed through and plundering the convoys of supply that they met.[69]

In late March 1675, the Mecklenburg infantry formed part of the Lower Saxon corps for guarding the town of Willstätt, on the right bank of the Rhine near Kehl and Strasbourg. This force was under Mecklenburg's *Oberstleutnant* Rolshausen. In August, Strasbourg's complaints about the

66 Georg Tessin, 'Mecklenburgisches Militär in Türken und Franzosenkriegen 1648–1718' in *Mitteldeutsche Forschungen*, band 42 (Cologne: Böhlau, 1966), p.74.

67 The name of the cavalry companies alluded to their function as a contingent for the *Reichsarmee* and the Lower Saxony Circle. Georg Tessin, 'Mecklenburgisches Militär in Türken und Franzosenkriegen 1648–1718' in *Mitteldeutsche Forschungen*, band 42 (Cologne: Böhlau, 1966), p.82.

68 'The Mecklenburg commander, *Obristleutnant* Vieregge, received orders to negotiate with the Imperial commissioners to take over the companies. The Margrave of Baden-Baden offered to temporarily take them into his service, but only until Mecklenburg could repay the money.' Georg Tessin, 'Mecklenburgisches Militär in Türken und Franzosenkriegen 1648–1718' in *Mitteldeutsche Forschungen*, band 42 (Cologne: Böhlau, 1966), p.83.

69 'The officers, dismissed by order of the Duke, followed them with the rest of the troops, joining with them in Nordheim, in Hannover. The deserters voluntarily returned to the companies waiting for the Duke's orders. Unexpectedly, they were not punished for desertion because they were not obliged to serve abroad and it was taken into account that they had deserted the allies because they had not received their pay but were willing to resume regular service at home.' Georg Tessin, 'Mecklenburgisches Militär in Türken und Franzosenkriegen 1648–1718' in *Mitteldeutsche Forschungen*, band 42 (Cologne: Böhlau, 1966), p.83.

subsistence of these troops forced the Imperial commissioners to move half of the troops from Willstätt. The Mecklenburg infantry remained under Strasbourg's subsistence until October, when the Republic refused to pay them into winter quarters, and thereby forcing Rolshausen to return home, but with only half of the original strength.[70]

In the spring of 1675, the Swedish invasion of Eastern Pomerania caused great concern in Mecklenburg. Both Schwerin and Güstrow were unable to muster their 600 horse and 1,068 foot established by the Circle assembly of March 1677. Moreover, in April, the Circle's members, with the Dukes of Mecklenburg among the first, rejected the Imperial claims to organise billeting in Lower Saxony. All 'foreign powers' were ordered to remove their troops, a move designed to evict the Brandenburgers from Mecklenburg and other Lower Saxon territories.[71] In May, Gustav Adolf of Güstrow and Christian Ludwig of Schwerin signed agreements with Celle and Wolfenbüttel, which would form their contingents by taking over Mecklenburg's share in exchange for subsidies. The deal was not a good one, because the Guelphs Dukes took more than their fair share. In addition to the payments for the troops, they demanded the supply of bread and fodder, and the provision of quarters.[72] Despite the presence of the Circle's troops, the war against the Swedes did not spare Mecklenburg and led to an increase in garrisons to counter the encroachments of Swedish and Danish troops. In 1679, Schwerin had a regular force comprising the mounted *Leibgarde*, the *Kreiscompagnie* of horse, and the garrisons of Schwerin, Dömitz and Rostock, in all 122 horse and 391 foot. Güstrow fielded the *Garde zu Pferd*, the *Leibgarde zu Fuß*, and the garrison of Rostock to a total of 90 horse, 310 foot and 11 artillerymen with other specialists.[73] In the following years, the strength continued to decrease, especially the company of *Garde zu Pferd*. In May 1684, the *Garde zu Pferd* of Mecklenburg-Güstrow numbered just 1 officer, 2 NCOs and 25 men, while the *Garde zu Fuß* had 2 officers, 3 NCOs, 4 corporals, 2 drums and 38 privates.[74]

New military engagements involved Mecklenburg in January 1686, when Duke Gustav Adolf of Güstrow agreed to hire 150 cavalry and 1,000 infantry to the Emperor under a special arrangement.[75] The Duke immediately began

70 Georg Tessin, 'Mecklenburgisches Militär in Türken und Franzosenkriegen 1648–1718' in *Mitteldeutsche Forschungen*, band 42 (Cologne: Böhlau, 1966), p.85.

71 Peter H. Wilson, *German Armies. War and German Politics, 1648–1806* (London: UCL Press, 1998), p.52. Both dukes of Mecklenburg had asked this in 1676 in an effort to avoid falling under Brandenburg influence.

72 On the other hand, secret clauses allowed part of the money paid by the territories to return to the Duke of Mecklenburg. The presence of forces belonging to a great power also offered the territory a degree of security that it would not have had if only its own forces were present. These resources enabled the Duke of Mecklenburg to modernise their fortresses. Georg Tessin, 'Mecklenburgisches Militär in Türken und Franzosenkriegen 1648–1718' in *Mitteldeutsche Forschungen*, band 42 (Cologne: Böhlau, 1966), p.85.

73 Klaus-Ulrich Keubke, *Kleine Militärgeschichte Mecklenburgs* (Schwerin: Stock & Stein, 1995), p.9.

74 Georg Tessin, 'Mecklenburgisches Militär in Türken und Franzosenkriegen 1648–1718' in *Mitteldeutsche Forschungen*, band 42 (Cologne: Böhlau, 1966), p.88,

75 Peter H. Wilson, *German Armies. War and German Politics, 1648–1806* (London: UCL Press, 1998), p.73.

to raise this considerable contingent but adjustments and modifications delayed the recruitment, and after 18 months the regiment was still only partially completed. On 17 June 1687, command was assigned to *Obrist* Ernst Christian von Österling, but as yet he could field only five companies, each of 125 rank and file, including six grenadiers. To this initial core, a further four companies were to be added in the autumn, along with three cavalry companies each of 66 men.[76] The infantry regiment comprised only musket-armed troops, with no pikemen; the grenadiers, lance corporals, and NCOs receiving flintlocks; bayonets were also issued to the whole regiment. On 1 May 1688, after further delays, the regiment marched to Hungary through Brandenburg and Silesia, where it was mustered by the Imperial commissioners on 2 June. The report recorded that the regiment had lost several soldiers through desertion. The *Oberstleutnant*'s company had barely a third of the establishment strength – investigations revealed that this was still incomplete when it left Mecklenburg – and it was noted that even the soldier's clothing was of poor quality.[77]

The march to Hungary continued in rainy weather, however desertions decreased when the regiment moved away from home, but at the same time the number of sick increased because of the unhealthy climate. In July, the infantry arrived on the Danube at Komárom, where the companies were embarked and transported to Peterwardein, and from there marched to Belgrade, besieged by the Imperial and Allied army under the Elector of Bavaria. The regiment, registered in the order of battle as *Kaiserlich-Mecklenburg*, barely fielded 25 or 30 men per company, but on 21 August it was sent to the infantry corps of *Generalwachtmeister* Wallis and deployed to the east of the city. The cavalry, which had continued overland, arrived before Belgrade on 31 August and was assigned to General Carafa's cavalry corps. There are no records of the Mecklenburgers' participation in the siege, however, and what remained of the infantry formed the garrison of Belgrade, where it remained until 31 October. On 1 November, the regiment numbered just 250 to 300 men, including the sick. They marched to the Danube, then into Moravia and Saxony, and finally crossed the border with Mecklenburg in January 1689. The survivors were divided into two companies and assigned to the existing garrisons. The cavalry entered the service of Brandenburg by an agreement signed on 25 April 1689.[78]

76 Georg Tessin, 'Mecklenburgisches Militär in Türken und Franzosenkriegen 1648–1718' in *Mitteldeutsche Forschungen*, band 42 (Cologne: Böhlau, 1966), p.85.

77 Georg Tessin, 'Mecklenburgisches Militär in Türken und Franzosenkriegen 1648–1718' in *Mitteldeutsche Forschungen*, band 42 (Cologne: Böhlau, 1966), p.89. For these reasons, the officer was dismissed.

78 Georg Tessin, 'Mecklenburgisches Militär in Türken und Franzosenkriegen 1648–1718' in *Mitteldeutsche Forschungen*, band 42 (Cologne: Böhlau, 1966), p.90.

Osnabrück

In 1650, an unusual disposition decided the destiny of the Prince-Bishopric of Osnabrück. In accordance with the provisions of Article XIII of the Treaty of Westphalia and the resolutions of the Nuremberg Execution, a *capitulatio perpetua osnabrugensis* (perpetual capitulation) established that the Prince-Bishopric of Osnabrück would be ruled alternately by a Catholic bishop elected by the cathedral chapter and a Lutheran bishop appointed by the Ducal House of Brunswick-Lüneburg. Therefore, upon the death of the Catholic Franz Wilhelm von Wartenberg in 1661, Ernst August, the youngest of the princes of Brunswick-Lüneburg, succeeded him. His long reign lasted until 1698, ruling the state alongside the newly established Electorate of Hannover.

The City of Osnabrück from a print dating to mid-seventeenth century. (Author's collection) The Bishopric remained to Ernst August even after he became Duke of Hannover in 1679. In 1698, after the death of Ernst August, the principality passed to the Catholic Bishop Charles Joseph of Lorraine.

In the late 1660s, the Italian historian Galeazzo Gualdo Priorato left his detailed accounts on the German states, including Osnabrück. He traced a positive picture of the principality celebrating it as the most fertile of Germany.[79] Until 1661, the state had had no regular troops except for the small palace corps of 12 *Trabanten* assigned to the residence of the Prince-Bishop. In 1662, Ernst August received three infantry companies from Duke August of Wolfenbüttel, which formed the core of the standing army.[80] Because of its geographical location, Osnabrück did not present any major vulnerabilities and its dual religious component sheltered it from neighbourly interference. No major fortress is mentioned and according to Gualdo Priorato the professional soldiers numbered about 500 in 1668, but some thousands of recruits could be gathered in a short time 'being Osnabrück a

79 Galeazzo Gualdo Priorato, *Relatione delle Corti e Stati .... e del Vescovato e Principato di Osnabruch* (Leyden, 1668), p.112.

80 Otto Elster, *Geschichte der stehenden Truppen im Herzogtum Braunschweig-Wolfenbüttel, 1600–1806*, vol. I (Leipzig, 1899–1901), p.76.

well-populated state.'[81] In the same year, the household troops comprised a company of 60 horse dressed in red.[82] By 1662, the foot formed one regiment of four companies under the commander of Johann Georg von Uffeln, and were assigned to the garrisons of the capital and of Fürstenau.[83]

Unlike the other Guelph princes, Ernst August did not join the Rhenish League, and took an active role in the Westphalian Circle. In 1664, he raised a cavalry company for the *Kreisregiment* Post, which marched to Hungary with the *Reichsarmee*.[84]

Despite the limited resources at his disposal, Ernst August participated in the trade of mercenaries and along with his cousin of Celle negotiated the hiring of troops with the Dutch Republic. In 1665, Osnabrück pledged to provide 1,500 horse and 2,000 foot against England and Münster, but the Peace of Cleves made the agreement no longer necessary. In 1666, Ernst August sent 840 horse and 1,000 foot to Bremen then under siege by the Swedes, and in autumn transferred them to the Palatinate, for the *Wildfang* War against Mainz. In 1668, the Prince provided one cavalry and one infantry regiment to the Dutch Republic, which retained this force until December, when it returned them to Osnabrück.[85] A further, limited, hiring of troops was concluded with the Republic of Venice in 1668. At the request of his cousin Georg Wilhelm of Celle, Ernst August mustered a battalion of foot under *Oberstleutnant* Degenfeld with 150 men from the regiment Uffeln and 150 new recruits. Only 15 returned to Osnabrück in early 1670.[86]

In the following decade, the regular troops increased with the formation of standing regiments of cavalry and infantry. Already in 1671, the Prince-Bishop had sent eight companies of infantry under *Obrist* Borch (OsI-3) to Wolfenbüttel for the siege of Brunswick. In 1674, Osnabrück joined Celle participating in the *Reichskrieg* against France. In 1674, about 1,500 horse and 3,000 foot joined the allies on the Upper Rhine, and the next year they formed the corps on the Moselle that fought at Conzer Brücke and Trier. In 1676, Spanish and Dutch subsidies allowed Ernst August to maintain 6,000 men in the field. In the winter 1676–1677 four cavalry regiments and four infantry regiments as well as three companies of dragoons were quartered in Brabant. The cavalry regiments had four companies while the infantry regiments had eight or nine companies.[87] The dragoons had been recruited in Flanders under *Obrist*, and later *Generalleutnant*, Jean-Charles de Louvigny,

81 Galeazzo Gualdo Priorato, *Relatione delle Corti e Stati .... e del Vescovato e Principato di Osnabruch* (Leyden, 1668), p.126.

82 Galeazzo Gualdo Priorato, *Relatione delle Corti e Stati .... e del Vescovato e Principato di Osnabruch* (Leyden, 1668), p.125.

83 Robert Sichart, *Geschichte der Königlich-Hannoverschen Armee* (Hannover, Hahn'sche Hofbuchhandlung, 1866), band 1, Band I, p.153.

84 See Bruno Mugnai, *W ars and Soldiers in the Early Reign of Louis XIV, volume 2: The Imperial Army 1657–1687* (Warwick: Helion & Company, 2019), p.287.

85 Georg Tessin, *Die Regimenter der Europäischen Staaten im Ancien Régime des XVI bis XVIII Jahrhunderts* (Osnabrück: Biblio Verlag, 1986), Teil 1, p.254.

86 Robert Sichart, *Geschichte der Königlich-Hannoverschen Armee* (Hannover, Hahn'sche Hofbuchhandlung, 1866), Band 1, p.361.

87 Robert Sichart, *Geschichte der Königlich-Hannoverschen Armee* (Hannover, Hahn'sche Hofbuchhandlung, 1866), Band 1, p.160: *Etat der Osnabrückschen Völker*.

who had served in the Spanish army of the Low Countries. On the campaign of 1677, Louvigny had command of the Osnabrück troops, which now also comprised a regiment of dragoons and a small artillery corps.[88] The infantry fought at the siege of Charleroi. The appointment of Louvigny had some repercussions among German officers. In particular, *Feldzeugmeister* Uffeln expressed his displeasure to the Prince, resigning in early 1678 and entering the service of Hamburg.[89]

The troops of Osnabrück continued to serve in the Spanish-Dutch Army of Flanders and on 14 August 1678, almost complete, they participated at the final Battle of Saint-Denis. The Peace of Nijmegen caused the disbanding of most of the troops, but Ernst August maintained in active service 2,893 men, who entered the army of Hannover in 1679.[90] The Prince-Bishop agreed to his officers requests that the regiments would not be disbanded.[91]

Osnabrück cavalry standards, 1670s. Left: red background with gold letters and fringes. Right: white background, gold circle, letters and fringes, natural eagle and bird on pale blue background. According to the arsenal's inventory, these and 22 other ensigns belonged to Ernst August's army, and when in 1679 he became Duke these followed the troops to Hannover. Unfortunately, attribution to regiments is uncertain and some standards could be ensigns from the age of Johann Friedrich.

Paderborn

The Prince-Bishopric of Paderborn belonged to the Westphalian Circle and, like the other German ecclesiastical territories, was at various times in personal union with other principalities. From 1650 to 1661, Prince-Bishop Dietrich Adolf von Recke ruled in Paderborn, succeeded by Ferdinand II

88 Robert Sichart, *Geschichte der Königlich-Hannoverschen Armee* (Hannover, Hahn'sche Hofbuchhandlung, 1866), Band 1, p.161.

89 Robert Sichart, *Geschichte der Königlich-Hannoverschen Armee* (Hannover, Hahn'sche Hofbuchhandlung, 1866), Band 1, p.154.

90 Robert Sichart, *Geschichte der Königlich-Hannoverschen Armee* (Hannover, Hahn'sche Hofbuchhandlung, 1866), Band 1, pp.168–170.

91 Georg Tessin *Die Regimenter der Europäischen Staaten im Ancien Régime des XVI bis XVIII Jahrhunderts* (Osnabrück: Biblio Verlag, 1986), Teil I, p.254.

Prince-Bishop Ferdinand von Fürstenberg (1626–1683), in a print from the *Monumenta Paderbornensia* (1672), after an engraving of Abraham Blooteling. (Author's collection)
Aware of the weakness of his state, Ferdinand remained as neutral as possible in military conflicts, but like the other members of his family was a supporter of France. Of great importance was his promotion of science and culture with works that contributed to the economic recovery of Paderborn.

of Fürstenberg until 1683, who was also Prince-Bishop of Münster from 1678.

After him, Hermann Werner von Wolff-Metternich zur Gracht ruled until 1704. The small principality was strategically unimportant and did not control any important locations or trade routes; sharing its borders with even smaller states, like Waldeck, Lippe and Corvey. Only Hessen-Kassel to the east and the Westphalian Duchy of Electoral Cologne were major principalities close to the Bishopric. As with other ecclesiastical principalities, after 1648 Paderborn regarded the position of the northwest German Catholic territories as vulnerable. The Treaty of Westphalia had sanctioned the secularisation of Minden and Magdeburg by Brandenburg and Bremen and Verden by Sweden. Understandably, these events caused great apprehension among those princes, such as the Bishops of Paderborn, who had no dynastic or territorial ties to the great ruling families of Germany. After the Westphalian Settlement, Paderborn's external politics remained aligned with that of most of the smaller states of the Empire and thus it kept a low profile. This was essentially focused on counterbalancing the influence of the larger armed states within the Empire's defence system through a policy oriented towards the association of states. The local economy had suffered considerably during the Thirty Years' War, and reconstruction after 1648 was delayed because Paderborn had to pay a large war compensation to Hessen-Kassel.

The first professional troops of Paderborn were recruited in 1664 for the contingent that the Westphalian Circle gathered for the war against the Ottomans in Hungary. This was a cavalry company and an infantry company, 58 horse and 102 foot, and were put into the regiments *Post zu Pferd* and *Uffeln zu Fuss*.[92] The bishop, as with many members of the Fürstenberg family, sided with France, but his support was little more than formal, because Paderborn continued a policy of appeasement while remaining an active member of the Westphalian Circle.

92 See Bruno Mugnai, *W ars and Soldiers in the Early Reign of Louis XIV, volume 2: The Imperial Army 1657–1687* (Warwick: Helion & Company, 2019), p.111.

In early 1672, Prince-Bishop Ferdinand entered the Marienburg Alliance with the Emperor, Mainz, Trier and Münster: an expedient to allow the option for a variety of negotiations. In the following spring, after the French invasion of the Dutch Republic, Paderborn responded to the Westphalian Circle request and sent 206 infantry to the newly raised *Kreisregiment* Waldbott, which was quartered in Cologne.[93] Meanwhile the Bishop did his utmost to maintain a relationship with France; in 1674 he had to pause any residual liaison with Paris, but even his support to the *Reichsarmee* was not always constant.

In 1676, Prince-Bishop Ferdinand raised a dragoon regiment and an infantry regiment and sent these to the allied army under Münster *General* Wedel in Verden-Bremen for service against Sweden. In October, both regiments were forced to take winter quarters in the Westerwald, where they remained until the summer of 1677. In September, the dragoons and infantry joined the German corps in Flanders in Dutch-Spanish subsidy. On 14 August 1678 they fought at Saint-Denis: the infantry was deployed in the first line with the Brandenburg and Osnabrück corps for the assault on the French left. The dragoons performed a secondary role in the cavalry reserve.[94] The Peace of Nijmegen closed the history of both units, which were disbanded in early 1679. The Ottoman emergence in Hungary reverberated in Paderborn, and in 1684, Bishop Hermann Werner raised three infantry companies which joined the Münster regiment Schwarz on the campaign. In January 1689, Paderborn entered the League of Augsburg along with the smaller principalities of the Westphalian Circle.[95]

93 Georg Tessin, *Die Regimenter der Europäischen Staaten im Ancien Régime des XVI bis XVIII Jahrhunderts* (Osnabrück: Biblio Verlag, 1986), Teil 1, p.254.

94 *Relacion de la Memorable Vitoria obtenida in Flandes .... y el socorro de la importante ciudad, y plaça de Mons* (Brussels, 1678), pp.8–9.

95 Richard Fester, *Die Armirten Stände und die Reichskriegsverfassung, 1681–1697* (Frankfurt am Main: Gebrüder Knauer (Druck), 1886), p.74.

Colour Plate Commentaries

Plate A – *Deutsche Allianz*, 1660-1664

1 – Pfalz-Neuburg, Infantry Field Officer, early 1660s.

This field officer, probably an *Obrist* or an *Obristleutnant* is a reconstruction from a portrait preserved in a private collection in Germany. The attribution to Pfalz-Neuburg is confirmed by the notes on the back of the painting of 'Düsseldorf, 1660'. The Franco-Dutch influence in men's fashion spread into West Germany as early as the 1650s. The short-sleeved coat typical of this period is an ideal compromise for the nobility between military dress and ruling class distinctive.

2 – Württemberg, Cuirassier Trooper, 1664

Leo Ignaz Stadlinger's book *Geschichte ders Württembergischen Kriegswesen von der Frühesten bis zurNneuesten Zeit* contains 36 colour plates illustrating Württemberg soldiers from 1638 to 1851. Despite the romantic style of the illustrations dealing with the uniform before 1700, many important details are accurately reproduced. This cuirassier is equipped in the standard South German cavalry style. The breast and back plates and the 'lobster-pot' helmet are painted black and are worn here over a very essential cloth *Rock*. This must have been the appearance of the Württemberg horsemen aggregated to the double contingent – *Reichsarmee* and *Deutsche Allianz* – sent against the Ottomans in Hungary.

3 – Electorate of Mainz, Pikeman, 1668

Although the iconography relating to the troops of the Mainz Electorate is almost nonexistent, some contemporary illustrations from the Rhineland show the main characteristics of the infantry in the 1660s. Undyed cloth, such as this grey-brown hue, was normally used for the cheap clothing of the largest part of any army of the time, namely the infantry. This pikeman, depicted in a German manual dating to 1668 has reduced his equipment to the essentials, putting aside the armour and helmet, which were certainly uncomfortable on marches and encampment.

Illustration from *Die Reconstructionen der Gimbelschen Waffensammlung* (Berlin: Ernst Siegfried Mittler und Sohn, 1902). In 1902 Karl Gimbel, retired lieutenant of the Royal Army of Württemberg, published a book with photographs of European arms and armour, which he had reconstructed from various textual and pictorial sources as well as from original items starting from Ancient Greece and running to the seventeenth century. Gimbel was an amateur historian, but being a military officer he did a thorough job and if his mannequins do not seem very life-like, they certainly look appealing. This figure represents a German *Schütze* dating to the 1650s–1660s. Apart from a few rough licences, such as the very long musket, narrow bandoleer and baldric, the reconstruction shows the universal characteristics of German military infantry clothing of those years. Note the fabric coat and sleeve seams covered by a fabric flap.

Plate B – The Three Brunswick, 1660s-1670s

1 – Hanover, *Öffener zu Pferde*, Trooper, 1668–72

Friedrich Schirmer, in the first volume of *Nec aspera Terrent! Eine Heereskunde der Hannoverschen Armee von 1631 bis 1803* relates that the cavalry wore a pale coloured broad-brimmed hat. According to the author, this would be a traditional distinctive of the cavalry from the Lüneburg Duchies until the next century. However, a documented delivery of black hats for the cavalry is dated to 1688. Further documents mention black hats until the end of the century. Schirmer also states that armour was abolished in 1693. The iron protectors or crosses (secrets) worn ***over*** the crown of the hat to protect against cuts to the head seem not to have been universal. Lüneburg was ideal for horse breeding, and it is not surprising that recruits provided their own horses, at a predetermined price.

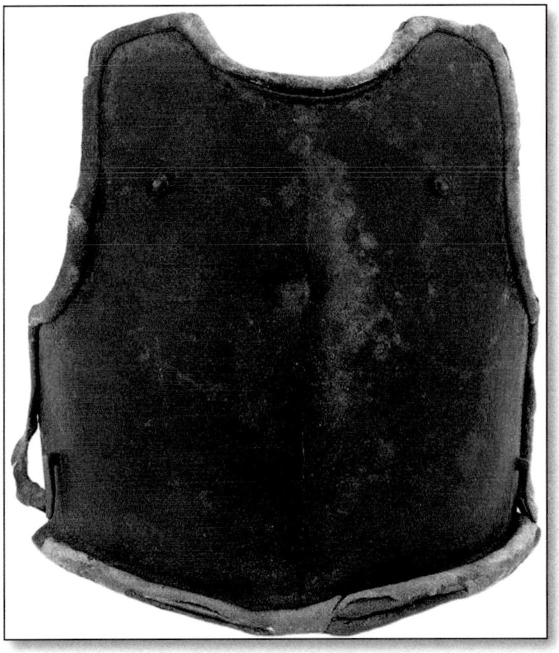

German or Austrian cavalry breastplate about 1650–1700 (Private Collection, Germany). This type of protection was widespread throughout Southern Germany and until the 1670s in Lower Saxony and Westphalia-Rhine. In these regions, the trend to abandon armour was influenced by the French, Spanish and Swedish cavalry.

A very fine example of boots for cavalry or dragoons manufactured in Germany, *c.* 1670–80 (Author's collection). Unfortunately, the boots have lost the spur-leather flap on the front of the foot, but are otherwise well preserved.

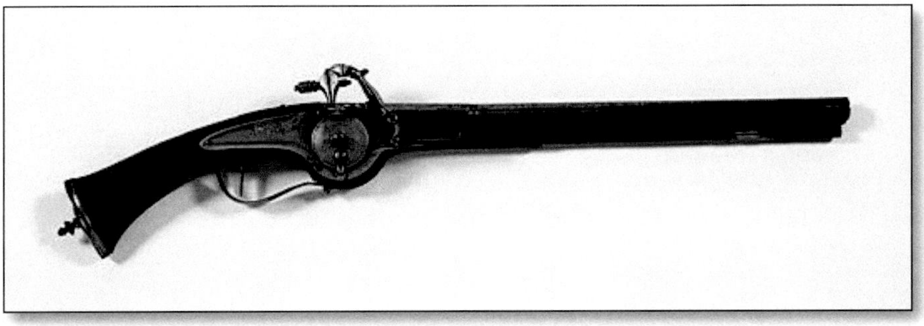

Wheelock pistol, Germany, 1660s (Private Collection, Italy). The barrel is signed I COMIN. The plate of the wheellock is finished in a point typical of the German pistols manufactured in South Germany. Almond-shaped pommel with moulded belt. Long shaft frame carved with a rosette on the screw-holder; the same rosette can be found on a Nuremberg pistol of the same period.

2 – Celle, *Leibregiment zu Fuss*, Pikeman. 1668

The uniforms of the troops of the two duchies of Lüneburg are known from as early as the 1660s thanks to the rich documentation preserved in the archives of Lower Saxony and in those of the Royal House of Hanover in England. This is almost unique in the context of seventeenth century Europe, with few exceptions. According to Robert Wilhelm Georg Sichart's *Geschichte der Königlich-Hannoverschen Armee*, red coats were introduced for the Celle infantry in the1660s. This pikeman is based on the figures carved on the gravestone of Josias von Waldeck, and from the accounts relating the final phases of the siege of Candia. According to the Venetian chroniclers, the pikeman replaced their weapons with shorter polearms such as spontoons and *corsesche*, the latter is depicted here. These weapons proved to be very effective for repulsing the Ottoman assaults, and for destroying the enemy approaches as well. According to contemporary reports, pikemen from the Guelph duchies did not wear armour after the 1650s.

Detail of the gravestone of Josias Waldeck, Celle, after 1670. The sculptures represent a cavalryman and a musketeer of Celle's army in the very early 1670s. The musketeer's coat is fairly simple and similar to the *Pyerock*, and comes down to below the knees. Some of the buttons, which could be of brass, are missing in the sculpture. Because of his equipment, not all of the buttons are visible but there must have been at least 24 down the front of the coat. The low pockets have six buttonholes but no visible buttons. The Swedish cuffs are split and folded back, without buttons. Breeches are fixed above the stockings as usual. The sword does not have a knuckle guard on the hilt as confirmed by some contemporary items preserved in Celle. Richard Knötel, who made his plate XIV/47 of *Grosse Uniformenkunde* on these figures, based the musketeer uniform on those of the Celle guards, whose colonel had been Josias von Waldeck, depicting the coat as red with black cuffs. The stockings are only partially covered by overstockings, which hang down loosely. As for the cavalrymen, his coat is probably of buffalo leather, with dark blue cloth cuffs applied, and worn over a cloth *Pyerock* – of red with dark blue Swedish cuffs in the Knötel's illustration. Were it not for the ammunition bag at the waist belt concealed by the bandolier, the style would be similar to that of the coeval German cavalry. In the style of the period, the neckcloth has a smaller accessory on top of it. Knötel shows for the musketeer the smaller neckcloth as red and the larger one as white; the horseman has a simple tied cravat of white with an additional red ribbon.

3 – Wolfenbüttel, Musketeer, 1675

The earliest mention of uniforms relating the infantry of Brunswick-Wolfenbüttel refers to the infantry companies in the Hungarian campaign of 1664, which are mentioned as the 'blue regiment'. A later description of the infantry companies gives better details. This comes from the 'Travel Diary' of Prince Albrecht of Sachsen-Gotha, who in May 1670 visited Wolfenbüttel.

He describes the garrison as consisting of five companies of 200–250 men, of which 50 carried out guard duty each day. They all wore grey coats with different facings. The colonel's company had cuffs of green, the major's company had red, blue for the third – the *Stückhauptman* (artillery captain), and yellow for the fourth, the colour of the fifth comopany's cuffs is not given. The companies probably were representatives of the regiments, an assumption supported by the statement that they were mostly corporals rather than privates.

A 1654 report records that pikes were carried by a third of the Wolfenbüttel infantry of each company. Elster mentions the pikes in 1663 for the companies which took part in the Hungarian campaigns, and these continued to equip the infantry until the 1680s. The same author, however, writes that the agreement made with the Dutch Republic in 1688 specifies that the infantry was to be armed only 'with good muskets and bayonets'.

Plate C – The Three Brunswick, 1680s

1 – Hannover, *Siegelberg zu Fuss* (BhI-9), Musketeer, 1685

In the 1660s, the infantry regiments of Hannover were known as the 'White', 'Red', 'Yellow' and 'Blue' regiments. Usually, this designation referred to the Colours, which were indeed in these hues but also referred to the uniforms as confirmed in the archival sources. As an example, when the regiment *Volalto zu Fuss*, also known as the *Weiss Regiment*, was originally raised in 1673, the capitulation specified: 'The *Schwadron* shall be dressed with light grey coats, green linings and facings, tin buttons, yellow leather breeches and black headwear.' In Hanover, the infantry continued to wear coats of grey, green or blue until the early 1680s. At this regard, Sichart quotes an order of the Duke dated 11 February 1680, which states that, except for the Life Guards, only two Hannoverian infantry regiments wore red coats. However, two years later the uniform for the infantry changed again. The contracts made with Venice in 1685–1687 also specify that the uniforms of the Hannoverian infantry regiment were to have been red, and in one case, red with blue facings for the regiment Podewils. In 1685, Hannover's commissioners put the condition for uniforms comprising a coat of red with blue cuffs and lining into a contract with Württemberg for the additional company enlisted there. Finally, the plan of the siege of Mainz in 1689, preserved in the Marburg Wilhelmshöher Kartensammlung, shows that all the Hanoverian and Celle infantry regiments were wearing red coats. Before 1682 and after 1695, the regimental commanders managed the purchase of uniforms directly. In the years from 1682 to 1695, the ducal administration ordered coats through three main suppliers: the *Hof Jud* Leffmann Behrens and the Hamburg merchants Johannes Overlaken and Jacob Schmidt. As for cavalry and dragoons, between 1682 and 1695, there is no evidence about the supply of uniforms by the ducal administration.

Sichart gives further accounts about the deliveries of scarves as a field sign. He states that in 1682 these were 'scarves of yellow canvas with fringes of the regiment's facing colour.' In 1685, the sources also refer to 'scarves of good yellow canvas and on both ends fringes of white, red and blue.' After November 1689, scarves are no longer mentioned in the deliveries. In addition to the uniform, the soldier received an overcoat or *Regenrock* (raincoat) made of undyed cloth. These were delivered to all regiments by the 1680s. The lining was generally in the facing colour for NCOs only.

In 1676 *Generalleutnant* Podewils introduced flintlocks. According to Schirmer, matchlocks were only done away with between 1676 and 1680. Sichart adds that the muskets were abolished in the camp at Leese in 1683, but this was valid only for the regiment Podewils according to Brandis. In 1684, following the example of Celle the year before, in Hannover a variable number of men in every company were selected as grenadiers and armed with three grenades each. Each soldier also had a small axe. Headwear is not mentioned but at this stage, the caps worn by grenadiers were in any case unofficial.

2 – Celle, *Bothmer Dragoner* (BcD-2), Private Dragoon, 1688

Celle introduced dragoons in 1671, and until 1688 no further unit was raised. According to Felix Leo Brandis, *Übersicht der Geschichte der Hannoverschen Armee von 1617 bis 1866*, the new regiment received a dark blue coat, probably to distinguish it from the existing regiment. As usual, the dragoon carried his ammunition under the saddle cover. The dragoon's smaller cartridge box was issued as supplies permitted, and often the infantry model was used instead

3 – Wolfenbüttel, *Holle zu Fuss* (BwI-5), Musketeer, 1689–1690

Information about the infantry of Wolfenbüttel suggests that Swedish (and Brandenburg) influence led to the adoption of the typical pattern in the late 1680s. The manufacture of the *Rock* required more cloth but it served to better protect the soldiers from the cold climate of Northern Europe. Moreover, the waistcoat improved the sanitary conditions of rank and file, and it was also functional in reducing wear on the *Rock*. According to the Elster, all Wolfenbüttel officers wore a heart-shaped red breast shield decorated either with the white horse of Lower Saxony or the crowned monogram of the reigning duke on a silver plate, or a completely silver shield with the same devices. These were presumably silver gorgets either red enamelled or completely silver. The officers also wore silver and yellow silk scarves.

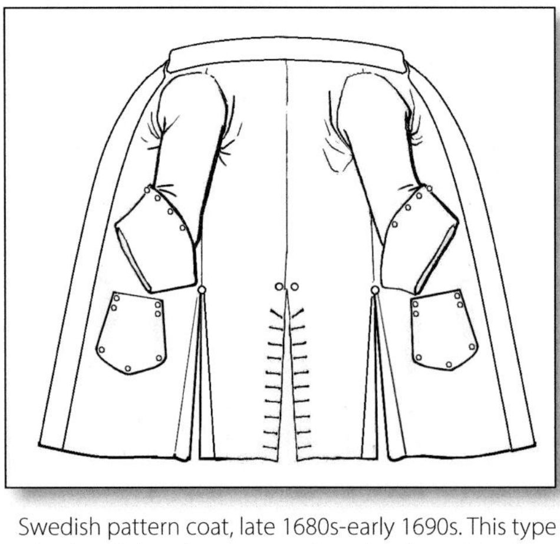

Swedish pattern coat, late 1680s-early 1690s. This type of *Rock* was common for the infantry of the North German states in imitation of the Swedish style coat, introduced in the 1680s. The cut prefigures the later uniforms of the infantry of Brandenburg-Prussia and also those of Wolfenbüttel, Mecklenburg and Holstein-Gottorf. Worn over a waistcoat, this item better protected the soldiers in the cold weather, and certainly it gave the soldier a much more practical and military appearance

Plate D – Hessen-Kassel and Hessen-Darmstadt

1 – Hessen-Kassel, *Ufm Keller zu Fuss* (HkI-3), Pikeman with *Kaputrock*, 1677

2 – Hessen-Kassel, *Prinz Carl zu Fuss* (HkI-9), Drummer, 1687

Carl von Stamford, in *Das Stehende Hessische Heer von 1670–1866*, recorded that since the 1670s the uniform of musketeers and pikemen had been the same. He also claims that the pikemen were equipped with armour and helmet, but some evidence suggests that metal protection was worn only in garrison. The infantry hired to Denmark in 1677 wore a blue *Rock*-coat to the knee, loose leather breeches, woollen stockings, black headwear and white cravat. As the contract expressly demanded that the soldiers have a raincoat, rank and file also received a *Kaputrock* for the winter campaigns. A supply contract dated 30 June 1681, stipulated that the *obrists* and the *Rentkammer* (war chamber) ordered cloth from the makers of Kassel. This was established again in 1683, with the recommendation that the cloth was of good quality, and would last at least two years, at an affordable price. The cost of the uniform and equipment was, of course, borne by the soldier who repaid the *Rentkammer* or the *obrists* with monthly deductions from his wages. According to Stamford, the contract of the regiment *Ufm Keller* specifies that the muskets were to be fitted with flint locks. It is unclear when exactly flintlocks were introduced, but the infantry raised by Hessen-Kassel for Hungary in 1685 was at least half equipped with flintlocks. The regiment *Prinz Carl*, raised for Venice in 1687, was completely equipped with flintlocks as required by the Republic. The privates carried a *Schweinsfeder*. Officers wore a coat with silver or gold lace and with a gorget; as usual, they were identified by scarves of white and red silk. The scarf appears to have been generally worn around the waist. Colours and drums were to be provided by the Landgrave, presumably with his Coat of Arms on them.

3 – Hessen-Darmstadt, *Leibgarde zu Fuss* (HdI-1), Musketeer, 1678

Dark blue uniforms had been issued to the infantry of Hessen-Darmstadt since the 1650s. A capitulation of 1677 specifies a blue *Rock* lined with bayes of different colours, a broad-brimmed hat and stockings of the same colour as the coat-lining, shoes, gloves, belts and cartridge pouches. According to Carl Christian Röder von Diersburg in *Geschichte des 1. Großherzoglich Hessischen Infanterie (Leibgarde) Regiments Nr. 115, 1621–1899*, 1899) dark blue coats with red cuffs and stockings were issued to the *Leibgarde zu Fuss* in 1660, and these colours continued to be worn in the following decades.

Plate E – Infantry, 1660s

1 – Frankfurt am Main, Militia's Officer, 1659–60

Based on a drawing by Maurice Leloir, this city militia officer wears a doublet and short open breeches of civilian dress. Only the scarf and the double-handed sword show him as a military man. However, in the Free Imperial City, militia for a long time did not wear an actual uniform, and officers, as usual, continued to dress according to their personal taste.

Officers and ensign of the City Militia of Frankfurt am Main, 1658–1660 after Maurice Leloire, *Histoire du Costume de L'Antiquité à 1914* (Paris: Henri Ernst, 1933). Three of these figures are dressed according to the style of the late 1650s; while the ensign wears a fashionable *justaucorps*.

2 – Lorraine, Infantry NCO, 1660–1664

Generally, in the 1660s and later, NCOs were not constrained to wearing the same uniform as the private soldiers. This figure is a reconstruction after contemporary images from Walloon-Flemish and French sources. Unfortunately, information on the uniforms of the Lorrainer infantry in the second half of the seventeenth century is very fragmentary. Certainly, uniform clothing for his army was the last concern of Duke Charles IV. The *Gazette de France* of 1653 describes the Lorraine infantry as heterogeneously dressed, and only officers and *sergeants* wore clothing looking 'appropriate to their status'. In 1667, a French officer describes the Lorraine infantrymen still dressed in 'outdated style', with clothing mostly of brown and dark grey.

3 – Palatinate, Musketeer, 1668–1669

According to Oskar Bezzel, *Geschichte des kurpfälzischen Heeres von seinen Anfängen bis zur Vereinigung von Kurpfalz und Kurbayern* (Munich: C.H. Beck, 1925), Elector Carl Ludwig required his officers to dress the infantrymen with dark blue coat and broad-brimmed, black hat. This private musketeer is a reconstruction after the drawings for the *Schola Militaris Moderna* by Johann Andreas Böckler.

Plate F – Infantry 1670–1680

1 – Baden (Swabian Circle), *Montfort zu Fuss* (BbI-1), Officer, 1672

The portrait of *Hauptmann* Georg Merius is the source for this figure. Brown coats were common in the Spanish Low Countries for both officers and men. Relations existing since the 1660s between the House of Baden-Baden and the Spanish Monarchy could have influenced the military dress of the Swabian principality.

2 – Osnabrück, *Leibregiment zu Fuss* (OsI-1), Musketeer, 1676

In *Geschichte der Königlich-Hannoverschen Armee* Robert Sichart gives some information about the uniforms of the Osnabrück troops. The *Leibregiment* received yellow coats in 1676, but the author does not add any further details about lining or other accessories. Thus this figure is a very partial reconstruction.

3 – Mecklenburg-Güstrow, Musketeer, 1672–75

In 1672, the Duke of Güstrow issued his infantry with uniforms of red cloth, while the Schwerin troops were dressed in grey. The Güstrow soldiers wore blue and yellow ribbons on their headwear and shoulders while those of Schwerin had red and white ribbons. In 1678 the Güstrow Company quartered in Rostock received grey coats again but with red lining, cuffs and stockings. In 1684 all the infantry of Güstrow were newly uniformed in light grey with blue facings and stockings. The drummers wore red coats. Pikes were only carried in the field, while in garrison all the infantry carried muskets.

Plate G – Hohenlohe Regiment, Greece, 1691–1694

In the 1694 painting illustrating the burial of Franceso Morosini in Napoli di Romania (modern day Naufplio in Greece), a large black and yellow striped colour with a central medallion, depicting presumably a Marcian Lion, appears in the background. The colours must have referred to some foreign regiment in Venetian service. In 1694, only three German mercenary regiments served in the Venetian army: *Waldeck*, *Bayreuth,* and *Hohenlohe*. Heraldic examination permits us to establish this flag as the Regimental Colours of the *Hohenlohe* regiment. The Count-Prince Johann Friedrich I von Hohenlohe raised 10 musketeer companies and 1 grenadier company to serve in the Peloponnese. Some documents preserved in the Hohenlohe family archive and in Venice reveal some aspects of the unit's organisation and dress. The regiment received equipment in Germany, but the uniforms were tailored on the Venetian mainland. Possibly, the ash grey coats with yellow cuffs and lining, manufactured in 1694 in Vicenza, could have been issued to this regiment when it returned from Greece. Yellow, black, and white designated the Hohenlohe House colours. Several early eighteenth century sources confirm the Austrian-Imperial influence on the equipment and dress of the Hohenlohe contingent. Such conjecture and some particular depictions, such as the officer in a complete yellow coat holding Morosini's sword on the pillow in the aforementioned painting, permit the reconstructed of the regiment's uniform.

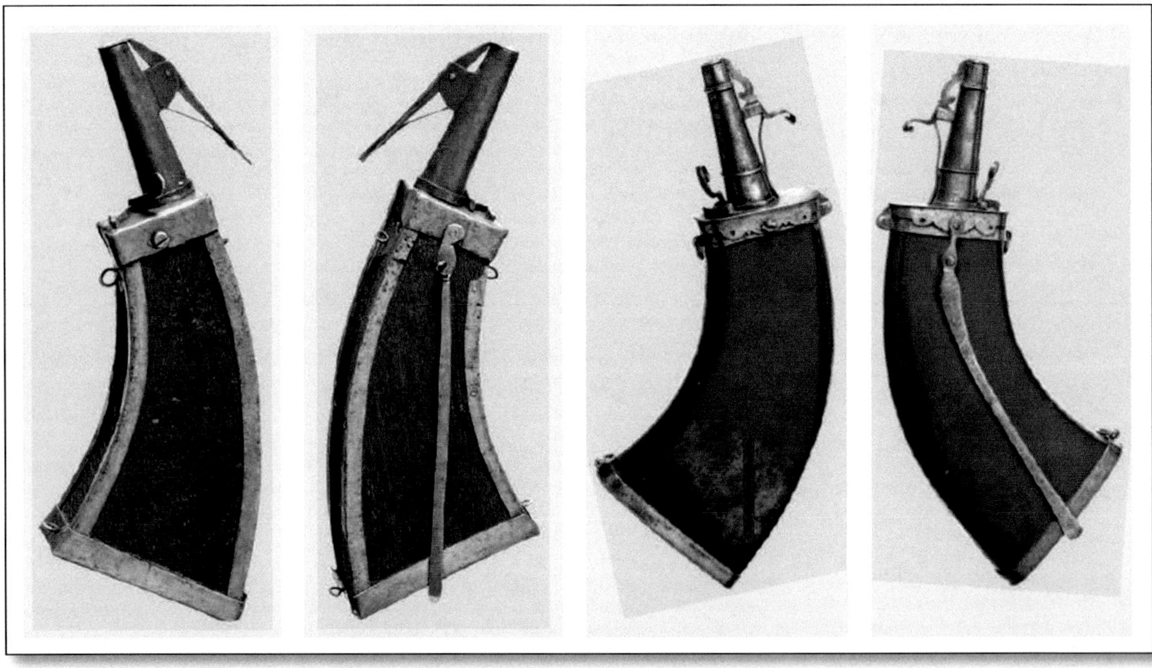

Powder Flask, Germany, Mid-Seventeenth Century (Private Collection, Germany)

Plate H – Cavalry, 1660s–1670s

1 – Mecklenburg-Schwerin, Trooper, 1664–69

The buff coat, or *Koller*, was the main item of uniform issued to the Mecklenburg-Schwerin cavalry since the 1650s. Some contemporary accounts confirm the same pattern until the early 1670s in Schwerin as well as in Güstrow. Klaus-Ulrich Keubke in *Kleine Militärgeschichte Mecklenburgs*, states that the Schwerin cavalry sent to France in 1672 had grey coats while the Lifeguard Company was in blue. The latter company carried a white standard with gold embroidery. By 1680, the *Garde zu Pferde* of Güstrow wore buff *Koller* again but with crimson cuffs laced in silver, leather breeches and black headwear with silver tape lace on the brim. Red cloaks with blue lining and collar were also issued. Saddle covers and pistol holster-covers were in crimson with white fringes. According to other sources, the cavalrymen wore the *Pyerock* instead of the cloak.

2 – Lorraine, German Cavalry Regiment, Trooper, 1672–78

The classic dress of the German heavy cavalry, consisting of *Koller*, back and breast and 'lobster-pot' helmet, identified the cavalrymen of the regiment raised east of the Rhine. From 1655 to 1668, Duke Charles IV recruited four cavalry regiments in Germany and a further two in 1675 and one of dragoons.

3 – Osnabrück, *Hitzfeld zu Pferde* (OsC-4), Trooper, 1674–75

Between 1673 and 1675, Prince-Bishop Ernst August of Osnabrück raised three cavalry and one dragoon regiment in anticipation of his participation in the war against France. Only the uniform of the two cavalry regiments is known, albeit summarily, but in all probability this conformed to that of the Celle cavalry, with which the Osnabrück contingent participated in the military campaigns from 1675 to 1678.

4 – Hessen-Darmstadt, *Riedesel zu Pferde*, Trooper, 1677

Friedrich Hild, in *Militärchronik des Großherzogthums Hessen von Anfang des Regierenden Hauses bis auf die neueste Zeit – 1567–1790* (Darmstadt: Friedrich Hild, 1828) notes that in 1677, the regiment received dark blue coats lined in grey-white. This referred only to troopers and NCOs, however, since the same author adds that the officers tailored the uniforms according to their own taste.

Plate I – Cavalry and Dragoons, 1680s–1690s

1 – Würzburg, *Truchsess Cuirassieren* (WzC-2), *Rittmeister*, 1683–85

Records and other information on the Würzburg cavalry uniforms state that these followed the Austrian and Southern Germany models. The regiment *Truchsess* passed into the Imperial Army in 1685, and a few years later the uniform is recorded as buff coat with black cuffs.

2 – Hessen-Kassel, *Prinz Philipp Dragoner* (BkD-1) Corporal, 1684

The three dragoon regiments of Hessen-Kassel wore colourful uniforms compared to the cavalry. In 1688 there were regiments with yellow, red and blue uniforms, later also grey-white, with saddle covers of the facing colour. The headwear had a white edging for NCOs. Because they were mounted

Officer's sword, probably German, *c.* 1650–1660. (Private Collection, Italy) Double-edged, slightly lenticular blade with decorative engraving on both sides and mottos under a Turk's hand with a sabre. Iron knuckle-bow hilt with ornamental finials, a crushed ball pommel and a parrying guard with an iron-driven guard plate. Cross guard end and winding missing, thumb ring on the back. Length 92cm.

Officer's sword, *c.* 1630–1660 (Private Collection, Italy). Double-edged, ridged blade with a Passau's wolf on both sides. Iron hilt engraved and punched with floral designs on the front. Iron knuckle-bow hilt with a large guard ring and openwork guard plate. Heart-shaped, ridged pommel with small pommel. Old moulded brass wire grip winding with Turk's heads. Cleaned, patina and stained on the back. Length 100.5cm.

infantrymen, the dragoons carried flintlocks and bayonets. As for the cavalry, the universal leather coat or *Koller* was gradually replaced by grey coats by the late 1670s. Breeches were of leather. In the same years, the 'lobster-pot' helmets were also replaced by the broad-brimmed hat, probably reinforced with an iron secret. Privates were still protected by a blackened cuirass in the 1670s and 1680s. Cuffed gauntlets of leather covered hands and the lower arm. Grey-white cavalry cloaks protected the horsemen against the rain and cold weather. The troopers were armed with the broadsword or *Pallasch*, suspended from a broad baldric. Two pistols and a carbine completed the armament. Behind the saddle a saddlebag containing the cloak was attached.

3 – Brunswick-Wolfenbüttel, *Lippe Dragoner* (BwD-3), Dragoon, 1688–89

In 1688, Hertzogs Rudolf August and Anton Ulrich recruited a regiment of dragoons after the last one had been disbanded three years before. At the siege of Mainz, a clothing reference states a red coat, but no mention is made of the lining colour, so it may be assumed that cuffs were also of red.

4 – The Palatinate, *Leibregiment zu Pferde* (kpc-i), Trooper, 1685–90

With the union of the Palatinate and Pfalz-Neuburg in 1685, the army was amalgamated with companies and regiments of the two states. With rank and file from Pfalz-Neuburg, the new cavalry *Leibregiment* was formed and quartered in Heidelberg and Düsseldorf. The uniform remained the one issued to the regiment of Pfalz-Neuburg in 1682.

Württemberg cavalry officer, Swabian *Kreisregiment* Hönstett, 1683, in a nineteenth century illustration from the Vinkhuijzen Collection of Military Uniforms (New York Public Library). Black headwear with red and white feather, blue-grey coat with white lining and cuffs laced in gold, white cravat and ribbons. The waist scarf is white, but it is likely that the officers of the Swabian Circle wore red, which was the distinctive colour of the *Reichsarmee*.

Plate J – Life Guards

1 – Lorraine, *Mousquetaires de la Garde* (loc-iii), 1664–69

There is some uncertainty about the year of formation of this company, but certainly the *Mousquetaires* became a prestigious unit of life guard. According to Jean-Charles Fulaine, in *Le Duc Charles IV de Lorraine et son Armée*, the uniforms was based on the one worn by the coeval French counterpart of the *Maison du Roi*, with red and yellow instead of blue and red. Despite the short existence of the company, the presence of a *maréchal des logis* and a *brigadier* emphasised the special status of the company, which was assimilated into the other mounted life guards. However, like their French model, it also performed service on foot. Although no trace of the company's role exists in the Lorraine archives, and virtually no information about the men who made up the company, the names of their wives and companions were constantly updated. In total, 56 female names are recorded, all residing in Nancy. The Duke showed interest in their plight as demonstrated by the affair of Suzanne Usurlot. She was the wife of musketeer Nicolas Ada, known as *La Plume*, who had been in the duke's service for 28 (or 30) years, had been wounded in the brief war against the Palatinate, and was hospitalised, infirm, in Bingen. Suzanne was alone in Nancy with five children and therefore sent a petition to the Duke for assistance. On 11 November 1668, the sovereign rewarded her with foodstuffs and a pension to be paid until *La Plume* recovered. In 1669, being the youngest unit of the life guard, the company was disbanded after Louis XIV reiterated the dissolution of the Lorraine Army. In a sign of protest against the disarmament imposed by Louis XIV, the duke had his Life Guards distributed with sticks instead of weapons.

2 – Hessen-Darmstadt, *Leibgarde zu Ross* (hdc-i), 1668

Occasionally, Galeazzo Gualdo Priorato provides interesting information about military uniforms in the 1660s. As for the life guards of Hessen-Darmstadt, he refers to *tomassine* of blue cloth lined with red with the livery of Darmstadt, presumably white-red-blue. The company was raised in 1648 and at several times the *Leibgarde zu Ross* were the only regular cavalry.

Zischägge/'lobster-pot' helmet, South German manufactured 1650–1660. (Private Collection, Germany)

3 – Celle, *Garde zu Pferd*, 1670–1675

Early sources states that the Household troops of Celle had worn carmine uniforms since the 1660s. The black facings remained the distinctive colour of the Celle mounted Life Guards in the next century. In the 1670s, back and breast armour was issued on campaign to troopers only.

4 – Württemberg, *Leibgarde des Herzogs* (wüc-i), 1673

According to Leo Ignaz Stadlinger, *Geschichte des Württembergischen Kriegswesens von der Frühesten bis zur Neuesten Zeit*, the only difference between the *Leibgarde* of the Crown Prince and that of the duke was that the former had black armour and helmet with brass accessories (gold for officers). Further distinctions were laces and fittings of bandolier and baldrics, of yellow for the duke's company, and of silver for the one of the crown prince. The standards also identified the companies; white with golden embroidery for the former, and silver for the latter.

Appendix I

The German Empire: The 'Immediate States' in 1649

Secular Electorates:

State:	Ruling Dynasty:	Domains in the *Reich*:	Extension in Geographic Square Miles:	Esteemed Population in 1648:
Bavaria	Bavarian Wittelsbach	Duchies of Bavaria and Upper Palatinate, County of Haag and Lordship of Mindelheim-Schwenk, and Wiesensteig	653.5	1,500,000
Brandenburg	Brandenburg Hohenzollern	Margravate of Brandenburg, Duchy of Pomerania, Duchy of Cleves, Counties of Mark, Ravensburg, Minden, condominium on the County of Hohnstein	651.8	1,280,000
Saxony	Wettin (Albertine Branch)	Duchy of Saxony, Margravate of Upper and Lower Lusatia, Landgraviate of Thuringia, Margravate of Meissen, counties* of Gommen and Burg	594	650,000
Palatinate	Wittelsbach-Simmern	Rhenish Palatinate, Principalities of Simmern and Lautern, Lordship of Ehrenfels; condominium on the principality of Veldenz and the county of Sponnheim	110.2	220,000

Ecclesiastical Electorates:

	State:	Ruling Prince:	Domains in the *Reich*:	Extension:	Population:[1]
CO	Cologne	Prince-Bishop Elector	Chapter of Cologne, Duchy of Westphalia, Prevostship of Recklinghausen	131.6	120,000
MA	Mainz	Prince-Bishop Elector	Chapter of Mainz, the town of Erfurt, part of the Lordship of Königstein	123.2	168,000
TR	Trier	Prince-Bishop Elector	Chapter of Trier, Abbey of Prüm, part of the Lordship of Lower Ysenburg and condominium of Merzig	121.2	145,000

1 Estimated population in the second half of the seventeenth century.

Secular Principalities:

	State:	Ruling Prince:	Domains in the *Reich*:	Extension:	Population:
1	Anhalt-Dessau	Princes (Ascanien)	Condominium on the Principality of Anhalt	48.6	64,000
2	Anhalt-Bernburg				
3	Anhalt-Harzgerode				
4	Anhalt-Köthen				
5	Anhalt-Zerbst		as above, and the Lordship of Jever		
6	Ansbach	Margrave (Franconian Hohenzollern)	Principality of Ansbach	62.7	122,000
7	Baden-Baden	Margrave (Zähringen of Baden)	Condominium on the Margravate of Baden, County of Eherstein, Prevostship of Ortenau, and condominium on the county of Sponnheim	35	47,000
8	Baden-Durlach	Margrave (Zähringen of Durlach)	Condominium on the Margravate of Baden, Margravate of Hochberg	29	36,000
9	Bayreuth	Margrave (Franconian Hohenzollern)	Principality of Bayreuth-Kulmbach	57.5	61,000
10	Braunschweig-Wolfenbüttel	Duke (Welfen of Brunswick)	Duchy of Wolfenbüttel, principality of Blankenberg, chapter of Walkenried	64.5	108,000
11	Hessen-Kassel	Landgrave	Principality of Hersfeld, condominium on the Landgraviate of Hessen, and on the counties of Henneberg and Schaumburg	129.5	156,000
12	Hessen-Darmstadt	Landgrave	Principalities of Homburg, condominium as above	79.5	92,000
13	Holstein-Gottorf	Duke	Condominium on the duchy of Schleswig-Holstein and the Lordship of Pinneburg	60	70,000
14	Holstein-Plön	Duke	Condominium on the county of Oldenburg, Lordship of Sodenburg and county of Rantzau	18	7.500
15	Lorraine	Duke (Guise)	Duchy of Lorraine, Margravate of Nomeny, County of Falkenstein and condominium of Merzig	327.9	400,000
16	Lüneburg Celle	Duke (Welfen of Lüneburg)	Principality of Celle, Duchy of Lautenburg, condominium on the county of Hoya	256.5	131,000
17	Lüneburg Calenberg	Duke (Welfen of Lüneburg)	Principalities of Calenberg and Grübenhagen, County of Diepholz, condominium on the Counties of Hoya and Hohnstein	133	148,000
18	Limburg-Styrum	Counts	Lordship of Gehmen	1	1,000
19	Mecklenburg-Güstrow	Duke	Principality of Güstrow, condominium on the Duchy of Mecklenburg and Ratzeburg	279.6	185,000
20	Mecklenburg-Schwerin	Duke	Principality of Schwerin, condominium on the Duchy of Mecklenburg and Ratzeburg		
21	Oldenburg	Duke (the King of Denmark from 1667)	Counties of Oldenburg and Delmenhorst, condominium on the duchy of Schleswig-Holstein and the Lordship of Pinneburg	124.6	50,000

22	Pfalz-Birkenfeld	Prince (Palatine Wittelsbach)	Condominium on the Principality of Veldenz and the County of Sponnheim	7	9,000
23	Pfalz-Neuburg	Duke (Palatine Wittelsbach)	Princupality of Neuburg, duchies of Jülich and Berg,	131.3	245,000
24	Pfalz-Sulzbach	Duke (Palatine Wittelsbach)	Principality of Sulzbach and condominium on the Principality of Veldenz	28.2	23,000
25	Pfalz-Zweibrücken	Duke (Wittelsbach-Zweibrücken – The King of Sweden from 1654)	Principality of Zweibrücken	36	35,000
26	Öst-Friesland	Prince	Principality of Öst-Friesland and Lordship on the Harlingerland	54	51,000
27	Sachsen-Coburg	Dukes (Ernestine-Wettin)	Condominium on the Ernestine-Thuringia territories and the County of Henneberg	121.2	176,000
28	Sachsen-Gotha				
29	Sachsen-Altenburg		as above, and the County of Sayn-Altenkirchen		
30	Sachsen-Weimar				
31	Sachsen-Lauenburg	Duke (Ascanien of Ratzenburg)	Duchy of Lauenburg	6	9,500
32	Tirol	Archduke (Habsburg)	Archduchy and County of Tirol	17.4	70.000
33	Württemberg	Duke	Duchy of Württemberg	151.5	120,000

Secular Lordships:

	State:	**Ruling Prince:**	**Domains in the *Reich*:**	**Extension:**	**Population:**
34	Aldenburg	Count	Lordship of Knipphausen	0,2	1,500
35	Arenberg	Duke	Duchy of Arenberg	8	2,700
36	Aspremont-Linden	Count	County of Reckheim	1.5	1,400
37	Auersperg	Prince	Principality of Thengen	0.5	400
38	Bentheim-Bentheim	Counts	County of Bentheim	16.75	12,000
39	Bentheim-Tecklenburg		a quarter of the County of Tecklenburg and three quarter of the Lordship of Rheda	3	4,800
40	Bentheim-Steinfurt	Count	County of Steinfurt	3.4	2,700
41	Bronkhorst.Gronsfeld	Count	County of Gronsfeld	1	900
42	Castell	Count	County of Castell	3.4	5,000
43	Croy	Duke	Lordship of Mylendonk	0.75	800
44	Detlev	Count	County of Rantzau	4.5	6,500
45	Dietrichstein	Prince	Lordship of Trasp	0.5	500

46	Erbach	Count	County of Erbach and and condominium on the Lordship of Breuberg	11.8	15,000
47	Freyberg	Baron	Lordship of Justingen	0.5	650
48	Fugger	Counts	Counties of Kirchberg and Weisserhorn, Lordships of Weisserburg and other in Swabia	13.2	12,500
49	Fürstenberg-Heiligenberg	Prince-Count	County of Heiligenberg, Lordships of Trochtelfingen and Jungnau	4	6,500
50	Fürstenberg-Mösskirch	Landgraves and Counts	Lordships of Mösskirch, Hausen and Grundelfingen	11.2	12,000
51	Fürstenberg-Stühlingen		Landgravate of Stühlingen and Baar	21	20,800
52	Geyer	Count	County of Geyer	2	2,000
53	Grafeneck	Baron	Lordship of Eglingen	1	1,400
54	Grotte	Baron	Lordship of Schauen	0.75	600
55	Hessen-Hanau	Count	Counties of Münzenberg and Lichtenberg	25	40,000
56	Hohenembs	Count	County of Hohenems	3.5	1,300
57	Hohenlohe-Öhringen	Counts	Condominium of the County of Hohenlohe	34.8	51,000
	Hohenlohe-Neunstein				
	Hohenlohe-Pfedelbach				
	Hohenlohe – Schillingfurst				
	Hohenlohe-Langenburg				
	Hohenlohe-Bartenstein				
58	Hohenzollern-Hechingen	Princes (Hohenzollern)	County of Hohenzollern	4.5	5,400
59	Hohenzollern-Sigmaringen		County of Sigmaringen and Lordship of Haigerloch	6	8,600
60	Holzapfel	Count	County of Holzapfel	3	3,000
61	Hillesheim	Count	Lordship of Reipoltskirchen	2	3,000
62	Kannitz	Count	County of Rietberg	4	6,500
63	Kirchberg	Count	County of Sayn-Hachtenburg	2	4,000
64	Königseck-Aulendorf	Counts	County of Königseck and Lordship of Aulendorf	5.5	1,600
65	Königseck-Rothenfels		County of Rothenfels	8.12	5,700
66	Kronberg	Count	County of Kronberg	0.8	900
67	Leuchtenberg	Landgrave (Wittelsbach)	Duchy of Leuchtenberg	4	2,600
68	Leiningen	Count (Old Branch)	Lordship of Westerburg and Schadock	2.5	3,500
69		Count (Jung Branch)	County of Leiningen and Lordship of Oberstein	11	12,000
70	Leyen	Count	Lordships of Hohen-Gerolsdseck	2.5	2.300
71	Liechtenstein	Prince	Lordships of Vaduz and Schellenberg	2.9	2,500
72	Ligne	Prince	Lordship of Fagnolles	0.25	300
73	Limpurg	Count	Lordships of Limpurg, Welzheim, Hausen and Sontheim	8	8,500
74	Lippe-Detmold	Count	Condominium on the County of Lippe	20	35,000
75	Lippe-Brack	Count			

<table>
<tr><td>76</td><td>Löwenstein-Rochefort</td><td>Count</td><td>Condominium on the County of Wertheim and on the Lordship of Bregenz</td><td>6.5</td><td>6,500</td></tr>
<tr><td>77</td><td>Löwenstein-Virneburg</td><td>Count</td><td>Condominium on the County of Wertheim, Lordship of Virneburg</td><td>6.5</td><td>7,000</td></tr>
<tr><td>78</td><td>Lobkowitz</td><td>Prince</td><td>Principality of Sternstein</td><td>2</td><td>1,500</td></tr>
<tr><td>79</td><td>Manderscheid</td><td>Count</td><td>Counties of Blankenheim and Gerolstein</td><td>7.5</td><td>7,500</td></tr>
<tr><td>80</td><td>Mark-Limay</td><td>Count</td><td>County of Schleiden</td><td>3</td><td>2,500</td></tr>
<tr><td>81</td><td>Metternich</td><td>Count</td><td>County of Winneburg and Beilstein</td><td>4</td><td>5,000</td></tr>
<tr><td>82</td><td>Mömpelgard</td><td>Count (Württemberg minor branch)</td><td>County of Mömpelgard</td><td>7</td><td>7,000</td></tr>
<tr><td>83</td><td>Montfort</td><td>Baron</td><td>Lordships of Tettnang and Argen</td><td>1.5</td><td>1,800</td></tr>
<tr><td>84</td><td>Nassau-Saarbrück</td><td rowspan="3">Counts (Nassau-Walram)</td><td>Counties of Saarbrück and Usingen, Lordship of Ottweiler</td><td>22</td><td>24,000</td></tr>
<tr><td>85</td><td>Nassau-Idstein</td><td>Lordships of Idstein, Wiesbaden and Lahr</td><td>12</td><td>13,500</td></tr>
<tr><td>86</td><td>Nassau-Weilburg</td><td>County of Weilburg, Lordships of Kirchenheim and Mehrenburg</td><td>12.20</td><td>33,000</td></tr>
<tr><td>87</td><td>Nassau-Dietz</td><td rowspan="5">Princes (Nassau-Otto)</td><td>Condominium on the County of Dietz</td><td>8</td><td>12,000</td></tr>
<tr><td>88</td><td>Nassau-Dillenburg</td><td>Principality of Dillenburg</td><td>12</td><td>19,000</td></tr>
<tr><td>89</td><td>Nassau-Hadamar</td><td>Principality of Hadamar and Lordship of Beilstein</td><td>6</td><td>9,000</td></tr>
<tr><td>90</td><td>Nassau-Orange</td><td>County of Mörs and Lingen, and condominium on the County of Dietz,</td><td>14.5</td><td>21,400</td></tr>
<tr><td>91</td><td>Nassau-Siegen</td><td>Principality of Siegen</td><td>14</td><td>20,000</td></tr>
<tr><td>92</td><td>Nesselrode</td><td>Baron</td><td>Lordship of Reichenstein</td><td>1</td><td>1,000</td></tr>
<tr><td>93</td><td>Nostitz</td><td>Count</td><td>County of Rieneck</td><td>1</td><td>700</td></tr>
<tr><td>94</td><td>Ortenburg</td><td>Count</td><td>County of Ortenburg</td><td>1.7</td><td>1,600</td></tr>
<tr><td>95</td><td>Öttingen-Baldern</td><td rowspan="3">Counts</td><td>Condominium on the County of Öttingen, Lordship of Dachstuhl</td><td rowspan="3">27</td><td rowspan="3">31,000</td></tr>
<tr><td rowspan="2">96</td><td>Öttingen-Spielberg</td><td rowspan="2">Condominium on the County of Öttingen</td></tr>
<tr><td>Öttingen-Wallerstein</td></tr>
<tr><td>97</td><td>Quadt</td><td>Baron</td><td>Lordship of Wickerad</td><td>1.5</td><td>1,200</td></tr>
<tr><td>98</td><td>Reuss-Plauen</td><td>Counts (Old Branch)</td><td rowspan="4">Condominium on the Counties of Reuss and Plauen, and on the Lordships of Gera, Schleitz, Lobenstein and Greitz</td><td rowspan="4">20</td><td rowspan="4">27,000</td></tr>
<tr><td rowspan="3">99</td><td>Reuss-Gera</td><td rowspan="3">Counts (Jung Branch)</td></tr>
<tr><td>Reuss-Schleitz</td></tr>
<tr><td>Reuss-Lobenstein</td></tr>
<tr><td rowspan="4">100</td><td>Salm-Salm</td><td>Prince-Count</td><td>County of Salm, Lordship of Anholt, and condominium on the Rheingravate and Raugravate</td><td>11.8</td><td>11,000</td></tr>
<tr><td>Salm-Dhaun</td><td rowspan="3">Princes</td><td rowspan="3">Condominium on the Rheingravate and Raugravate</td><td rowspan="3">7.5</td><td rowspan="3">7,500</td></tr>
<tr><td>Salm-Grunbach</td></tr>
<tr><td>Salm-Stein</td></tr>
</table>

101	Schwarzenberg	Prince	Principality of Schwarzenberg-Seinsheim, Landgravate of Klettgau, Lordship of Gimborn and Neustadt	15	19,000
102	Schwarzburg-Sonderhausen	Counts	Condominium on the County of Schwarzburg and Hohnstein	15.6	23,000
103	Schwarzburg-Rudolstadt			17.6	25,000
104	Schaumburg-Lippe	Count	Condominium on the Counties of Schaumburg and Lippe	8.5	10,000
105	Schönborn	Count	Lordship of Wiesentheid	3.2	3,300
106	Sinzendorf	Counts	Burgavate of Rheineck, Lordships of Tannhausen and Warthausen	1.9	2,000
107	Solms-Brauenfels	Count	Condominium on the County of Solms, three quarter of the county Tecklenburg and one quarter of the Lordship of Rheda	9.1	9,500
108	Solms-Laubach	Counts	Condominium on the County of Solms	4.7	6,000
109	Stolberg	Counts	Condominium on the County of Königstein	2.2	2,400
110	Tilly	Counts	Lordship of Breiteneck	0.5	1,000
111	Traun-Abensberg	Baron	Lordships of Egloff and Siegen	1.3	750
112	Truchsess-Waldburg	Count	County of Waldburg	20.5	16,000
113	Veelen	Count	Lordship of Bretzenheim	1	900
114	Waldbott-Bassenheim	Baron	Lordships of Ollbrück, Bassenheim and Pyrmont	1	1,000
115	Waldeck	Prince (Branch of Eisenberg) Prince (Branch of Wildungen)	Counties of Waldeck and Pyrmont, Lordships of Wittem, Eiss and Schlenacken	21.1	23,000
116	Wartenberg	Counts	County of Wartenberg	2	1,300
117	Wied	Count (Branch of Runkel)	County of Kriechingen, condominium on the Counties of Wied and Nieder-Ysenburg	8	13,000
		Count (Jung Branch)	Condominium on the County of Wied	3	6,000
118	Wittgenstein	Count (Old Branch)	Condominium on the County of Wittgenstein, Lordship of Homburg	9	8,500
		Count (Jung Branch)	Condominium on the County of Wittgenstein	5	7,000
119	Wolfstein	Count	Lordships of Sulzburg and Pyrbaum	2	2,300
120	Ysenburg	Counts	Condominium on the Counties of Upper and Lower Ysenburg	10.7	21,000

Imperial Knigthsips (*Reichsritterschaft*)

	Ritterkreis	Canton:	Extension:	Population:
121		Danube		
122		Heggau, Algau and on Bodensee		
123	Swabia	Neckar, Schwarzwald and in the Ortenau	70	80,000
124		on Kocher		
125		im Kreichgau		
126		Odenwald		
127		Steigerwald		
128		im Gebirg		
129	Franconia	Altmühl	80	100,000
130		Baurach		
131		Rhönwerra		
132		Oberrhein		
133	Rhenish	Mittelrhein	11	45,000
134		Niederrhein		

Ecclesiastical Lordships and Abbeys:

	State	Ruling Prince:	Extension:	Population:
Mb	Magdeburg[2]	Prince-Archbishop	38	25,000
Sa	Salzburg	Prince-Archbishop	171	85,000
Au	Augsburg	Prince-Bishop	43	46,000
Ba	Bamberg	Prince-Bishop	65	91,000
Be	Besançon	Prince-Bishop	9.6	8,000
Bs	Basel	Prince-Bishop	13.5	28,500
Bx	Brixen	Prince-Bishop	17	13,000
Ei	Eichstädt	Prince-Bishop	20	28,000
Fr	Freysing	Prince-Bishop	15	15,000
Hi	Hildesheim	Prince-Bishop	40	61,000
Ko	Konstanz	Prince-Bishop	5	5,500
Lü	Lübeck	Prince-Bishop	6.6	40,000
Li	Liège	Prince-Bishop	105	110,000
Mü	Münster	Prince-Bishop	220	250,000
Os	Osnabrück	Prince-Bishop	56	82,000
Pa	Paderborn	Prince-Bishop	15	30,000
Ps	Passau	Prince-Bishop	50	47,000

2 Annexe to Brandenburg in 1689.

Re	Regensburg	Prince-Bishop	4.1	15,500
Sp	Speyer	Prince-Bishop	28	25,000
St	Strasbourg	Prince-Bishop	13.5	20,000
Tr	Trent	Prince-Bishop	75	74,000
Wo	Worms	Prince-Bishop	3.5	14,000
Wü	Würzburg	Prince-Bishop	96	150,000
135	Berchtesgaden	Prince-Abbot	10	10,000
136	Buchau	Prince-Abbot	1.7	1,500
137	Corvey	Prince-Abbot	5	5,000
138	Ellwangen	Prince-Abbot	6.7	9,000
139	Essen	Prince-Abbot	3	4,000
140	Fulda	Prince-Abbot	32.5	45,000
141	Lindau	Prince-Abbot	0.5	300
142	St. Blasien	Prince-Abbot	4.5	3,700
143	St. Gallen	Prince-Abbot	0.5	400
144	Kempten	Prince-Abbot	16	21,000
145	Ochsenhausen	Prince-Abbot	4	4,000
146	Stavelot and Malmedy	Prince-Abbot	3	3,500
147	Thorn	Prince-Abbot	1.5	1,500
148	Werden	Prince-Abbot	1	2,500
149	Quedlinburg	Prince-Abbess	14.3	8,382
150	Cornelius-Münster	Prevost	2	4,000
151	Elchingen	Prevost	2.5	2,000
152	Gengenbach	Prevost	1	750
153	Kaisersheim	Prevost	3	3,000
154	Marchtal	Prevost	3	2,800
155	Odenheim	Prevost	2	2,000
156	Ottobeuren	Prevost	5	6,000
157	Petershausen	Prevost	1.5	1,700
158	Reggenburg	Prevost	2.5	2,400
159	Roth	Prevost	1.5	1,400
160	Salmansweiler	Prevost	4.5	4.500
161	Schussenried	Prevost	2	1,500
162	Ursperg	Prevost	1.7	1,800
163	Yrsee	Prevost	2	2,200
164	Weingarten	Prevost	7.5	6,500
165	Weissenhau	Prevost	1	700
166	Wettenhausen	Prevost	2	2,500
167	Baind	Abbess	0.1	100
168	Burscheid	Abbess	1	1,000
169	Elten	Abbess	0.5	800

170	Gutenzell	Abbess	1.6	1,000
171	Hegbach	Abbess	1.7	1,400
172	Rothmünster	Abbess	1.5	1,500
-	The Teutonic Order	-	15.5	22,000
-	The St. John Order of Malta	-	2	3,000

Imperial Free-Cities and Villages:

City:	**Extension:**	**Population:**
Aalen	1	2,000
Aachen	1	13,000
Augsburg	2	30,000
Biberach	2.5	5,000
Bopfingen	0.75	900
Bremen	4.7	60,000
Buchau	0.25	600
Buchhorn	0.5	500
Cologne	1	27,000
Dinkelsbühl	1	4,000
Dortmund	0.75	5,500
Esslingen	0.75	5,000
Frankfurt am Main	4	25,000
Friedberg	1	1,500
Gengenbach	0.5	300
Giengen	0.25	1,000
Gmünd	3	3,000
Gosslar	0.5	4,000
Hall	6	9,000
Hamburg	6.4	98,000
Heilbronn	1.8	5.500
Illkirch	1	2,500
Isni	1	1,000
Kaufbeuren	2	3,500
Kempten	0.75	1,800
Königshofen	1.1	1,500
Landau	1.3	1,900
Leutkirch	1	9,000
Lindau	2	2,400
Lübeck	6.26	40,000
Memmingen	2	5,500

Mühlhausen	4	7,500
Nordhausen	0.5	5,000
Nördlingen	1.5	4,000
Nuremberg	20	40,000
Offenburg	0.25	2,000
Pfullendorf	1	2,000
Ravensburg	2.5	3,000
Regensburg	1	11,000
Reutlingen	1	5,000
Rostock	5.6	18,000
Rothenburg	6	13,000
Rothweil	4	7,000
Schweinfurth	2	3,000
Speier	0.5	3,400
Strasbourg	4.5	22,000
Überlingen	1.25	3,500
Ulm	14	10,000
Wangen	1.5	2,000
Weil	0.25	900
Weissenburg	1	3,200
Wetzlar	0.5	3,500
Wimpffen	0.25	1,400
Windsheim	1	2,000
Worms	1	4,000
Zell am Hammersbach	1	2,500

45 further Imperial Free-Villages and Free-Communities.
Geographic Square Miles; 1 GSM = 3.442 Square Kilometres.

Bibliography

Archival Sources

Bayerische Bavarian Staatsarchiv and Kriegsarchiv
Niedersachsen Hauptstaatsarchiv Hannover (NSHa)
Hessisches Staatsarchiv Marburg
Landesarchiv Sachsen-Anhalt: *Abteilung Dessau*
Münster State Archive, *Archiv Galen*

Contemporary Sources

Anonymous, *Relation des violences exercées au Palatinat, à la fin de l'année 1673 & au commencement de 1674* (Cologne: 1675).

Anonymous, *Neben-Ordonnanz In dem Hertzogthumb Württemberg: Nach der allgemeinen, de dato Wien, den 11. Septembris diß Jahrs, außgegangenen und Publicirten Käyserl. Ordonnanz: und darauff von deß Hochlöbl. Schw äbischen Cräyses Ständen, [et]c. erfolgtem Schluß, eingerichtet* (Stuttgart: 1677)

Anonymous, *Historisch, Merkwürdige Beyträge zur Kriegs-Geschichte des Grossen Churfüsten Freidrich Wilhelms in der Lebenbeschreibung Otto Christoph Freyherrn v. Sparr* (Stendal, 1793).

Beck, Wilhelm, *Die neuere Kriegsgeschichte der Hessen: in Beschränkter Beziehung auf den izt bestehenden Landgräflich Hessischen Kriegsstaat, vom Anfang seiner Errichtung bis zum Jahr 1730* (Marburg: 1790),

Chapuzeau, Samuel, *Rélation De L'Estat Present De La Maison Electorale Et De La Cour De Baviere* (Paris: 1673).

Gualdo Priorato, Galeazzo, *Relatione della Corte e Stati del Serenissimo Ferdinando Maria Elettore di Baviera* (Leyden: 1668).

Gualdo Priorato, Galeazzo, *Relatione delle Corti e Stati delli Serenissimi Landgravii d'Hassia in Kassel e Darmstadt, contenente anche le relationi della Città e Repubblica di Colonia, del Vescovato e Principato di Herbipoli, dell'Arcivescovato e Principato di Magonza, dell'Arcivescovato et Elettorato di Colonia, del Vescovato e Principato di Munster, del Vescovato e Principato di Osnabruch* (Leyden: 1668).

Gualdo Priorato, Galeazzo, *Relatione degli Stati del Serenissimo Filippo Guglielmo Duca di Juliers, Neuburg, etc.* (Cologne: 1668)

Gualdo Priorato, Galeazzo, *Relatione del Governo, e Stato delle Città Imperiali di Norimberg, Augusta, Ulm e Francoforte* (Cologne: 1668)

Gualdo Priorato, Galeazzo, *Relatione della Corte e Stati del Serenissimo Gustavo Adolfo Duca di Meckelemburg* (Cologne: 1669)

Gualdo Priorato, Galeazzo, *Relatione degli Stati del Serenissimo Christiano Alberto duca di Holstein e Schlesvvic* (Cologne: 1669)

Gualdo Priorato, Galeazzo, *Relationi delle Città Imperiali & Anseatiche di Colonia, Lubecca, Bremen, & Amburgo, (…) delle Corti e Stati de' Serenissimi Elettor di Baviera, e de' Langravi d'Hassia in Kassel e Darmstadt* (Bologna: 1674)

Gualdo Priorato, Galeazzo, *Vita et azzioni di Guglielmo Quinto, principe landgravio d'Hassia* (Vienna: 1674)

Gude, Heinrich Ludwig, *Nachricht von der Stadt Bremen* (Halle:1700)

Gude, Heinrich Ludwig, *Nachricht von der Stadt Hamburg* (Halle: 1701)

Gude, Heinrich Ludwig, *Staat der Chur und Fürstlichen Hauser Braunschweig-Lüneburg* (Halle: 1701)

Gude, Heinrich Ludwig, *Staat der Fürsten zu Anhalt mit einem Anhang von Herzogtum Sachsen-Lauenburg* (Halle, before 1708)

Gude, Heinrich Ludwig, *Nachricht von der Stadt Lübeck* (Halle, before 1708)

Gude, Heinrich Ludwig, *Staat der Marck-Graffen von Baden-Baden und Baden-Durlach* (Halle, before 1708)

Gude, Heinrich Ludwig, *Staat von Chur-Pfalz* (Halle, before 1708)

Gude, Heinrich Ludwig, *Des Hochfürstl. Landgrafs. Hessischen Staats* (Halle, before 1708)

Gude, Heinrich Ludwig, *Staat der Fünff Teutschen Erb Bischöffe als des Erb Bischöffen und Chur-Fürsten zu Mainz, Trier und Köln, dann der Erb Bischöffen zu Salzburg und Besançon. Ingleichen des Hoch Meisters Teutschen Ordens* (Halle, before 1708)

Gude, Heinrich Ludwig, *Staat der Herzoge von Mecklenburg* (Halle, before 1708)

Gude, Heinrich Ludwig, *Staat der Herzogthümer Schleswig-Holstein und des bishoffthums von Lübeck* (Halle, before 1708)

Gude, Heinrich Ludwig, *Staat der Herzoge von Württemberg* (Halle, before 1708)

Meinardus, Oskar (editor) *Protokolle und Relationen der Brandenburgische Geheimen Rathes aus der Zeit der Kurfürsten Friedrich Wilhelm*, bande I-VII (Leipzig: Hirzel, 1889–1919)

Pufendorf, Samuel von, *An Introduction to the History of the Principal Kingdoms and States of Europe, translated by Jodocus Crull* (Frankfurt am Main: Friedrich Knocken, 1695)

General Sources

Ackermann, Jürgen, *Verschuldung, Reichsdebitverwaltung, Mediatisierung*, from the series *Schriften des Hessischen Landesamtes für Geschichtliche Landeskunde, Das Beispiel der Grafschaft Ysenburg-Büdingen 1687–1806* (Marburg: Selbstverlag des Hessischen Landesamtes für geschichtliche Landeskunde 40, 2002)

Aretin, Karl Otmar, von, *Das Altes Reich, 1648–1806* (Stuttgart: Klett-Cotta, 1993)

Eickhoff, Ekkehard, *Venedig, Wien und die Osmanen: Umbruch in Südosteuropa, 1645–1700* (Munich: Klett-Cotta, 1973)

Luard, Evan, *The Balance of Power: The System of International Relations, 1648–1815* (London: Palgrave Macmillan, 1992)

Dollinger, Philippe, *Die Hanse* (Stuttgart: Alfred Kröner, 2012)

Dotzauer, Winfried, *Die deutschen Reichskreise 1383–1806* (Stuttgart: Franz Steiner, 1998)

Duchhardt, Heinz, *Altes Reich und europäische Staatenwelt, 1648–1806* (Munich: De Gruyter Oldenburg, 1990)

Whaley, Joachim, *Germany and the Holy Roman Empire. Vol. 2: from the Peace of Westphalia to the Dissolution of the Reich. 1648–1806* (Oxford & New York: Oxford University Press, 2012)

Wilson, P. H. and Evans R. J. W. (eds), *The Holy Roman Empire, 1495–1806: A European Perspective* (Leiden & Boston: Brill, 2012)

Zürcher, Erik-Jan (ed.), *Fighting for a Living. A Comparative History of Military Labour 1500–2000* (Amsterdam: Amsterdam University Press, 2003)

German Military History

Belaubre, Jean and Golberg, Claus-Peter, *Les Armées qui Combattirent Louis 14: Le Cercle du Rhin Supérieur*, (Paris: Privately Published, 1974)

Bredow, Claus von, *Historische Rang-und Stammliste des Deutschen Heeres* (Berlin: Biblio Verlag, 1905)

Brunner, Karl, *Der Pfälzische Wildfangstreit unter Kurfürft Karl Ludwig (1664–1667)* (Innsbruck: Wagner´schen Universität-Buchhandlung, 1896)

Dalwigk zu Lichtenfeld, Friedrich Freiherr von: *Geschichte der Waldeckischen und Kurhessischen Stammtruppen des Infanterie-Regiments von Wittich, Nr. 83. 1681–1866* (Oldenburg: Publisher not given, 1909)

Fester, Richard, *Die Augsburger Allianz von 1686* (Munich: Rieger, 1893)

Fester, Richard, *Die Armirten Stände und die Reichskriegsverfassung, 1681–1697* (Frankfurt am Main, Gebrüder Knauer (Druck), 1886)

Fiebig, Ewald, *Unsterbliche Treue. Das Heldenlied der Fahnen und Standarten des Deutschen Heeres* (Berlin: Wilhelm Andermann,1936)

Flurschütz da Cruz, Andreas, *Der Krieg der Anderen. Venedig, die deutschen Reichsfürsten und die Anfänge internationaler Subsidienprojekte in der Frühen Neuzeit* (Paderborn: Brill Schöningh 2024)

Goerlitz, Walter, *History of the German General Staff, 1657–1945* (New York: Barnes & Noble, 1995)

Janke, Arthur, *Die Belagerungen der Stadt Trier in den Jahren 1673 bis 1675 und die Schlacht an der Conzer Brücke am 11. August 1675* (Trier: Lintz,1890)

Knötel, Herbert and Richard: *Mittheilungen zur Geschichte der Militärischen Tracht – Beiträge zur Uniformkunde*, (Rathenow: Max Babenzien, 1892)

Knötel, Richard, *Die Grosse Uniformenkunde*, Bande I–XVIII (Rathenow: Max Babenzien, 1890-1914)

Knötel, Richard and Sieg, Herbert, *Farbiges Handbuch der Uniformenkunde. Die Entwicklung der Militärischen Tracht der Deutsche Staaten, Österreich-Ungarns und der Schweiz bis 1937* (Stuttgart: W. Spemann, 1985)

Koch, Jochen, *Johann Philipp Winheim, Kriegskommissair der Bayreuther Regimenter im 'Grossen Türkenkrieg (1687–1695) und späterer Reichspostmeister in Coburg (1698–1717)* (Regensburg: Roderer, 1998)

Köcher, Adolf, *Geschichte Von Hannover Und Braunschweig 1648 Bis 1714*, bande I-III (Leipzig: Hirzel, 1884–1895)

Köppen, Fedor von, *Heerschau über die Kriegsvölker Europa's* (Hamburg: Hamburger Wissenschaftliches Antiquariat Fritz, 1890)

Kraus, Jürgen (ed.), *Vom Bunten Rock zum Kampanzug* (Ingolstadt: Bayerischen Armeemuseums, 1987)

Lezius, Martin and Knötel, Richard, *Die Entwicklung des Deutschen Heeres von Seinen Frühesten Anfängen bis unsere Tage in Uniformtafeln* (Berlin: Verlag für Militärgeschichte und Deutsches Schrifttum,1936)

Lundquist, Karl Gustav, *Sveriges Krig Med Staden Bremen Och Politik I Samband Darmed Aren 1665–1666* (Stockholm: Edm. Janse, 1893)

Meier-Wilcker, Hans (supervisor) Papke, Gerhard & Petter, Wolfgang (eds), *Deutsche Militärgeschichte, 1648–1939*, Band I (Munich: Bernard & Graefe, 1983)

Nolan, Cathal J. (ed.), *Wars of the Age of Louis XIV, 1560–1715. An Encyclopedia of Global Warfare and Civilization* (London & Westport: Greenwood Press, 2008).

Parrot, David, *The Business of War: Military Enterprise and Military Revolution in Early Modern Europe* (Cambridge: Cambridge University Press, 2012).

Redlich, Fritz, *The German military enterpriser and his workforce: a study in European economic and social history*, vols I-II (Wiesbaden: Steiner Verlag, 1964–5).

Schnur, Roman, *Der Rheinbund von 1658 in der deutschen Verfassungsgeschichte* (Bonn: Röhrscheid, 1955).

Tessin, Georg, *Die Regimenter der Europäischen Staaten im Ancien Régime des XVI bis XVIII Jahrhunderts* – Teil 1 (Osnabrück: Biblio Verlag, 1986)

Wilson, Peter H., *German Armies. War and German Politics, 1648–1806* (London: UCL Press, 1998)

Wilson, Peter H., *Iron and Blood. A Military History of the German-speaking Peoples since 1500* (London: Penguin Books, 2022)

Ansbach-Bayreuth

Bezzel, Oskar, *Die Haustruppen des letzten Markgrafen von Ansbach-Bayreuth unter preußischer Herrschaft* (Munich: C.H. Beck, 1939)

Baden-Baden and Baden-Durlach

Beese, Christian, *Markgraf Hermann von Baden (1628–1691), General, Diplomat und Minister Kaiser Leopolds I* (Stuttgart: Veröffentlichungen der Kommission für Geschichtliche Landeskunde in Baden-Württemberg, Band 121 1991)

Bavaria

Gold, Winfried, Das *Zeitalter Max Emanuels und die Türkenkriege in Europa 1683–1687* (Munich: Nusser, 1976).

Hoffmann, Anton, *Das Heer des Blauen Königs. Die Soldaten des Kurfürsten Max II. Emmanuel von Bayern. 1682–1726* (Munich: Piloty & Loehle, 1909)

Hüttl, Ludwig, *Max Emanuel. Der Blaue Kurfürst 1679–1726* (Munich: Süddeutscher Verlag, 1976)

Junkelmann, Markus, *Kurfürst Max Emanuel von Bayern als Feldherr* (Munich: Herbert Utz, 2000)

Kraus, Jürgen, *Bayerische Fahnen: Die Fahnen und Standarten des Bayerischen Heeres vom 16. Jahrhundert bis 1918* (Vienna: Verlag Militaria, 2017)

Kühlmann, Hermann, *Geschichte der Bayrischen Fahnen und Standarten, Textband II, Das Zeitalter des Absolutismus 1679–1777* (Munich: unpublished manuscript, 1959)

Münich, Friedrich, *Geschichte des Königlich-Bayerischen I. Chevaulegers-Regiments Kaiser Alexander von Rußland. 1: Die Stämme des Regiments (1645–1682): gleichzeitig ein Beitrag zur ältesten bayerischen Heeres-Geschichte von 1611–1682* (Munich, 1862)

Münich, Friedrich, *Geschichte der Entwicklung der Bayerischen Armee seit zwei Jahrhunderten (1618–1818)* (Munich: Biblio Verlag, 1864)

Staudinger, Karl, *Das Königlich Bayerische 2. Infanterie-Regiment, Kronprinz 1682 bis 1882* (Munich: In Kommission bei Kommission bei R. Oldenbourg1882)

Staudinger, Karl, *Geschichte des Kurbayerischen Heeres Insbesondere unter Kurfürst Ferdinand Maria, 1651–1679* (Munich: J. Lindauer, 1901)

Staudinger, Karl, *Geschichte des Kurbayerischen Heeres unter Kurfürst Max II Emanuel, 1680–1726* (Munich: J. Lindauer 1904)

Brandenburg

Bleckwenn, Hans, *Unter dem Preußen-Adler. Das brandenburgish-preußische Heer, 1640–1807* (Munich: Bertelsmann, 1978)

Carsten, Francis L., *The Origin of Prussia* (Oxford: Oxford University Press, 1979), (Italian Edition, Bologna: Il Mulino, 1982)

Ciriacy, Ludwig Friedrich von, *Chronologische Übersicht der Geschichte der Preußischen Heers Dessen Stärke, Verfassung und Kriege seit den Letzen Kurfürsten von Brandenburg bis auf die Jetzigen Zeiten* (Berlin: Mittler, 1820)

Craig, Gordon A., *The Politics of the Prussian Army, 1640–1945* (Oxford: Oxford University Press, 1964. Italian Edition, Bologna: Il Mulino, 1984)

Crouzas, Adolph von, *Die Organisationen des Brandenburgischen und Preußischen Heeres von 1640, sowie Neuzeitig Diejenigen des Norddeutschen Bundes und Deutschen Reichsheeres,* vol. I (Berlin: F. Riemschneider, 1873)

Förster, Friedrich, *Friedrich Wilhelm, der Grosse Kurfürst, und seine Zeit* (Berlin: Salzwasser Verlag, 1885)

Friedrich, Karin, *Brandenburg-Prussia, 1466–1806: The Rise of a Composite State.* Studies in European History Series. (Houndmills: Palgrave Macmillan, 2012)

Gansauge, Hermann von, *Das Brandenburgisch-Preussische Kriegswesen um die Jahre 1440, 1640 und 1740* (Berlin: Mittler, 1839)

Groehler, Olaf, *Das Heerwesen in Brandenburg-Preußen von 1640 bis 1896. Das Heerwesen* (Berlin: Brandenburgisches Verlagshaus, 2001)

Guddat, Martin, *Handbuch zur preußischen Militärgeschichte 1688–1786,* (Hamburg: Mittler, 2011)

Hirsch, Ferdinand, *Urkunden und Achtenstücke zur Geschichte des Kurfürsten Friedrich Wilhelm von Brandenburg* (Berlin: Reimer, 1902), bande XVII-XVIII

Hüttl, Ludwig, *Friedrich Wilhelm von Brandenburg, der Große Kurfürst, 1620–1688* (Munich: Süddeutscher Verlag, 1981)

Jany, Curt, *Geschichte der Königlich Preußischen Armee bis zum Jahre 1807*, vol. I (Berlin: K. Siegismund,1928)

Kinkenborg, Melle, *Fehrbellin: Nach Berichten und Briefen der führende Männer* (Leipzig: R. Voigtländers verlag, 1913)

Köppen, Fedor von & Knötel, Richard, *Preussens Heer in Bild und Wort, 1619–1889* (Glogau: Carl Flemming, 1900)

Malinowsky, Louis von & Bonin, Robert von, *Geschichte der Brandenburgisch-Preussischen Artillerie*, vols I-III (Berlin: Duncker & Humblot, 1842)

Merta, Klaus-Peter, *Das Heerwesen in Brandenburg-Preußen von 1640 bis 1896. Die Uniformierung* (Berlin: Brandenburgisches Verlagshaus, 1991)

Müller, Heinrich, *Das Heerwesen in Brandenburg und Preussen 1640–1806. Die Bewaffnung* (Berlin: Brandenburgisches Verlagshaus, 1991)

Mülverstedt, Georg Adalbert von, *Die Brandenburgische Kriegsmacht unter dem Großen Kurfürsten* (Magdeburg: Baensch, 1888)

Müsebeck, Ernst Friedrich Christian, *Die Feldzüge des Grossen Kurfürsten in Pommern 1675–1677* (Hamburg: von der Ropp,1897)

Opitz, Eckardt, *Österreich und Brandenburg im Schwedisch-Polnischen Krieg 1655–1660: Vorbereitung und Durchführung der Feldzüge nach Dänemark und Pommern* (Boppard: Harald Boldt Verlag, 1969)

Ortenburg, Georg, *Die Brandenburg-Preußische Armee in Historischer Darstellung* (Berlin: Deutsche Gesellschaft 1898)

Redlin, Karl, *Fahnen und Standarten der Brandenburg-preußischen Armee 1623–1713* (Berlin: Privately Published, 1971)

Pelet-Narbonne, Gerhard, *Geschichte der Brandenburg-preußischen Reiterei, Teil I. Die alte Armee* (Berlin: E.S. Mittler und Sohn, 1905)

Rocholl, Heinrich, *Der Große Kurfürst von Brandenburg im Elsass 1674–1675* (Strasbourg: Karl J. Trübner, 1877)

Various, *Stammliste der königlich preußischen Armee seit dem 16ten Jahrhundert bis 1840* (Berlin: C.S. Mittler, 1840)

Brunswick-Lüneburg-Celle and Brunswick-Lüneburg Hannover (Calenberg)

Brandis, Felix Schütz von, *Übersicht der Geschichte der hannoversche Armee von 1617 bis 1866* (Hannover & Leipzig: Hahn, 1903)

Decken, Friedrich von der, *Beiträge zur Hannoverschen Geschichte unter der Regirung Herzogs Georg Wilhelm (1649–1665)* (Hannover: Hahn'sche Hofbuchhandlung, 1839)

Kohler, H., 'Der französische-Niederländische Krieg von 1672 bis 1679 und der Anteil der Truppen des Gesamthauses Braunschweig-Lüneburg an diesen Kriegen' in *Braunschweigisches Magazin* (1Brunswick: 1838), s. 4

Leonhardt, H. H., *Die hannoversche Armee. Ihre Tradition und ihr Wandel im Laufe der Kriegsgeschichte, 1636–1866* (Hannover: Culemannsche Verlagsanstalt, 1966).

McMillin, Teresa S., *Guide to Hannover Military Records, 1514–1866, on Microfilm at the Family History Library* (Inverness, IL: Lind Street Research, 2014)

Poten, Bernhard von, *Die Generale der Königlich-Hannoverschen Armee und ihrer Stammtruppen* (Berlin: Ernst Siegfried Mittler und Sohn, 1903)

Reitzenstein Johann Freiherr von, *Die Uniformbilder in der Armee-Ehrenhalle des Vaterländischen Museum in Celle* (Celle: W. Ströher, 1914)

Schirmer, Friedrich, *Nec Aspera Terrent! Eine Heereskunde der Hannoverschen Armee von 1631 bis 1803*, vol. 1 (Hannover: Helwing, 1929)

Schirmer, Friedrich, *Das Celler Soldatenbuch, Ein Beitrag zur Geschichte des Standorts Celle* (Celle: Pohl, 1937)

Schirmer, Friedrich, 'Die Braunschweig-Lüneburgische Infanterie von 1660–1714' in *Die Zinnfigur*, 5 1930 (Berlin: 1930), pp.110–111

Sichart, Robert Wilhelm Georg von, *Geschichte der Königlich-Hannoverschen Armee*, Band I (Hannover, Hahn'sche Hofbuchhandlung, 1866)

Schwenke, Alexander, *Geschichte der hannoverschen Truppen in Griechenland 1685–1689, zugleich als Beitrag zur Geschichte der Türkenkriege. Nach archivalischen Quellen* (Hannover: Hahn 1854)

Wissel, Friedrich von, *Geschichte der Errichtung Sämmtlicher Chur-Braunschweig-Lüneburgischen Truppen* (Celle: Johann Dieterich Schultze,1786)

Brunswick-Wolfenbüttel

Elster, Otto, *Geschichte der stehenden Truppen im Herzogtum Braunschweig-Wolfenbüttel, 1600-1806*, band I (Leipzig: Heinsius, 1899)

Faber, Annette, '… und besahe, was noch denckwürdiges darinne wahr. Zum Aufenthalt Prinz Albrecht von Sachsen-Gotha in Wolfenbüttel und Braunschweig in Mai 1670' in *Braunschweigisches Jahrbuch für Landesgeschichte* (Wolfenbüttel: Jahrbücher des Braunschweigischen Geschichtsvereins, 2004), Band 85, pp.77–99

Venturini, Carl, *Umriss einer pragmatischen Geschichte des Kriegswesens im Herzogtum Braunschweig* (Magdeburg: Publisher not stated,1837)

Electorate of Cologne and Liège

Goorts, Roeland, *War, State and Society in Liège. How A Small State of the Holy Roman Empire survived the Nine Year's War (1688–1697)* (Leuven: Leuven University Press, 2019)

Lonchay, Henri, *La principauté de Liège, la France et les Pays-Bas au XVIIe et XVIIIe siècle. Étude diplomatique* (Brussels, 1891).

Hessen-Kassel

Böhme, Uwe Peter, *Hessisches Militär Die Truppen der Landgrafschaft Hessen-Kassel 1672–1806* (Kassel: Vogel-Druck, 1986)

Dechend, Hans, *Geschichte des Füsilier-Regiments v. Gersdorf (Kurhess.) Nr.80 und seines Stammregt. von 1631–1900* (Marburg: Elwert, 1901)

Ditfurth, Max Freiher von, 'Die Hessen-Kasselsche Kriegsmacht unter dem Landgrafen Karl bis zum Frieden von Ryswick 1697' in Zeitschrift *für Hessische Geschichte*, band VIII Neu Serie – 1860

Lettow-Vorbeck, Friedrich von: *Geschichte des Füsilier-Regiments v. Gersdorff Nr. 80 und seines Stamm-Regiments, des kurhessischen Leibgarde -Regiments von 1631–1913* (Marburg: N.G. Elwert, 1913)

Stamford, Carl von, *Die Feldzüge der Regimenter Ufm Keller und von Hornumb von Hessen-Kassel in dem Reichskriege Gegen Schweden, auf Schonen und auf Rügen; 1677 und 1678* (Kassel: Freyschmidt 1862)

Stamford, Carl von, *Das Stehende Hessische Heer von 1670–1866* (Kassel: 1899–1900)

Strieder, Friedrich Wilhelm, *Grundlage zur Militär-Geschichte des Landgräflich Hessischen Corps* (Berlin: Publisher not Specified, 1798)

Freyschmidt, August, 'Die Hessen-Kasselsche Kriegsmacht unter der Landgraf Karl bis zum Frieden von Ryswick 1697', in *Zeitschrift des Vereins für Hessische Geschichte und Landeskunde*, vol. VIII (Kassel: 1860), pp.109–215

Various, *Stamm-und-Rang-Liste des kurfürstlich Hessischen Armee Corps von 16ten Jahrhundert bis 1866* (Kassel: Gg. Francke und Ponnaz. 1866)

Hessen-Darmstadt

Beck, Fritz, *Geschichte des Großherzoglich Hessischen Feldartillerie-Regiments Nr. 25 und seiner Stämme, 1460–1883* (Berlin: Siegfried Mittler und Sohn, 1884)

Beck, Fritz, *Geschichte der Großherzoglich Hessischen Fahnen und Standarten* (Berlin: Mittler, 1895)

Beck, Fritz, *Die alten Hessen-Darmstädtischen Reiterregimenter bis zur Errichtung des 1. Großherzoglich Hessischen Dragoner-Regiments Garde-Dragoner-Regiment Nr. 23 1609–1790* (Darmstadt: Wittich, 1910)

Hild, Friedrich *Militär-Chronik des Großherzogthums Hessen von Anfang des Regierenden Hauses bis auf die neueste Zeit*, vol. I (1567–1790), (Darmstadt: Friedrich Hild, 1828)

Keim, August von, *Geschichte des 4 Großherzoglich Hessischen Infanterie-Regiments Großherzogin (Prinz Carl) Nr. 118 und seiner Stämme* (Berlin: E.S. Mittler und Sohn 1879)

Röder von Diersburg, Carl Christian, *Geschichte des 1. Großherzoglich Hessischen Infanterie (Leibgarde) Regiments Nr. 115*, 1621–1899, (Berlin: Ernst Siegfried Mittler & Sohn, 1899)

Holstein-Gottorf

Knüppel, Günter, *Das Heerwesen der Fürstentums Schleswig-Holstein-Gottorf, 1600–1715* (Neumünster: Karl Wachholtz, 1972)

Rode, Friedrich Carl, *Kriegsgeschichte Schleswig-Holsteins* (Neumünster: K. Wachholz 1935)

Free Imperial Cities

Brumshagen, Andree, *Das Bremer Stadtmilitär 1618–1810: zur Bedeutung und Funktion des Soldaten in der reichsstädtischen Gesellschaft* (Bremen: Staatsarchiv Bremen, 2010)

Galperin, Peter, *In Wehr und Waffen – Wehrbürger, Söldner und Soldaten in Oldenburg und den Hansestädten* (Stuttgart: Motorbuch, 1983)

Gény, Joseph, *Die Fahnen der Strassburger Bürgerwehr im 17. Jahrhundert* (Strasbourg, J.H.E. Heitz, 1902)

Kracauer, I., 'Das Militärwesen der Reichsstadt Frankfurt am Main im 18. Jahrhundert' in *Archiv für Frankfurts Geschichte und Kunst* 12 (Franfkfurt am Main, 1920) pp.1–180

Kraus, Jürgen, *Das Militärwesen der Reichsstadt Augsburg 1548–1806* (Augsburg: Stadtarchiv, 1980)

Kraus, Jürgen, *Die Fahnen und Uniformen der Reichsstadt Augsburg 1545–1806*, Veröffentlichungen des Bayerischen Armeemuseums Nr. 7 (Ingolstadt: Bayerisches Armeemuseum, 1983)

Muhsfeld, Theodor, 'Das Hamburgische Militär' in *Zeitschrift fur Hamburg Geschichte,* vol. 14 (Hamburg, 1909)

Schwark, Thomas, *Lübecks Stadtmilitär im 17. und 18. Jahrhundert, Untersuchungen zur Sozialgeschichte Einer Reichsstädtischen Berufsgruppe. Veröffentlichungen zur Geschichte der Hansestadt Lübeck,* Reihe B, 18 (Lübeck: Schmidt-Röhmhild, 1990)

Kurpfalz (the Palatinate)

Bezzel, Oskar, *Geschichte des Kurpfälzischen Heeres von Seinen Anfängen bis zur Vereinigung von*
Kurpfalz und Kurbayern, vol. I (Munich: Lindauer LTR-Verl, 1925)

Lorraine

Clement, Arnaud, *Les Familles d'Ancienne Chevalerie de Lorraine* (Nancy, 2015)

Fulaine, Jean-Charles, *Le Duc Charles IV de Lorraine et son Armée* (Metz: Editions Serpenoise, 1997)

Mainz

Guhrauer, Gottschalk Eduard, *Kur-Mainz in der Epoche von 1672,* (Hamburg: Perthes, 1839)

Kahlenberg, Friedrich P., *Kurmainzische Verteidigung Einrichtungen und Baugeschichte der Festung Mainz im 17. und 18. Jahrhundert* (Mainz: Stadt Mainz Stadtarchiv 1963)

Mentz, Georg, *Johann Philipp von Schönborn: Kurfürst von Mainz, Bischof von Würzburg und Worms: 1605–1673,* vols I-II (Jena: Fischer, 1896–9)

Schlösser, Susanne, "...die Stadt Mainz fühlte indessen die Bedrückungen sehr hart...' Die Festung Mainz und ihre Auswirkung auf den Alltag der Bevölkerung im 17. und 18. Jahrhundert' in *Mainzer Geschichtsblätter,* Heft 7: (Mainz: Die Wacht am Rhein, 1992), pp.9–24

Mecklenburg-Schwerin and Mecklenburg-Güstrow

Keubke, Klaus-Ulrich, *Kleine Militärgeschichte Mecklenburgs* (Schwerin: Stock & Stein, 1995)

Tessin, Georg, 'Mecklenburgisches Militär in Türken und Franzosenkriegen 1648–1718' in *Mitteldeutsche Forschungen,* band 42 (Cologne: Böhlau, 1966), pp.4–203

Tessin, Georg, 'Mecklenburgische Uniformen vor 1718' in *Zeitschrift für Heereskunde* (Hamburg: Deutsche Gesellschaft für Heereskunde 1980), pp.75–77

Münster

Alpen, Johann von, *Decadis de Vita et Rebus Gestis Christophori Bernardi Episcopi et Principis Monasteriensis,* 2 vols, (Münster, 1694–1703)

Bönninghausen, Clemens Maria Franz von, Die *kriegerische Tätigkeit der münsterschen Truppen: 1651–1800* (Harvard: Harvard University Press, 1978)

Depping, Georges Bernard, *Geschichte des Krieges der Münsterer und Cölner im Bundnisse mit Frankreich gegen Holland in den Jahren 1672, 1673 und 1674* (Münster, Theissing, 1840)

Kohl, Wilhelm, *Christoph Bernhard von Galen. Politische Geschichte des Fürstbistums Münster* (Münster: Regensburg Verlag, 1964)

Meeter, E., *Geschiedenis van het Belag van Groningen in 1672* (Groningen, 1839)

Tessin, Georg, 'Beiträge zur Formationsgeschichte des Münsterischen Militärs. Überarbeitet und ergänzt von Hans-Joachim Behr', *in Westfälische Forschungen. Mitteilungen des Provinzialinstituts für westfälische Landes und Volksforschung des Landschaftsverband Westfalen-Lippe*, vol. 32 (Münster: Aschendorffsche Verlagsbuchhandlung, 1982)

Various, 'Die Geschichte des Emslandes im Rahmen der allgemeinen deutschen Geschichte: 2. Der erste holländische Krieg 1665–1666' in *Emlandsbuch 1928 – Ein Heimatbuch für die Kreise Weppen, Aschendorf, Kümmling* (Osnabrück: 1928), pp.6–10

Various, 'Die Geschichte des Emslandes im Rahmen der allgemeinen deutschen Geschichte: 5. Der zweite holländische Krieg. 1672–1674' in *Emlandsbuch 1928 – Ein Heimatbuch für die Kreise Weppen, Aschendorf, Kümmling* (Osnabrück: 1928), pp.13–17

Various, 'Die Geschichte des Emslandes im Rahmen der allgemeinen deutschen Geschichte: 6. Die Teilnahme Christoph Bernhards von Galen an dem gegen die Franzosen 1674 und gegen die Schweden 1675 erklärten Reichskriege' in *Emlandsbuch 1928 – Ein Heimatbuch für die Kreise Weppen, Aschendorf, Kümmling* (Osnabrück:1928), pp.18–21

Verspohl, Theodor, 'Das Heerwesen des Münsterschen Fürstbischofs Christoph Bernhard von Galen 1650–1678', in *Beiträge für die Geschichte Niedersachsens und Westfalens*. 18. Heft (Münster: Universität Münster, 1909)

Zeigert, Dieter, 'Die Artillerietruppe des Fürstbistums Münster 1655–1802. Erster Teil: Errichtung, Organisation und Einsatz der Artillerie unter Fürstbischof Christoph Bernhard von Galen (1650–1678). Ein kurzer Streifzug durch die Geschichte der Artillerie bis zum 17. Jahrhundert' in *Westfälische Zeitschrift*, 134, (Paderborn: Bonifatius GmbH 1984), pp.9–106

Pfalz-Neuburg

Beitelrock, Johann W., *Geschichte des Herzogtums Neuburg oder der jungen Pfalz* (Aschaffenburg: Wailandt, 1866–67)

Lipowsky, Felix Joseph, *Geschichte der Landstände von Pfalz-Neuburg* (Munich: Lentner,1827)

Saxony

Bauer, Frank, 'Zur Organisation und Struktur der kursächsischen Armee an der Wende vom 17. zum 18. Jahrhundert' in *Sächsische Heimatblätter* Nr. 5 (Leipzig: Zentrum für Kultur//Geschichte Niederjahna, 1983), pp.224–271

Beust, Friedrich von, *Feldzüge des kursächsischen Armee*, bande I (Erfurt: Sächs. 1801)

Friedrich, Wolfgang, *Die Uniformen der kurfürstlich Sächsischen Armee, 1683–1763* (Dresden: Beyer, 1998)

Friesen, Ernst von, 'Das Defensionwesen im Kurfürstenthume Sachsen', in *Archiv für die Sächsische Geschichte*, 1 (Dresden & Leipzig: 1863), pp.194–228

Schorr, Dan, *The Saxon Army, 1700–1721* (Matthews: Editions Brokaw, 1987)

Schuster, Oskar & Francke, Friedrich August, *Die Geschichte der Sächsische Armee von der Errichtung bis in die neueste Zeit: Unter Benutzung handschriftlicher und urkundlicher Quellen*, vol. I (Leipzig: Verlag von Duncker & Humblot,1885)

Thenius, Walter, *Die Anfange des stehenden Heerwesen in Kursachsen unter Johann Georg III. und Johann Georg IV* (Leipzig: Quelle & Meye 1912)

Querengässer, Alexander, *The Saxon Mars and His Force. The Saxon Army during the Reign of John George III 1680–1691* (Warwick: Helion & Company, 2019)

Saxon Duchies

Jacobsen, Roswita & Brandsc, Juliane, *Friedrich I, von Sachsen-Gotha und Altenburg. Die Tagebücher 1667–1686* (Weimar: Hermann Böhlaus Nachfolger, 2011)

Thiele, Andrea, 'The Prince as Military Entrepreneur? Why Smaller Saxon Territories Sent «Holländische Regimenter» (Dutch Regiments) to the Dutch Republic', in J. Fynn-Paul (editor) *War, Entrepreneurs, and the State in Europe and the Mediterranean, 1300-1800,* (Leyden-Boston MS: Brill, 2014) History of Warfare, Volume: 97, pp. 170-192.

Trier

Janke, Arthur, *Die Belagerungen der Stadt Trier in den Jahren 1673 bis 1675* (Trier: Lintz: 1890)

Kentenich, Gottfried, *Geschichte der Stadt Trier: von ihrer Gründung bis zur Gegenwart; Denkschrift zum 100jährigen Jubiläum der Zugehörigkeit der Stadt zum preussischen Staat* (Trier: Interbook, 1915)

Württemberg

Andler, Rudolph von, 'Die Württembergischen Regimenter in Griechenland, 1687–89', in *Württembergische Vierteljahreshefte für Landesgeschichte* XXXI (Stuttgart: Uhland'schen Buchdruckerei1922/4), pp.217–279

Menzel, Rudolf, *Geschichte des Infanterie – Regiments Kaiser Wilhelm, König von Preußen (2. Württembergischen) Nr. 120, 1673–1909* (Stuttgart: Uhland'schen Buchdruckerei1909)

Schempp, Adolph von, *Der Feldzug 1664 in Ungarn unter besonderer Berücksichtigung der herzoglichen wiirttembergischen Allianz- und schwâbischen Kreistruppen* (Stuttgart: Kohlhammer, 1909)

Stadlinger, Leo Ignaz, *Geschichte des Württembergischen Kriegswesens von der Frühesten bis zur Neuesten Zeit* (Stuttgart: Druck und Verlag der K. Hofbuchdruckerei zu Guttenberg 1856)

Wilson, Peter H., *War, State and Society in Württemberg, 1677–1793* (Cambridge: Cambridge University Press, 1995)

Wunder, Bernd, *Frankreich, Württemberg und der Schwäbischen Kreis während der Auseinandersetzung über die Reunionen (1679–97)* (Stuttgart: Kommission für geschichtliche Landeskunde in Baden-Württemberg, 1971)

Würzburg and Bamberg

Caspary, Hermann. *Staat, Finanzen, Wirtschaft und Heerwesen im Hochstift Bamberg (1672–1693)* (Bamberg: Historischer Verein, 1976)

Hagen, Eduard, *Die Fürstlich Würzburgische Haus Infanterie von ihren Anfängen bis zum Beginn des Siebenjährigen Krieges 1636–1756* (Munich: Lindauer,1910)

Kopp, Walter. *Würzburger Wehr: eine Chronik zur Wehrgeschichte Würzburgs* (Würzburg: Freunde Mainfränkischer Kunst und Geschichte, 1979)

Articles

Brandão, Jack, 'The First German Reich: between the Thirty Years' War and the Crisis of the 17th Century' *Lumen et Virtus, Revista Interdisciplinar de Cultura e Imagen*, vol. X, no.25, August 2019 (Brazil: Jackbran Consult Ltda, 2019) pp.144–165

Franzkowiak, Andreas and Wenzel, Chris: 'Keramikgranaten aus Ingolstadt – Ein außergewöhnlicher Fund' in: *Waffen und Kostümkunde – Zeitschrift für Waffen und Kleidungsgeschichte*, vol. I (Heidelberg: Universitätsbibliothek Heidelberg, 2018), pp.65–80

Grotefend, Wilhelm, 'Schrautenbach-Weitolshausen, Ludwig Balthasar von' in *Allgemeine Deutsche Biographie*, bande 54 (Leipzig: *Bayerische Akademie der Wissenschaften*, 1908), pp.181–183

Hirsch, Ferdinand, 'Die Armee des Grossen Kurfürsten und Ihre Unterhaltung während der Jahre 1660–86' in *Historischer Zeitschrift*, LIII (Oldenburg: Walter de Gruyter,1885), pp.240–289

Jakobs, Rainer, 'Braunschweigisches Militärwesen 1641–1714. Heeresorganization in Spannungsfeld von landständischer Verfassung und Fürstlichem Absolutismus', in *Braunschweigisches Jahrbuch für Landesgechsichte*, 81 (Wolfenbüttel: Braunschweigischer Geschichtsverein, 2000), pp.29–75

Kortzfleisch, Gustav von, 'Der Oberelsässische Winterfeldzug 1674–75 und das Treffen bei Türckheim nach archivalischen Quellen bearbeitet' in *Beiträge Landes und Volkskunde Elsass-Lothringen*, XXIX Heft (Strasbourg, 1904)

Langer, Heinrich & Dudás, Janos, 'Die Kämpfe in Ungarn 1684 bis 1686 und die Rückeroberung Budas im Spiegel des Theatrum Europaeum' in *Acta Historica Academiae Scientiarum Hungaricae*, bande 34, nr 1 (Budapest: Akadémiai Kiadó, 1988), pp.17–25

Marr, Anton, 'Der Feldzüg im Jahre 1675 in Deutschland. Nach Österreichischen Originalquellen' in *Österreichische Militärische Zeitschrift*, (Vienna: Kaiserl. Koenigl. und Hof und Staatsdruckerei), bande III 1839, p.267–293, band IV 1840, p.137–170

Marr, Anton, 'Der Herbstfeldzug Montecuccolis gegen Condé, 1675 am Rheine und an der Mosel. Nach Österreichischen Originalquellen', in *Österreichische Militärische Zeitschrift*, vol. II (Vienna: Kaiserl. Koenigl. und Hof und Staatsdruckerei, 1842), p.129–152

Marr, Anton, 'Der Feldzüg 1676 in Deutschland mit Benützung Österreichischer Originalquellen', in *Österreichische Militärische Zeitschrift*, vol. III (Vienna: Kaiserl. Koenigl und Hof und Staatsdruckerei,1844), pp.11–26

Münter, Otto, 'Die Waldeckische Truppen von 1681–1750' in *Geschichtsblätter für Waldeck,* 71 (Waldeck: Wilhelm Bing, 1983), pp.179–208

Schröder, Martin, 'Die bewegte Bellona: die kursächsische Durchzug- und Marschorganisation am Beispiel eines braunschweig-lüneburgischen Durchzugs von 1685', in *Militärgeschichtliche Zeitschrift*, 77 (Oldenburg: Walter de Gruyter, 2018), 1, pp.1–36

Tessin, Georg, 'Reichsarmee und Allianzkorps im Türkenfeldzug 1663/64', in *Zeitschrift für Heereskunde*, VII, (Hamburg: Deutsche Gesellschaft für Heereskunde, 1983)

Tessin, Georg, 'Die Deutschen Regimenter der Republik Venedig', in *Zeitschrift für Heereskunde*, X (Hamburg: Deutsche Gesellschaft für Heereskunde, 1982)

Thiele, Andrea, 'Von Kundschaftern und Kundschaft. Soldatenhandel und Wissenszirkulation zwischen Sachsen-Gotha und den Niederlanden im 17. und 18. Jahrhundert' in O. Kann and M. Schwarz (eds), *Militär und Gesellschaft in der Frühen Neuzeit. Themenheft Militärisches Wissen vom 16. bis zum 19. Jahrhundert* Nr22 (Potsdam: Universitätsverlag Potsdam, 2011), pp.153–172.

Varga, János, 'Die Beteiligung kurbayerns und des fränkischen Reichskreises am Großen Türkenkrieg 1683–1699' in *Ungarn-Jahrbuch 27* (München: Zeitschrift für interdisziplinäre Hungarologie 2004), pp.321–330

Wilson, Peter: 'The German Soldier Trade of the Seventeenth and Eighteenth Centuries. A Reassessment' in *The International History Review*, vol. 18, no.4 (London: Routledge & Co., 1996), pp.757–792

About the author

Bruno Mugnai was born in Florence in 1962 and still lives there with his partner Silvia. Active for years as a historical researcher and illustrator, he is the author of several titles published by, among others, the Historical Office of the Italian Army and Helion & Co. His books focus on the historical periods and geographical areas of his interest – the ancient Italian states, Central and Eastern Europe in the sixteenth, seventeenth, and eighteenth centuries, and South America after the conquest. He is a member of 'La Sabretache', the Society for Military History Studies, and of the Italian Society of Military History. As an illustrator, he collaborates with important Italian and foreign specialists, and with the Stibbert Museum of Florence. Bruno is a Rugby Football Union enthusiast, who still believes in an Italian Grand Slam in the Six Nations Tournament.

Other titles in the Century of the Soldier series

No 38 ***Wars and Soldiers in the Early Reign of Louis XIV:*** *Volume 1 - The Army of the United Provinces of the Netherlands, 1660–1687*

No 39 ***In The Emperor's Service:*** *Wallenstein's Army, 1625–1634*

No 40 ***Charles XI's War:*** *The Scanian War Between Sweden and Denmark, 1675–1679*

No 41 ***The Armies and Wars of The Sun King 1643–1715:*** *Volume 1: The Guard of Louis XIV*

No 42 ***The Armies Of Philip IV Of Spain 1621–1665:*** *The Fight For European Supremacy*

No 43 ***Marlborough's Other Army:*** *The British Army and the Campaigns of the First Peninsular War, 1702–1712*

No 44 ***The Last Spanish Armada:*** *Britain And The War Of The Quadruple Alliance, 1718–1720*

No 45 ***Essential Agony:*** *The Battle of Dunbar 1650*

No 46 ***The Campaigns of Sir William Waller***

No 47 ***Wars and Soldiers in the Early Reign of Louis XIV:*** *Volume 2 - The Imperial Army, 1660–1689*

No 48 ***The Saxon Mars and His Force:*** *The Saxon Army During The Reign Of John George III 1680–1691*

No 49 ***The King's Irish:*** *The Royalist Anglo-Irish Foot of the English Civil War*

No 50 ***The Armies and Wars of the Sun King 1643-1715:*** *Volume 2: The Infantry of Louis XIV*

No 51 ***More Like Lions Than Men:*** *Sir William Brereton and the Cheshire Army of Parliament, 1642–46*

No 52 ***I Am Minded to Rise:*** *The Clothing, Weapons and Accoutrements of the Jacobites from 1689 to 1719*

No 53 ***The Perfection of Military Discipline:*** *The Plug Bayonet and the English Army 1660–1705*

No 54 ***The Lion From the North:*** *The Swedish Army During the Thirty Years War: Volume 1, 1618–1632*

No 55 ***Wars and Soldiers in the Early Reign of Louis XIV:*** *Volume 3 - The Armies of the Ottoman Empire 1645–1718*

No 56 ***St. Ruth's Fatal Gamble:*** *The Battle of Aughrim 1691 and the Fall Of Jacobite Ireland*

No 57 ***Fighting for Liberty:*** *Argyll & Monmouth's Military Campaigns against the Government of King James, 1685*

No 58 ***The Armies and Wars of the Sun King 1643-1715:*** *Volume 3: The Cavalry of Louis XIV*

No 59 ***The Lion From the North:*** *The Swedish Army During the Thirty Years War: Volume 2, 1632–1648*

No 60 ***By Defeating My Enemies:*** *Charles XII of Sweden and the Great Northern War 1682–1721*

No 61 ***Despite Destruction, Misery and Privations..:*** *The Polish Army in Prussia during the war against Sweden 1626–1629*

No 62 ***The Armies of Sir Ralph Hopton:*** *The Royalist Armies of the West 1642–46*

No 63 ***Italy, Piedmont, and the War of the Spanish Succession 1701–1712***

No 64 ***'Cannon played from the great fort':*** *Sieges in the Severn Valley during the English Civil War 1642–1646*

No 65 ***Carl Gustav Armfelt*** *and the Struggle for Finland During the Great Northern War*

No 66 ***In the Midst of the Kingdom:*** *The Royalist War Effort in the North Midlands 1642–1646*

No 67 ***The Anglo-Spanish War 1655–1660:*** *Volume 1: The War in the West Indies*

No 68 ***For a Parliament Freely Chosen:*** *The Rebellion of Sir George Booth, 1659*

No 69 ***The Bavarian Army During the Thirty Years War 1618–1648:*** *The Backbone of the Catholic League (revised second edition)*

No 70 ***The Armies and Wars of the Sun King 1643–1715:*** *Volume 4: The War of the Spanish Succession, Artillery, Engineers and Militias*

No 71 ***No Armour But Courage:*** *Colonel Sir George Lisle, 1615–1648 (Paperback reprint)*

No 72 ***The New Knights:*** *The Development of Cavalry in Western Europe, 1562–1700*

No 73 ***Cavalier Capital:*** *Oxford in the English Civil War 1642–1646 (Paperback reprint)*

No 74 ***The Anglo-Spanish War 1655–1660:*** *Volume 2: War in Jamaica*

No 75 ***The Perfect Militia:*** *The Stuart Trained Bands of England and Wales 1603–1642*

No 76 ***Wars and Soldiers in the Early Reign of Louis XIV:*** *Volume 4 - The Armies of Spain 1659–1688*

No 77 ***The Battle of Nördlingen 1634:*** *The Bloody Fight Between Tercios and Brigades*

No 78 ***Wars and Soldiers in the Early Reign of Louis XIV:*** *Volume 5 - The Portuguese Army 1659–1690*

No 79 ***We Came, We Saw, God Conquered:*** *The Polish-Lithuanian Commonwealth's military effort in the relief of Vienna, 1683*

No 80 ***Charles X's Wars:*** *Volume 1 - Armies of the Swedish Deluge, 1655–1660*

No 81 ***Cromwell's Buffoon:*** *The Life and Career of the Regicide, Thomas Pride (Paperback reprint)*

No 82 ***The Colonial Ironsides:*** *English Expeditions under the Commonwealth and Protectorate, 1650–1660*

No 83 ***The English Garrison of Tangier:*** *Charles II's Colonial Venture in the Mediterranean, 1661–1684*

No 84 ***The Second Battle of Preston, 1715:*** *The Last Battle on English Soil*

No 85 ***To Settle the Crown:*** *Waging Civil War in Shropshire, 1642–1648 (Paperback reprint)*

No 86 ***A Very Gallant Gentleman:*** *Colonel Francis Thornhagh (1617–1648) and the Nottinghamshire Horse*

No 87 ***Charles X's Wars:*** *Volume 2 - The Wars in the East, 1655–1657*

No 88 ***The Shōgun's Soldiers:*** *The Daily Life of Samurai and Soldiers in Edo Period Japan, 1603–1721 Volume 1*

No 89 ***Campaigns of the Eastern Association:*** *The Rise of Oliver Cromwell, 1642–1645*

No 90 ***The Army of Occupation in Ireland 1603–42:*** *Defending the Protestant Hegemony*

No 91 ***The Armies and Wars of the Sun King 1643–1715:*** *Volume 5: Buccaneers and Soldiers in the Americas*

No 92 ***New Worlds, Old Wars:*** *The Anglo-American Indian Wars 1607–1678*

No 93 ***Against the Deluge:*** *Polish and Lithuanian Armies During the War Against Sweden 1655–1660*

No 94 ***The Battle of Rocroi:*** *The Battle, the Myth and the Success of Propaganda*

No 95 ***The Shōgun's Soldiers:*** *The Daily Life of Samurai and Soldiers in Edo Period Japan, 1603–1721 Volume 2*

No 96 ***Science of Arms: the Art of War in the Century of the Soldier 1672–1699:*** *Volume 1: Preparation for War and the Infantry*

No 97 ***Charles X's Wars:*** *Volume 3 - The Danish Wars 1657–1660*

No 98 ***Wars and Soldiers in the Early Reign of Louis XIV:*** *Volume 6 - Armies of the Italian States 1660–1690 Part 1*

No 99 ***Dragoons and Dragoon Operations in the British Civil Wars, 1638–1653***

No 100 ***Wars and Soldiers in the Early Reign of Louis XIV:*** *Volume 6 - Armies of the Italian States 1660–1690 Part 2*

No 101 ***1648 and All That:*** *The Scottish Invasions of England, 1648 and 1651: Proceedings of the 2022 Helion and Company 'Century of the Soldier' Conference*

No 102 ***John Hampden and the Battle of Chalgrove:*** *The Political and Military Life of Hampden and his Legacy*

No 103 ***The City Horse:*** *London's militia cavalry during the English Civil War, 1642–1660*

No 104 ***The Battle of Lützen 1632:*** *A Reassessment*

No 105 ***Monmouth's First Rebellion:*** *The Later Covenanter Risings, 1660–1685*

No 106 ***Raw Generals and Green Soldiers:*** *Catholic Armies in Ireland 1641–1643*

Polish, Lithuanian and Cossack armies versus the might of the Ottoman Empire

No 108 ***Soldiers and Civilians, Transport and Provisions:*** *Early Modern Military Logistics and Supply Systems During The British Civil Wars, 1638-1653*

No 109 ***Batter their walls, gates and Forts:*** *The Proceedings of the 2022 English Civil War Fortress Symposium*

No 110 ***The Town Well Fortified:*** *The Fortresses of the Civil Wars in Britain, 1639-1660*

No 111 ***Crucible of the Jacobite '15:*** *The Battle of Sheriffmuir 1715*

No 112 ***Charles XII's Karoliners Volume 2*** *- The Swedish Cavalry of the Great Northern War 1700-1721*

No 113 ***Wars and Soldiers in the Early Reign of Louis XIV:*** *Volume 7 - Armies of the German States 1655–1690 Part 1*

No 114 ***The First British Army 1624–1628:*** *The Army of the Duke Of Buckingham (Revised edition)*

No 115 ***The Army of Transylvania (1613–1690):*** *War and military organization from the 'golden age' of the Principality to the Habsburg conquest*

No 116 ***The Army of the Manchu Empire:*** *The Conquest Army and the Imperial Army of Qing China, 1600–1727*

No 117 ***French Armies of the Thirty Years' War 1618–48***

No 118 ***Soldiers' Clothing of the early 17th century:*** *Britain and Western Europe 1618–1660*

No 119 ***Novelty and Change:*** *New research, ideas, thoughts and interpretation on the British Civil Wars and the military history of the 17th century*

No 120 ***Peter the Great's Disastrous Defeat:*** *The Swedish Victory at Narva, 1700*

No 121 ***Royalist Newark, 1642–1646:*** *Sieges and Siege Works*

No 122 ***The Battle of Fribourg 1644:*** *Enghien and Turenne at War*

No 123 ***Science of Arms:*** *The Art of War in the Century of the Soldier, 1672 to 1699: Volume 2: Cavalry, Artillery & the Conduct of War*

No 124 ***Supplying the New Model Army:*** *Logistics, arms, ammunition, clothing, victuals and the matériel of war, 1645–1646*

No 125 ***Wars and Soldiers in the Early Reign of Louis XIV:*** *Volume 7 - Armies of the German States 1655–1690 Part 2*

SERIES SPECIALS:

No 1 ***Charles XII's Karoliners:*** *Volume 1: The Swedish Infantry & Artillery of the Great Northern War 1700–1721*

For the complete range of Century of the Soldier titles please go to
www.helion.co.uk/series/century-of-the-soldier-1618-1721.php